James Brown worked on the NME, founded *loaded*, *Jack* and *Leeds, Leeds, Leeds* magazines, and was Editor-in-Chief of British *GQ*. He is a media entrepreneur and journalist and hosts a weekly show on talkSPORT. He is now down to three matches a week.

ABOVE HEAD HEIGHT

A FIVE-A-SIDE LIFE

JAMES BROWN

Quercus

First published in Great Britain in 2017 by Quercus.
This paperback edition published in 2018 by

Quercus Editions Ltd
Carmelite House
50 Victoria Embankment
London EC4Y 0DZ

An Hachette UK company

A CIP catalogue record for this book is available
from the British Library

PB ISBN 9781786481788
EBOOK ISBN 9781786481771

Picture Credits
p.vi © Travis Hodges
p.245 © Jimmie Gregory
p.309 © John Riordan

10 9 8 7 6 5 4 3 2 1

Typeset by Jouve (UK), Milton Keynes

Printed and bound in Great Britain by Clays Ltd, St Ives plc

For my dad, Ray Brown, who came to watch all my middle
school games, and my favourite players, then and now,
Allan Clarke and Marlais Brown.

Goal hanging.

Contents

Introduction

I would like to say that this book is a journey into the world of five-a-side and amateur football, but if it in any way resembles how I play football it will be less a journey and more a quick sprint forward past one player, a shot powering high and wide, and then a long walk back into my own half.

I've used the word 'my' because I am writing it, but I don't believe the book is just about me. It is the autobiography of an amateur footballer, but it's not so much my story as our story. I've written it for all of us who run late out of the office or the home, wearing or clutching a bag of hastily assembled, mismatched kit, thinking, 'Shit, I forgot my water,' and wondering if we've remembered the £7 subs that is the entry fee for our hour of living dreams. And hang on, have we got the right boots for the surface we'll be playing on?

We are the men – and increasingly women – who disappear for an hour or so and come back looking like we've been chased by bulls, starved of water and oxygen, and collapse like a wet cardboard box awaiting the attention of a loved one, a pint (whether beer or orange juice and lemonade) or an approving post-match comment from a mate. 'That shot in the first half was amazing,' is the best it gets. 'Don't forget we've got people coming for lunch and we're going to get the curtains in ten minutes,' is the worst.

This is a book about dreams so long-standing that they have become ingrained in our lives. Dreams are often referred to as 'unattainable' or 'pie in the sky', but while dreams are elusive for many, for the keen five-a-side player, the Sunday footballer, the true amateur, they are lived week in, week out.

When I say five-a-side I should remind you that I mean any level of regular play on anything that isn't grass and involves fewer than eleven players on each side.

It's not just playing but watching too. I can watch games anywhere. When I used to visit my former in-laws, Roger and Cheryl, in Swansea I'd find myself down on the Mumbles Road walking the dog and avidly watching student matches. I once went to see a team called Cherry Burton in Hull because a mate, Swift Nick, was playing; another team-mate was a young guy called Paul Heaton, who subsequently sent me a demo tape of his unsigned band, The Housemartins. Although I would never deliberately travel to go and see this standard of football, I find it hard not to slow down and watch.

Five-a-side players are the true footballers. As kids many of us dreamed of playing football professionally, but unlike professionals we actually get to play football for ever (or for as long as our bodies will allow). Most of the former professional footballers I know or have met (and my fascination with their lives means I've met a lot) stop playing when they stop earning.

We play football for love, not money. We play it for life and we play it everywhere. Our kit is damp. Our boots and trainers are full of tiny black rubber pellets, the soles caked with sand. Our legs are a leopard's back of bruises. Our shirts are tight around the belly. Our heroes' names are plastered across our shoulder blades. Our showers are too cold in winter and too hot in summer. Our used sports bags stay unpacked in the hall. Our water bottles are under the kitchen sink. Our post-match warm-down takes place in the pub. As does the match analysis. Our warm-up is non-existent and involves just a few seconds of a stretch that was in fashion fifteen years ago. Pre-match we're hoping we are picked on the same side as certain players. Our performance is patchy and maybe not what it used to be. But we think we played great. It's sporting karaoke, a time and place to live out our dreams.

Comedian and author David Baddiel summed it up perfectly when I asked him what the hell we were doing chasing a ball around late on a Tuesday night: 'It's partly about football – it's amazing how football sticks with you, how you never quite give it up, whatever else you give up with age – and partly about being with men. As you get older it's quite hard to have mates, I think, or at least to hang out with your mates like you did when you were a kid, or maybe in your twenties. You have to have a reason to do it, to take you away from family and work, etc. So football does that, provides a reason, and then makes its own history, stuff you can talk about nostalgically. The number of times we've had the same conversations at the curry house afterwards . . . it's the creation of a little culture.'

We are amateur five-a-side footballers, we are the game. Now excuse me while I go and find a white T-shirt and a dark T-shirt, because the bloke who's picking me up has been waiting patiently outside in his car for ten minutes and we're going to be late for kick-off.

Real Hackney. L-R: Sunderland Graham, Fashionable Frank, Derby Dave, James Kyllo, Gary Graham King, Peter Berlin, Tooting Tim.

We Cremated James Yesterday

For the last few decades James has organized our regular Wednesday night and Sunday morning football games. Amateur football is a strange brotherhood – whether, as in our case, it's midweek indoor five-a-side or outdoor Sunday nine-a-side. Artificial surfaces, artificial dreams. Grown men still imagining they're playing for their childhood teams.

I've rarely seen the men alongside me at the crematorium in non-football clothes before, never mind funereal black. We normally wear a mixed bag of old club shirts (Derby County, Arsenal, Spurs, Chelsea, Charlton) and thinning, well-washed T-shirts that are unfaithful to their original colours.

I don't know many of the men's surnames. Instead, they're known by a series of poor tags that aren't even nicknames – Sunderland Graham, Beardy Dave, Tall Ben, Little Ben. I've only been to the houses of two of them and I don't know what half of them do for a living or what their wives are called. I know some of their children – but only because we've been playing long enough for nippers who occasionally watched from the sidelines ten years ago to turn into young men who play regularly and bring some youth and ability to an ageing team. I occasionally come across the players in real life and what surprises me is that they're wearing long trousers, not shorts.

The thing that binds everyone who plays five-a-side is the same thing that made us, as kids kick a ball in the playground at school, in the streets as it got dark and in the park at weekends. It's the overwhelming desire to stay true to that feeling you get when you score or tackle or pass and it prompts a round of applause and you are, just for a moment, Allan Clarke or Thierry Henry or whoever your childhood hero was. It's not televised, so there's only word-of-mouth proof, but even crap amateur players can score world-class goals.

Five-a-side runs as an unusual parallel to the rest of our lives. Come rain, shine, birth, divorce and even death, we show up and play.

When news came that James had died, I tried to explain our connection to my girlfriend, who had met him maybe twice in a decade, a passer-by on the street. He wasn't a close friend but he was a good friend. A nice, genuine guy. I'd attended his birthday dinner at his favourite curry house in the summer. When I heard I just sat in a state of shock and then went out to walk in the park where I used to bump into him weekly, riding his bike round the ponds.

I'd first met him thirty years earlier on a musician friend's doorstep; I'd attended his birthday dinner in the summer. How do you approximate the familiarity that comes from seeing someone twice a week at football for seventeen years?

These regular fixtures have lasted much longer than all my jobs and almost twice as long as my longest relationships. Despite occasional flare-ups on the pitch, they've remained more good-natured, more consistent and less painful than following the teams we support.

They offer windows into the personalities of the people you share the pitch with. Every regular five-a-side player with an eye for the game can describe in clear detail the playing styles of his or her own teammates. We've enjoyed and endured them for what seems like for ever: the sharp shooter; the late tackler; the on-pitch organizer who doesn't do what he asks others to; the one who produces almost accidental brilliance from nowhere; the one who shows up and plays in what looks like your grandma's slippers; the ones who can't run any more because their chests or their legs are letting them down.

There's more: the angry player who's calm off the pitch; the lazy, selfish player who won't go in goal; the person who runs round and round in circles, not hearing the pleas for passes from everyone around him; the grown man who will kick a fourteen-year-old; the player who thinks he's still as good as he was ten years ago; the generous, hard-working, selfless player; and the player who's a long way from a natural but turns up and does his best.

This last description suited James Kyllo. He was ungainly – not, you suspect, someone who played as a kid – but there were few things better than seeing James edge in from the far wing at a corner and celebrate an unexpected goal with almost childlike glee. A man who never expects to score looks great when he does, running away to his own half while pumping his fists in a mixture of happiness, sense of achievement and disbelief. That was our friend James.

Importantly, James was the man who booked the pitches, collected the money and, in his own statistically fascinated way, took charge of a long-running series of annual tables, awarding individual players points for victories or losses. This tended to create more competitive tension than is necessary in a friendly game – but it felt fantastic the year I came top.

James Kyllo was a tall, large, quiet man, well read and endlessly enthusiastic about music. He rode a bicycle in massive army shorts, sandals and a fleece. The newer Sunday footballers who joined us over the years would never have guessed that he had been a punk rocker and was one of the invisible mainstays of Creation Records – a pillar around which the excess and success of Oasis and Primal Scream thrived. But then Creation founder Alan McGee couldn't believe James was a long-standing Sunday footballer when I rang to tell him of James's unexpected death and to ask him to pass on the news to his record label colleagues.

It was only with James's passing that I realized what a strange, open-ended family exists on these small AstroTurf and wood-panelled pitches. It's the same the country over.

The Sunday after he died, we gathered around the centre circle and stood for what seemed like five minutes' silence. No one arranged it. Just amateur footballers honouring one of our own.

Goals Are My Business

You start with one-a-side as a toddler, work up the scale as a kid to two-a-side (which is called Wembley and also involves a neutral goalie), then three-a-side in PE or the playground, and then in the street or park it escalates, with more and more players hitting anything up to fifteen-a-side, after which you snap back down to eleven in your school team and Sunday league teams. Finally, as work and life and social drift kick in as you get older, you snap down to a weekly five-a-side.

Well, that's roughly how it went for me (with a twelve-year break when I went for a very long night out). The newer generations who have grown up with specialist five-a-side centres like Goals and Powerleague will able to play five-a-side for life. If this is you then make sure you get a Five for Life tattoo. Somewhere visible.

I can remember quite clearly the first time I went onto a football pitch to play football. It was behind the primary school in Collingham, right in the heart of the professional-footballer belt. Three England and Scotland internationals lived in the village. My house backed onto the pitch, although I've no memory of there ever being any games there. All the football action took place out in the street, The Avenue, where our family friend and opposite neighbour was the Leeds United and England striker Allan Clarke.

It was his number 8 I had sewn onto the back of a white football shirt with matching white shorts and thick heavy white socks. On my feet I had my first pair of football boots, which had come from the little shop at the top of the road. These boots are a link to a time that is long gone now. They had no brand, no markings, no words, no colours: just a pair of black ankle-high football boots. You could have demolished buildings with them.

One of my parents mentioned the boots in the shop, so as a curious pre-school football fan I went up to take a look. Sure enough, on the top of a wire rack in front of the counter with the old-fashioned push-button till, there was a pair of rigidly upright boots. This was about 1969, but they looked like they'd been made in 1959. Even Dead Shot Keen, the ghost in Billy's Boots in *Tiger and Jag* comic, would probably have thought they looked old.

My dad didn't have any interest in football, so this probably seemed like a solution. It ticked my box of wanting some and didn't involve any extravagant investment. To see a pair like this now, you'd need to go to a football museum. The leather came up to the ankle, it was hard and tough, and the boots reared up to show the sole and front of the studs at the front. Even professionals didn't wear things like this. I don't think anything like it had been worn since the early 60s – the 1860s. Anyway, a bad workman blames his tools, but I managed to roll that ball through the big white goalposts, so they did their job.

I didn't wear them across the road when my mum went in for a coffee with Sniffer's wife, Margaret, and his dog Pelé. The Clarkes were happy for me to take his England caps out of his cabinet and put them on my head. I was in his kitchen when he came back from England's unsuccessful defence of the World Cup in Mexico 1970. One time he opened his bag and gave me his mud-splashed LUFC number 8 soccer tags. He took my autograph book and filled it with absolute legends: Bremner, Giles, Hunter, Gray, Madeley, Cooper, Revie – all of them.

This was a huge influence on the rest of my life, actually being with my hero as a little kid. It made me believe anything was possible. It wasn't another world on a screen, somewhere else; it was here. A great striker, the Leeds United number 8. He would cement my bond with the club and the sport for life. I read his book, *Goals Are My Business*, and I intended to make them mine too.

The Headingley Wallers

My five-a-side life starts against the red-brick walls of the Leeds 6 streets you see during Test Matches at Headingley. If you could go up a block when the camera pans over the Kirkstall Lane end and zooms in on the large terrace ends beyond the stand, you'd find our street pitches.

There were three sets of goals on terrace ends where the three streets, Estcourt Avenue, Headingley Avenue and Headingley Mount, are dissected by Canterbury Drive. If you went to university in Leeds, it's highly likely you either lived in these streets or knew someone who did. Throughout my adult life I've been credited with magical abilities for predicting the addresses of ex-students who told me they went to university in the city. Back in the 1970s those streets had as many families living in them as students, if not more.

Nowadays the streets are empty of kids and families and it's almost 100 per cent students. The bushes at the front of the house I grew up in have been dug up and the garden concreted over. The back gardens have been sold to developers for flats. The corner wall we sat on is still there, but in the summer the area is like the *Mary Celeste*. Back then the streets weren't plastered with 'To Let' signs, as they are now, and the terrace ends were sprayed with goalposts.

Further along Canterbury Drive, where it met Ash Road and the road turned from tarmac to gravel, there was another set of goals and, more importantly, just where the road ended there was the open green space at the bottom of the woods by Queenswood Drive that led up to Beckett Park.

This rough area bisected by a gravel track had three major functions throughout the year. Every August it would be where we hurled sticks at the giant horse chestnut trees to get conkers. Every November it was where we chumped for and built the local bonfire. And for the rest of the year it was where we would play big matches until it turned dark. When that happened the games were partially illuminated by the slight glow of the number 56 bus terminus, which acted as a poor substitute for floodlights.

Conkers, bonfire, football – what more could you want? It was bumpy underfoot, balls got lost in weeds by the wall or flew down onto the main road, but it was a place where great goals were scored and dreams and great saves were made. Just up behind it, between the start of the woods and Ash Road, was a large stone house with an immaculate grass five-a-side-sized pitch next to it. We'd sit on the wall and stare at it for hours, but it just looked too pristine to go on. No one ever used it. Its presence was a total mystery.

These streets were the pitches of my youth. In the summer holidays and at weekends, if numbers were strong enough, we'd walk or cycle through those woods and play in Beckett Park on the grass. I played in these areas between the ages of five and fourteen, from 1971 to 1980. As far as I know, this is the first recorded information about these vitally important fixtures, teams and stadiums.

The Headingley streets between Ash Road and Kirkstall Lane were overrun with kids, absolutely packed, which meant you could pretty much play football constantly. Every day of the year, rain and snow aside, from the moment you got in from school till the time your parents would start worrying about you, because it was two hours after dark and, if you hadn't changed, your school trousers would be ruined. It was constant football day and night, on mud and gravel or tarmac and paving stones.

If you stood in the street with a ball other kids would just show up.

The thump of ball on wall worked like Ron Burgundy's Viking horn on the news team. Only there'd be no horn, just the smack smack smack of a ball being 'Lorimer!-ed' against a wall. Or you might be the one arriving late and the others would already be there, scuffling between one pavement and the other, twisting and turning, pushing the ball and then hammering it 'into' the red-brick goal that had been sprayed long ago and was now fading, or had been freshly chalked out.

I could stand on Canterbury Drive from our corner of Headingley Avenue and look down towards the bottom of the woods six streets away to see where a game was going on. Nobody ever said no to you joining the game, you just showed up, were given or chose a side and joined in. If you had any sense you'd judge who had the best players before you even got there and join them without discussing it. Failing that, you'd just join the team your best mate was on, the one who you knew would pass to you. That's assuming the other team weren't already shouting for you to join them.

This wasn't confined to childhood. While I was writing this book my mate David Smith said, 'At the Talacre Centre in Kentish Town, back when teams were chosen at random based on shirt colour, before we started actually picking sides, people used to turn up with both shirts in the car and hide behind the bushes to see who was wearing what, and then select which side they wanted to be on based on who was already in that colour.' Some things don't change.

Back in Leeds 6 in the mid-1970s, joining an existing game in the streets simply involved both teams shouting, 'Us, us, us, kicking that way!' It also seemed compulsory, expected even, that as soon as you joined a game you'd just charge straight into the action and go for the ball. A tangle of pumps, monkey boots, school shoes, adidas T-shirts, flared jeans or shorts.

There were cheap unbranded trainers from a local Asian clothes shop on North Lane, trainers you could peel the front rubber off. No one was wearing branded trainers in 1974. Unless they were Dunlop Green Flash tennis shoes. We hadn't even seen branded trainers. Adidas, Puma, Gola and Patrick made boots, but so did Woolworths.

The balls weren't a million miles away from the balls professionals use now, though. They were very light, made of plastic, and would swerve like crazy when you hammered them, whooshing past a dumb-founded goalkeeper with his feet stuck rigid to the tarmac.

There were all sorts of balls on the go: gold and black rubbery ones that were really quite squeezable to the touch; really, really light orange and black ones, fly-aways, which you could win on a 10p stall at a school fair; heavier plain white plastic ones that you could still use for a bit even if they'd been bitten by a dog or punctured beneath a mov-ing car.

Then there were the summer balls you brought back from beach holidays in Filey, tattered old 'proper leather balls' or 'pills' discarded by adults in the park. The polished sheen had been kicked off these and all that was left were tatty cloth panels hanging off the weight of the bladder inside. Some of these battered and bruised old balls would last for what seemed like ever. There were orange plastic Frido training balls that were great for curling.

The king of the street football was the Wembley Trophy, which was made of heavier red plastic, giving it more resistance to anything it was kicked against, and allowing you to keep it down at kid height. We practised an unofficial below-head-height simply because to start hammering it high in the air increased the likelihood that it would land in a garden or backyard, with the ensuing ball search interrupting play, or even crash through a window, like my friend the late Johnny Martin accidentally did with a perfect volley through the glass into the kitchen of 30 Estcourt Avenue.

The Wembley Trophy was brick-coloured with moulded panel lines you could fill in with pen after you'd written your name and 'LUFC

RULE' on it. For aficionados of 1970s nostalgia, the Wembley Trophy is up there in the Top Ten street toys with Clackers and the Space Hopper, but they outlasted both of those. It was the ultimate durable street football. If you had a Wembley Trophy in play it felt like a better game. There was less unpredictability in your shooting and it was easier to keep hold of in goal – although saving a full blast from close range would sting the palms, especially if there were bits of grit stuck in the ball. There's a company selling Wembley Trophies online now, but football nostalgia expert Derek Hammond, editor of the *Got, Not Got* books, and I have both scoured their site and photographs and don't think they're the same as the originals. There'll be originals somewhere, though, sitting on a shelf in an advertising agency next to a *Six Million Dollar Man* board game and a *Star Wars* toy, or resting flat and forgotten at the back of some grandad's garage in Guiseley.

For a very short while there were also lightweight white plastic balls with Leeds United players' names and faces on it: a marketing idea from the inventor of the famous LUFC sock tags, the legendary 'You Are the Ref' illustrator Paul Trevillion. No one in their right mind would use one of these to play football. The cheapness of the product meant a few boots and it would shrink, taking Bremner, Reaney or Giles's faces with it. The rarity meant they were difficult to replace. I saw them booted high into the stands at Elland Road when my grandad took me to a night game one time and we were so high up in the stands the players and the balls seemed a mile away.

I never remember a time without footballs. Even if you were miraculously short for a while you could use a tennis-er, but it would only be a matter of minutes before someone would bring their proper ball and you'd trade up.

The terrace ends on Canterbury Drive meant you could just go out into the street with a ball on your own, because every good shot would be rewarded with an equally good bounce back. Get on a good run and you could just be hammering the hell out of them. Strangely, no one whose walls we were booting the ball against ever came out and complained. Just booting a ball against a wall solo killed time until someone else showed up. Most of us had brothers and sisters, so you'd rarely start with just one.

You could practise headers against the wall but you'd usually only manage three before the momentum ended. Volleys were a big part of the day and a scorching volley no one but a passer-by could see would still be announced with a scream of, 'LORIMER!', 'GILES!', 'CLARKE!', 'CRUYFF!' or 'BREMNER!' The same applied for tennis in the summer. A line drawn at hip height across the wall would give you your own red-brick game of squash or tennis and with that you had your own Centre Court and commentary with Borg, McEnroe or Connors playing Năstase or Ashe.

The location allowed us to develop street techniques. Hitting your shots low without catching the kerb was an art form. Chipping the keeper meant he couldn't run back and push it over the sprayed crossbar, because he'd just clatter into the wall where the goal line should have been. A ball played towards the keeper that rebounded off the kerb he was stood on would draw him out and allow you to chip the ball over him. It was simple stuff.

Some street skills didn't really play any part in the game itself. They make a point nowadays of saying an athlete needs to have practised 10,000 hours to get to the top, but back then we didn't need a sports psychologist to explain that if you just stood on one path and chipped the ball on to the opposite kerb endlessly you could perfect the bounce back so it would land right back at your feet again or even in your hands.

Once you'd tired of that after, ooh, a couple of hundred days, you could do the same with throw-ins. The simple joy of seeing the ball accelerate off the sharp edge of the kerb, increasing its momentum and coming straight back to you, was thrilling.

When my eldest son, Marlais, was about eight I took him out into our north London street to practise this. It was a lot more difficult with the amount of cars everywhere, but it still felt great when either of us hit the edge just right. Significantly, when we tried this there was never anyone else playing anything in the street, with or without a ball. On the grass across the main road and behind the shops in front of the flats, yes, but the roads full of town houses were kid-free. More than one driver sped through, scowling at us like we were mad.

This is the root of my five-a-side life, the terrace ends and the kids in Headingley. The walls were our goals and if we went up to as many as five-a-side we'd switch playing directions and play along instead of across the road, putting bricks into cardboard boxes to use them as one goalpost with a lamp post as the other. Or coats, random traffic cones, even a ball with a shirt draped over it, which sat like a pregnancy bump in the road, we used whatever was around.

Forty years on I can remember the names of sixty kids who lived in those streets. They normally came in twos or threes, but the Catholic and Asian families had more. Sixty is a massive squad to choose from, even Real Madrid don't have a first-team squad that size, but that's what we had. I have no idea what most of those sixty are doing now. Some, like Micky Hughes and John Cassidy, have reappeared in twenty-first-century style on Facebook and Twitter. One, Hughie, is a priest, and another, Johnny, died young. Others are very much alive and I remember their names: Mick and Paul Birch, Pete Masters, Si Holmes, Ken Brown, Craig Roy, Phil and Richard McStay, Johnny, Chris, Paul and Rob Munden. Then there were Paddy Matthews, Chris Nelson, Johnny Martin, Ian Ginner, Arthur Brownbridge, Suresh and Parish Chohan, Peter Salter, the Walkers, the Andersons, the Baileys, the Marsdens, and Bapty and Gummy. Plus my sister Sally, who became Alex, a keen street footballer, ahead of her time. There were the kids who came from further away, like Johnny Paynter, the Mone brothers, the Nortons, plus the ones whose surnames have gone with the years, like Richard, Gareth and Nickie. And finally there was a kid called Keith Rawnsley, who organized boxing matches in his backyard at Langdale Terrace and once fell spectacularly from the top of a tree in the woods and broke his collar bone while the rest of us were hanging about on a rope swing.

In real life now we're all older than our dads were then, but when I recall those names I see streets of kids playing football, riding bikes, hanging around up trees, sitting on garage roofs and draped over stone walls like a Bayeux Tapestry of street football. We were fuelled by Limeade, Dandelion and Burdock, Calypso Jubblies, Tizer (the Appetizer), Hubba Bubba, Bubblicious, Texans, Twix, Mars Bars, Chipmunk and Tudor Crisps, McCowan's Highland Toffee, Mojo Chews, Penny Chews, Black Jacks and Fruit Salads, ice pops and the shit-hard bubblegum that came with football cards and Bazooka Joe. No one wanted or wore a baseball cap apart from Bazooka Joe.

For a more substantial meal you could buy bread rolls and small loaves to go with all the sweets from Don Hammond's shop. Take them home and attack them with jam. Or have fish and chips and scraps from Andrew Warbie's dad's chip shop on North Lane. We had no need for sports nutritionists – we were all as fit as we needed to be and we were all as good as our last game/goal/save. Fat people were old, thin people were young and fat young people were goalies.

These roads weren't tiny Kray Twins-style Bethnal Green alleys, they were wide streets with enough space for the car owners to park well away from where the kids played football. There was nothing famous about them, but years before George Orwell had once stayed on our street for a while, at his sisters', while working on *The Road to Wigan Pier*.

Apart from the ebb and flow of people having to go in for their tea, nothing would stop us really. A car passing slowly through our midst would prompt everyone to pause and slowly edge out of its way, whoever was on the ball carefully dragging it under his feet. For a moment it would be quiet, a pause in play, and then as the car drove through – either rolling over our goalposts or swerving round them – the ball would be carefully dragged back underfoot to exactly where it had been and we would all just kick off again with animated screams for passes. A tiny bit of stop motion prompted by a car.

People on bikes were tolerated but barely paused for. If we were waiting for a ball to be retrieved from a garden or a backyard, or a goalie had it in his hands and a cyclist emerged, we'd wait and shout, 'Ninety miles an hour!' or 'Get off and milk it!', but if we were in the thick of the action they'd have to chance their luck. There were probably better routes than through fifteen kids in the middle of a match, and people took them.

During Test Matches the streets were rammed with cars, so we would move to the bottom of the woods. If that had been parked over we'd head to the park, and if that had been converted into a free car park our attentions would turn to joining the cricket crowds by nicking over the wall into the rugby ground via a lamp post halfway down the ginnel by the Turnways.

We'd walk across the Leeds Rugby League ground stands into the adjoining cricket ground and head straight out of the gate again, selling the pass outs to a late-arriving adult for less than the cost of a full-price ticket, and then head back in via the same lamp post or under the broken barbed wire at the corner of the ground opposite the North Lane Baptist Church to do it again.

It was in this church hall at Cubs that we played crab football, where you'd sit down on your arse and then push yourself up with your arms and legs and crawl around upside down, hopefully booting the ball high and goalwards in a strange crustacean version of five-a-side.

Back on the street, the only other moving thing that caused us to stop was Flash Harry, a mysterious man in a long grey mac, with a black fringe splayed across his frowning brow, who looked like Bryan Ferry. He'd hustle through our game on the opposite pavement to where the goals were. Heading who knows where. No one knew much about Flash Harry. Even the kids who lived in his street didn't.

In the way that rumours bestow glory on the mysterious, it was suggested that he'd been a great artist who had gone mad. He certainly looked troubled, not that anyone would ever do anything to him. He was an exotic local in that he was an adult who never spoke, smiled or looked happy – pretty much what my girlfriend says about me now, come to think of it.

Unlike other adults, he wouldn't try and show any solidarity with us by tackling the ball or booting it back to us. He'd walk on through quickly and we'd just stop and watch him go.

He was here, there and gone. A bit like some of the shit Serie B signings Massimo Cellino made in his first year at Leeds United. There was never any suggestion of perversion about this isolated loner, as there undoubtedly would be today. No one's parents warned us away from him or anything.

Flash Harry wasn't the only peculiar person we'd see roaming the streets of Headingley. Occasionally a grown man in a grey Buffalo Bill cowboy outfit, with holstered pistol and whip, could be seen moseying on down Headingley Lane into town past Paraphernalia, the joss sticks and sheepskin coats shop my mum worked at, and Mr Natural, two belated attempts to capture a bit of 1960s San Francisco in Leeds 6.

These interruptions were the pitch invaders of their day and, them aside, it would take a lot to truly break up or finish a game. There was one major annual interruption, though, and that was the arrival of the street cricket season. This would begin with a simple sighting of a couple of kids with wickets, tattered pads, spiky batting gloves, a Corky ball and bats heading up to Beckett Park, optimistically hoping to attract people for a game.

Living within West Indies crowd roaring distance of Headingley made it impossible to ignore the cricket season, and why should we? It felt like our duty to replicate the sporting seasons and in reality all we needed for cricket was a bat and a tennis-er and a fielder stood in front of all the various gardens on the junction of Langdale Avenue and Canterbury Drive, where wickets had been chalked onto the lamp post outside Stuart Anderson's house.

This crossroads position gave you about 80 per cent of a normal cricket field to bat into, apart from long leg, which was occupied by Stuart's house. Play would occasionally be interrupted by someone pulling a wheelie on a racing bike with cow-horn handlebars. Somehow, this never happened in football – I guess it was easier to impersonate Evil Knievel in the middle of a tarmac cricket field than among a huge mass of kids kicking at a Wembley Trophy and screaming, 'Man on!'

It was during this period that I played my first school games at Bedford Field Middle School, Woodhouse. We had a home and an away fixture against Blenheim and I scored the only goal in the home 1–0 victory. The sense of excitement when my first goal flew off my boot over the other players and into the massive net was immense, and then as I walked off hearing an adult saying, 'That goalscorer is some player.'

Seeing my dad come to watch every game, even though he didn't like football, was a boost. I was picked to play in the year above straight away. They had a full season of fixtures, but I was so tiny my heavy rugby shirt hung through the bottom of the shorts I'd tucked it into. The arrival of the new light nylon kits, Crystal Palace's white with the blue and red slashes, prompted the PE department to give us all an old blue version of the same kit that they no longer needed. Football kits were so rare in those days I wore it everywhere.

At Bedford Field we had a tough, gritty, sandy all-weather pitch that was so rough it was a no-weather pitch. Brutal, no one ever did any sport on it; the tarmac was softer. The only good thing that ever happened on that all-weather pitch was on late-arrival prefect duty with the gorgeous Elizabeth Conway. It was our turn to sit there for a week and write down the names of latecomers while everyone else was in assembly. On a really foggy morning we left the command post and walked out into the mist and had a snog, at 9.10 a.m. I'd still take that now if it was on offer. With her.

As I progressed through those four years of middle school we had two stars in the team. There was a kid called Matthew Cooper, who had one blinding season of dribbling past all the opposition. He was so thrilling to watch that the kids on the sidelines would chant 'Super Cooper' en masse every time he got the ball, as if it was at Elland Road. People were actually showing up just to watch Super Cooper. The other star was Shay Glennan, a Gypsy kid who rarely attended school and could sometimes be seen sitting on top of a tall abandoned red-brick terraced house overlooking the playground. Shay was a Brummie with thick black hair and he was a great player. He moved like he was running through sherbert but he still beat his man. He was almost as famous for his football as he was for his extensive leaves of absence. He was the George Best of Woodhouse.

Can Five-a-side Be Beautiful?

If you want to seek out natural beauty, one of the last places you'd go looking is a sunken gym on a dark rainy Wednesday night in Hoxton, east London. Scores of latte bars, pop-up shops and cupcake cafés may have sprouted from the square at the heart of this jumbled part of the city, and inspired gentrification across Britain from Manchester to Margate, but by night in the drizzle off the main street you still see it for what it once was – and for some still is: a cluster of ageing tower blocks and maisonettes.

Where shotguns were once sawn off, handguns are now couriered by pre-teens, crack pipes are still sucked and factory-farmed chicken bones are fried, chewed on and spat out for rats. I've nothing against the place, I've lived either side of it for decades. It is what it is. When I'd started to deal with my post-*loaded* magazine addiction problems, people helped me stay clean from drink and drugs here, I put my kid in nursery here and I played football once a week for a long time here. I didn't feel any need to 'discover it' once the music and art crowd moved in for good.

In the late 1990s, though, rumours of its rough and ready appeal prompted fashion-conscious people to sell perfectly nice flats in Notting Hill when Hollywood mainstreamed it and decamp to this rough little patch of the capital above Shoreditch and Old Street. I couldn't believe it. None of my mates who grew up around Pitfield Street wanted to live anywhere near there; in fact they wanted to move as far away as possible.

It wasn't long before some of the newcomers from Notting Hill sold up and set off again for the leafier streets of Stoke Newington or Crouch End. You can have as many pop-up shops as you like now, but Mugging Mondays in 1999 never proved popular. It's become a lot more inviting and comfortable for newcomers and visitors now, art galleries with craft beers replacing rough drinkers on the canal, art bookshops sitting alongside bookies, but some old memories live on.

One night about a decade ago I went back to a flat at the top of one of the tower blocks with a funny Italian woman I met in a bar, and hung out with her until she nodded off on her own secret heroin stash. As she slept I opened her windows and looked out over the jewel-lit London night and realized that probably the further away you were from Hoxton the better it looked or sounded.

Six months later I asked my mate (who'd introduced me to the girl) how she was and he replied, 'Oh, she committed suicide. I didn't tell you because I thought you'd be upset.'

For every new bar, nightclub or coffee shop there was another grim story like that. When I was getting clean from my active addiction, I'd made a lot of friends from round there and life in the flats was still very different from life in the artists' warehouses.

As my Mum also died of an overdose, the Italian girl's death was often on my mind as I'd head down to the heart of Hoxton to play football. It was a constant reminder of how five-a-side had given me a new focus and the potential consequences of relapse. Hoxton has changed massively, its reborn social atmosphere has influenced inner-cities across the country, but no, it is not a place to seek out natural beauty. It may be a distorted Brechtian Utopia for some, but at ground level it can still feel like a trap. But that is where we head every Wednesday – to a two-pitch polished-floor gym sunk well below street level, where ceiling lights illuminate a half-used car park and a bike rack cluttered with wheel-less orphaned frames.

At one end of Falkirk Street is the main Kingsland Road, which was, for a while, the Highway of Hipsterdom between Shoreditch and Dalston. The Hipsters must have moved on now, though, as I haven't seen anyone riding a penny farthing, dressed as a lion tamer in Stoke Newington for almost a year now. They've migrated south to some other former dump, like Deptford or Peckham: places the black cabs would never take you home to in the 1980s, places once only known outside of London because of the comedy of Del Boy and the tragedy of Damilola. I know Peckham's changed since I lived there in the mid-80s because I drove through it recently and the chip shop had a handwritten window statement about the purity of their deep-frying oil, saying it was made of acorns or something.

At the western end of Falkirk Street, Hoxton, is the chicken shop where schoolgirl Agnes Sina-Inakoju was gunned down and killed in 2010, innocently caught in an inter-gang drive-by. Shot in the neck with a sub-machine gun by two guys in their early twenties on pushbikes who are both now serving thirty-two-year minimum sentences. In the tragic, stupid and pointless Olympics, that's a moment that would have taken gold, silver and bronze. It's unnerving, children getting shot on the street we play five-a-side on. You'd think from reading the *Evening Standard* that the gangsters had put down their guns to pick up their mini-lattes and were all going out with heiresses.

In between these two streets is our pitch. The building is as unspectacular as the physiques of our playing squad. Naked, we look like something Lucian Freud might have painted. But we show up every week in haphazard football gear, all shapes and sizes, kit and men. And here beneath the bright lights I can confidently say that you will find beauty, albeit only occasionally. If I was making this claim in a brochure aimed at attracting paying visitors I'd be on shaky ground and many guests would leave disappointed, true, but I do believe five-a-side can be beautiful. And not just because of my own ludicrous and ill-founded high opinion of myself.

Turn off Falkirk Street into the sports centre car park, park your car or chain your bike, negotiate the electric doors and walk into wonderland where dreams are lived and clean sheets shattered. Inside, a guy in a pale blue polo shirt pleasantly nods hello from behind a low reception desk covered in leaflets and forms. He knows his shift is almost over, just our game to go then he lock up and knock off.

Beyond him is a closed café bar for the college the gym is a part of. To his left is a cabinet that holds cups and awards for work with the London 2012 Paralympics. To our left as we head towards the changing rooms we can look down onto the first pitch, where the *Green Soccer Journal* staff are finishing their game. The clock is closing in on 9 p.m. but there's no let-up in pace. Nice kits, fast angular passes, four-a-side, four touches from goalie to goal. Twenty years younger than us. Peter Sutcliffe beards. The *GSJ* game is how it is for a lot of young men yet to hit the wall around thirty-one. How it should be (not the beard bit).

Beyond them on our pitch a basketball match is raging end to end. They're still going strong, competing to the last. Unlike in the same closing minutes of our games, no one is just dawdling around, too fucked to run, and importantly they have the correct number of players per team. Subs and other players are slumped round the edge, swigging water on a raft of sports bags.

At the doorway alcove where the chest-high wall splits the two pitches in half, five or six men are already assembled in Everton, Sunderland, Liverpool, Charlton and Leeds kits, ready to come onto the two pitches the moment the clock hits 9. Most of them are from the game I play in, keen to get going, like bargain hunters on Boxing Day. We get on well with our regular neighbours on the pitch next door, sometimes extending to player swapping, which is the football equivalent of wife swapping. No, sorry, no it's not. We lend if we have too many players and they don't have enough.

At one point in our game's history, as you passed this view from reception you'd bump into people on their way to a room to do capoeira, the half dance, half martial art, but that stopped a while back now. Maybe they moved on to half knitting, half didgeridoo. I imagine capoeira recruitment among the young took a bit of a hit when that video of the kick-boxer knocking out the cartwheeling capoeira fighter with one punch went viral. Still, as a discipline it looked weirdly cool and vaguely interesting – maybe even spiritual. A martial art performed to music from Brazil? I can see why people would go for something like that. God only knows what they must have thought of a sport as traditional and nylon-orientated as five-a-side. I wonder what it would be like to play five-a-side every week to Latin music, something with true rhythm, an idea they considered during the 1970s in the NASL. I only played along to music once, at Vince Power's Phoenix Festival, and it sounded superb despite only being a Stone Roses tribute act.

Where is this magic you speak of? I didn't say magic, I said beauty. The beauty takes place on the shiny wooden floors with the multi-sports coloured line markings, in the space between the two short and long ragged goalposts. It exists, I've both felt it and seen it.

It comes with motion and it can come to one player alone or between two people or three, four or even the whole team, all five of us. And by us I mean you as well as us. It is purely based on the movement of the ball, where it goes and how it gets there and what happens to it along the way.

For me, the ball should always be moving. If it was meant to stand still it would be a cube not a sphere. The beauty comes in small ways: a pass across a crowded D, a cushioned flick that releases an accelerating attacker or a perfect one-two that leads to the devastating simplicity of a three-pass goal.

And it comes when you run. With the ball. Around the opposition, ignoring your own teammates, head down and body swaying. You drag the ball back from the man right in front of you, then roll it forward as your body weight angles your shoulders down, across and ahead in a diagonal away from his outstretched foot. You guide the ball with the outside of the foot and then just head for the space between the players. Swerving, accelerating, making sure they see your body and not the ball. It's a slalom but you are in control, not gravity, and you race for that space across the last defender until he can't reach you because he's static and you're gliding through. Then, when you're there, instinct and angles take over and you cut the ball back across the keeper into the huge space he's left exposed behind him or power it into the near corner with a ferocity that frightens him.

Pushing the ball through that Z move always feels good. Taking it at left back, then moving diagonally across the pitch with only momentum and opportunity to assist you. Then finishing with accuracy and confidence. It's surprising, when you have the fitness to do this, how often it becomes playable as the opposition back off to mark others instead of closing you down. Get a measure of the opposition, know you can take them on and finish the move, and you're there. The repeated beauty of a punishing stream of goals follows. There was a time – when I didn't look like I'd eaten a cauldron – I could do this all match long.

The fastest goals are sharp, snappy and involve the minimum of running and passes. They always look both unstoppable and impressive. It is their economy and simplicity that give them their beauty. The ball is either delivered down the wing, crossed and finished in three passes from start to end or concertinas across the axis of an X with a simple one-two before being dispatched.

Sometimes the opposition is perfectly placed to move the ball fast against you like that and it's crushing to be on the receiving end. Particularly if you're caught by the counter attack straight after your own goalscoring effort, momentarily lulled into complacency by celebration and satisfaction.

Those goals that just slice you apart are five-a-side at its greatest. In a good game they are frequent, as both teams take possession and bring the ball out and instinctively execute winning move after move. The ball is only surrendered because it's being picked out of the opposition's net. To do this you need not only the right personal fitness and sympathetic teammates to interact with but also, importantly, the right number of teammates. Too often in the pick-up games there are too many players for the size of the pitch and numerically imbalanced teams.

Goalkeepers in five-a-side rarely give us beauty so much as spectacular planning or improvisation: a raised leg that stops a penalty in the centre of the goal, diverts the ball up over head height and out of play. A scrabble across a mat or hard floor that allows a fingertip touch to direct the ball to safety away from crossing the line. These are applauded, but somehow they are considered make-do rather than magnificent.

A simple side-footed return pass of a one-two – or, as the Dutch call it, a wall pass – can feel beautiful. Angling the position of the foot so you don't even add to the force of the ball, other than to knock it back into the path of the advancing player. In a busy, cluttered game, with ten men on a pitch, more than forty shots on targets and seventeen-odd goals, such a minute interaction might go unnoticed, but the player feels it. The teammate who has instigated the move welcomes the ball back exactly where they are rushing to, where they need it to be.

It's crowned by the shot and goal that follow, and that's where everyone's attention lies. But the scorer and the passer know that simple reading of the weight of the incoming ball and the angled foot, allowing it to feed back out, were measures of technical efficiency and instinctive beauty. Yes, I know I am only describing a one-two. But if beauty is simplicity, then just putting your foot into the path of a ball can give you that.

How the ball enters the net can be beautiful too. Power is impressive, but so are precision and cunning. The ball that steals across the goal, gently dipping past the falling, dumbfounded keeper's hands, and spins into the net is wonderful. Those mini-seconds when everyone stops to wonder if it will keep spinning and creep in, or flatten out, hit the post and come back to the keeper; the line of the D preventing you from doing anything but watch and gasp or shout. Those moments are fantastic, but there's no time to prolong the appreciation.

People see beauty in art and literature and they're right to. It expresses or calms the pain or curiosity they have for life, themselves or the world, but in almost every case art and literature are created by the individual rather than the group. In the fast rollerball world of five-a-side, the beauty can come purely from the individual – you've seen the childhood solo goals of Ronaldinho or Maradona on sketchy film on YouTube – but more often than not, along that short burst of adrenalin and action that results in the ball in the net, someone else helped that ball along the way, changed its direction, cushioned it back.

Even if it is just a quick roll-out from the keeper that gives you a one-second advantage against the opposition, that second you're mentally ahead of the other side is the second where the goal comes from, while they're still wondering what happened.

There is no preplanning, no rehearsal, no time spent doing demos for an amazing goal, be it solo or the result of teamwork. All you have is hunger, energy, muscle and mental memory. Memory that goes back to that pass or shot in a street or a park or a school playground years and years before.

That is where beauty lies. In the instinct and the ability for the amateur player to do something that impresses, sometimes astounds, his friends, teammates and opposition. And it's a passing, fleeting experience, because no one but the participants are watching these games, no one is filming indoor five-a-side. They should be, because with more phone clips of skills and goals and fouls from competitive amateur eleven-a-side games going viral online, the proof is there that goals scored by street dreamers like us are as likely to amaze people as the ones scored on TV by guys on £100,000 a week.

Anyone with the right ambition can score a goal of beauty. Maybe not to order, maybe not every week, but given the right circumstance they can. The circumstances being luck, timing, momentum and aggressive desire to just knock the opposition down a peg, wipe out the scores and rewrite them with you one goal up.

You have got to want to dominate the opposition with your ability on those indoor pitches, to show that not only is it easy for you to score an amazing goal but also, no matter what they can muster as a whole team, you will step up as an individual again and put the ball in their net once more. Make them bend over and pull it out, smeared in reluctance, embarrassment, disappointment or mild midweek fury. When you are attacking with that cocky desire and confidence, when you know you can glide through whatever blockade they attempt to put in front of you, that is when the beauty comes.

A top professional once pointed out that the best way to practise penalties is without a goalkeeper, because the goalkeeper is irrelevant if you can place it fast and accurately enough into the furthest reaches of the goals. Do that and it will be impossible for him to stop the ball.

The same applies with that dribble that transcends the ordinary stop-start nature of a fractured wing game, a dribble that flows through the space in the middle of the pitch to register a resounding goal that demoralizes the opposition as much as it inspires your own team.

You do not see the opposition, you do not even need to see them. You just need to know where the space is and how to weave through it, keeping the ball ahead but with you until you push it free and shoot it beyond their keeper.

Do that and you have your beauty in five-a-side. And if you want to see great five-a-side goals week in, week out in the professional game just watch Messi, Özil, Mahrez and Suarez score great five-a-side goals with their teammates at the top of their game. From the street to the gym to stadiums around the world, you can see the raw invention. And that's exactly what you need on a pitch that is as small and packed and sometimes rigid as a bar football table: a freestyle player who will do something that creates the beauty. And you know that can be you.

Headers and Volleys Meets *Enter the Dragon*

For the pre-Powerleague generation the simplicity of the games we played in the street and the use of the walls are two of the main reasons adults love five-a-side so much. Street and playground games are the seeds of the five-a-side world.

I firmly believe that apart from the social and competitive elements of five-a-side it's partly a yearning for the freedom of childhood that drives men out of the house or workplace weekly and onto the five-a-side pitches.

Tom Findley, who I've played with on and off over the last ten years, tells me the reason he looks forward to five-a-side every Friday is that it keeps him together fitness-wise for the rest of the week, knowing he's got to go out and test himself against the same people he's played with for decades. That's a valid point, but I think the draw is as emotional as it is physical. We still want some of our childhood.

Maybe it's just me who longs for a rerun of childhood, and with good reason, but in the same way a middle-aged guy with a family might go to a gig three times a year when he used to go once a month, so a weekly five-a-side game is a reduced version of the daily games we played in the playgrounds and streets of our childhoods.

The affection held for that time of our lives runs deep, as do the memories. Back then there were no twenty-five-year mortgages, no redundancies, no technological shift away from traditional industries, no leaking roofs to fix, no bosses or clients being a pain, no complicated personal relationships to balance or untangle, no divorces (or at least not our own), no cars to insure, no real concerns about health or diet, no waistline to worry about.

These are the responsibilities and challenges of everyday adult life, but as children we had none of them. On a typical day out in the street, the biggest challenge you might have to face was having to play Headers and Volleys with someone who couldn't chip the ball in the air properly. Or playing with someone who might insist on taking their ball in with them when it was time for their tea. 'Ah, come on, leave it here!'

Headers and Volleys is a familiar old street game, as are Wembley, Wembley Double, Cuppy and Kerby. All got plenty of mentions when I tweeted for clarification on what people out there call Wall-y or Spot. (I have to spell Wall-y like, that even though I appreciate it looks like the Pixar film *WALL•E*, but if I lose the hyphen we're left with Wally and no one wants to admit they spent most of their childhood playing a game with the same name as a Del Boy Trotter insult.) It only took this one question to prick the memories of hundreds of football fans. Answers included Slam, Donkey Slam, Donkey, Spot, Spot On, Wall-y, Wall Ball, 5 Alive, Five and Out, 5 Lives, Lives (each person had three), One Touch, One Touch Wall, One Touchy, Tappy Once, Bad Eggs, Bangers, Boggle, Rebounds, Bouncebacks, Squash, Soccer Squash, Hitty Affy (Scotland) and Names (Dublin). Alex Winters told me in Cardiff they called it Cooler and another tweeter spelt it Koola. We clearly all had different names for it, but everyone was playing it.

If you grew up in lush green meadows chewing grass stalks or tending sheep, or spent your schooldays on a desert island fantasizing about shipwrecked girls or up a tree pretending to be Tarzan, I'll explain what Wall-y is and then you'll see the link between this simple repetitive game and five-a-side.

Wall-y had a few basic rules that seem to have been roughly stuck to wherever it was played across this nation. A number of kids would take it in turns to boot the ball at a designated wall. The wall could be on a terrace end or perhaps in a schoolyard, a community centre or church hall, or garage doors. It didn't really matter so long as it had space in front of it for kids to congregate. More recently, in his pre-teen years, Marlais and I would play it against the metal goalposts on the playing field near where we spent ours weekends, awarding different points for posts, crossbar and net stanchion.

If you didn't manage to hit the wall with your one-touch shot you lost a life. If you lost three lives you were out. This would continue until it came down to two players and then one winner. The sharper the angle at which you managed to get the shot away, the more punishing the follow-up shot would be for the next shooter. If you got really close and could just skim the wall, there was a chance the ball would fly for miles and be impossible for the next player to return. The only way to deal with such a shot was to get right up against the wall at the other end of the house and hit it straight back at the wall as soon as it rebounded.

The rules dictated that you could only hit the ball once on your turn. What happened when you were out is where my regional Twitter feed-back diverged. Games in some areas involved a punishment section where kids would have the ball booted at them as they bent over against the wall. Others would just be booted up the arse and legs by the rest of the players. The other move you could make on your turn was to fire the ball at another player. If you hit them they were interfering with play and they'd lose a life.

Any amount of cunning could be used to get someone near enough the ball for you to boot it at them. Of course, they knew that and would approach it like a matador does a bull, trying to swerve out of the way. If they succeeded and you missed them the ball would fly off in a different direction from the wall and you'd be a life down. If you hit them they'd be a life down, not to mention rubbing wherever you'd hit them with the ball.

One tweeter, @cotardelli, reminded me that a really unlucky player could find his ball behind the goal and have to try 'a banana shot' round. This was certainly possible in our area, where the camber of the road would mean the ball fired at an acute angle to the wall could slowly roll back into the bottom of Back Headingley Avenue, the back road where people left their bins, bikes and washing.

The gutters could be a dead end as far as Wall-y went, because if they settled in there, even the ones opposite the wall, you'd have to scuff your shoe over the top of the ball to get it to bounce up with any momentum. The kerb prevented you from getting behind the ball, so it would be the scuff, a mad attempt at booting it from the side or even back off the kerb it was nestling against.

All of these Wall-y angles meant that we were constantly trying to assess angles and direction and weight of shots and passes, which is the closest some of us came to trigonometry and was a skill that would be vital later on if you were to prosper in five-a-side, particularly in using the gym walls for one-two passes back to yourself.

This game is still played, but in significantly reduced numbers. I've only seen one game in years and that, in a weird case of synchronicity, was while writing this chapter. I was going to collect my little boy from nursery and there were two twelve-year-old girls in the flats kicking a ball to each other, one more assured than the other, and then they started playing Wall-y off a tiny wall that supported an iron staircase, although the more talented player was hitting it with less spite than we used to use, when the aim was to make the next shot for the opposition as hard as possible.

Once the teatime lure of fish fingers, peas and chips had thinned the numbers and you were down to just three of you, Headers and Volleys was the perfect game. You'd have one kid against the wall in goal, one in the centre of the goal area looking to strike and one out on the wing ready to pass them in.

The winger would chip them in onto the preferred foot or head of the striker, who would invariably strike the ball just a few feet from the keeper, who had already curled into a protective ball to keep his face away from the volley.

Played right, with a good skill balance between the three players, this game could feature some of the greatest volleys never to be caught on camera. Headers weren't bad too, but usually involved waiting for a really light fly-away ball to hang in the air against the wind and then be headed back across the goal from the way it came.

The glory of a well-executed header or volley means this simple game, while no doubt flouting the below-head-height rule of five-a-side, could knit two players together into one assist-and-score unit. Both kids would be commentating, with scant regard for the likelihood of the line-up, 'Eddie Gray chips it in for Cruyff, who hammers it past Clemence!'

Johan Cruyff's influence on kids of the 1970s could regularly be seen and heard during games of Headers and Volleys. Although it was better to attempt flying volleys on grass or mud than over tarmac, kerb and paving stone.

Thankfully for the young stars of Headingley, we had plenty of grass five minutes up the road on our bikes at Beckett Park. Beckett Park is a lush green communal park with loads of trees young enough to make good goalposts and loads of space for as many different games as you wanted. If you could be arsed and there were enough of you, it was worth going up there for a 'big game'.

When Cruyff karate-kicked a goal for Barcelona against Atlético Madrid in the 73–74 season, he created a new way of attacking that allowed us kids to mix the martial arts moves of Bruce Lee with the ball-playing skills of our volleying heroes. Headers and Volleys Entered the Dragon.

Plenty of kids had attempted mad shots before, but Cruyff did so in a proper match and scored. It was a licence to ignore the foot-up rule and for a while you'd find yourself in attacks resembling martial arts street battles.

If you were in goal and saw the opposition winger tearing down the right wing to your left, you could bet your last bit of pocket money that when a ball came in at what used to be head height, you'd turn to see the flying foot-up stance of a Shaolin karate monk shouting, 'Haaaiii Karate!' after the TV advert for the fragrance of the same name. As far as I know, professional players didn't yell, 'Haaaiii Karate!' when going in to volley a ball home. It would be like Bruce Lee shouting, 'Maaan on!' while booting a ball for a football-orientated fragrance aimed at the Far East.

The underlying fault line that ran through the whole history of Headers and Volleys was that most people were better at heading and volleying than they were crossing, which meant that the attacker would invariably miss a bad cross and land on the keeper, like Peter Sellers's combative manservant Kato landing in an umbrella stand.

For every good cross you received, whether in the street or in the park, there would be three crosses that never achieved any height or ended up either behind the striker or too far in front of him to attack, so the keeper could just catch it or watch it sail by.

If you were half decent you could chip beautiful balls up endlessly for someone to keep slicing them so far wide they didn't even hit the wall and ended up in Kev Devers's backyard.

I'm not bad at crossing a ball now, but in the first years in the school team any corner I took would just fire along the ground into the first defender. I actually got a nice genuine round of applause from team-mate Gary Burton the first time I put a cross in high enough for him to head a goal.

At street or park level, though, with lighter balls, the crosses were headed and volleyed home (or not) all day long. To have crosser and striker in a state of mutual understanding is vital not only to this street game but also to a good five-a-side team. I frequently find myself thinking back to those days when the cross would fade and die before I could volley it, usually when a poor ball has just been intercepted by the opposition during a Wednesday night five-a-side game.

Pleasingly, Headers and Volleys – or Bonehead as tweeter Rich Reardon called it, or Lewy Gammy, as Sam P told me it was known in Wakefield – is a game still enjoyed by professionals. In 1996 I drove up to Sutton Coldfield for *loaded* to interview Aston Villa captain Andy Townsend, who was enjoying a period of success with club and adopted country, Ireland. As I waited for the boys in claret and blue to come in from the misty training ground, I found Townsend, Steve Staunton and Dean Saunders round the front of one of the changing rooms, covered in mud, enjoying a game of Headers and Volleys.

Saunders in particular was slamming in some great scissor kicks, acrobatic volleys and diving headers. He was like a performing seal jumping for fish. All three of them were having a great time and it was a pleasure to see that the completed cross level was nearer 90 per cent than the 25 per cent I'd been used to as a kid.

This was a glimpse of the great joy it must be to be a professional player: 'What do you do all week?' 'I play Headers and Volleys and then at the weekend we have a match.' Great life.

I was out one night with a chap called Chris Palmer when Headers and Volleys also came up in the conversation. Chris was the director of the 'If Carlsberg Did Pub Teams' advert. ICDPT is one of the greatest football-related adverts ever, and there are plenty to choose from. If it was fun to watch you can imagine what fun it was to make. If you've not seen it this is what happens: a bunch of real Three Lions legends Stuart Pearce, Jack and Bobby Charlton, Peter Reid, Bryan Robson, Des Walker, Shilts and more jump into a van to go and play a Sunday league fixture for a pub. Meanwhile Chrissy Waddle attempts to jump into the back of the van, which is forever being driven just that little bit forward; the laughter at this from inside the van is genuine. They overtake Peter Beardsley, who is cycling there on his drop-handle racer. There's something reassuringly satisfying about seeing these true greats in vintage England kit, even though, or perhaps because, they are from different generations.

In the dressing room Bobby Robson is giving the Three Lions a team talk when Stuart Pearce's phone goes off. I think this was ad-libbed by Pearce and Robson, as his phone did actually go off and interrupt filming, and Chris kept it in the final ad to give it that genuine sense of disbelief, camaraderie and fun.

In the commercial the lads run out to the shock of the opposition and win the game despite their age. Chris told me that after the filming wrapped most of the legends went off to get changed but he watched in awe as World Cup-winning dynamo Alan Ball and former European Player of the Year Chrissy Waddle took it in turns to chip balls in for Bobby Charlton to smash into the back of a net guarded by Peter Shilton. This impromptu game of Headers and Volleys from ex-pros who'd been pretending to be a pub team was a true reversal of normal behaviour.

Back in the streets of Leeds 6 – as everywhere else across the nation – we didn't have to dream of playing at Wembley. All you needed to play the game Wembley was a handful of your mates. Wembley was the street version of the FA Cup. It involved one goalkeeper and every other man for himself, tasked to score a goal to qualify for the next round, and the last man not to score was out. This went on until it was a two-man final and the winner was rewarded by going in goal. Which to me never seemed like much of a reward. If there were too many kids you'd pair up for Wembley Doubles. This involved the same rules but featured loads of teams of two scrabbling around to get the ball and score.

The dominant players would immediately chase after the ball and find themselves at the centre of endless tackles, while the clever players were goal hanging waiting for the weak shot or loose ball to come their way so they could just beat the keeper close in. While everyone else was standing round with their hands on their thighs and their heads hanging down, knackered from the massively lengthy tackling session.

Wembley Doubles is the closest street game comparison to my Wednesday night game, which is often overcrowded, with players diving in left, right and centre, holding on to the ball too long and then looking up in disbelief when they lose it to the opposition.

In a game of Wembley the kerb would be the last line of defence and the goalie wouldn't really care who scored. He wasn't on anyone's team and the sooner it was over the sooner he could play out again. Wembley Doubles allowed for one-twos, good communication and joint celebrations, all aspects of a decent five-a-side game. The only difference being that after a goal in five-a-side you don't go and sit on a small wall with your mate, swig Vimto from a can and then try and spell out your initials on the floor with spit dangling from your gob.

There is one other major similarity between five-a-side and kids' street football that I haven't mentioned yet and that is the two unavoidable obstacles that absolutely stop play. In a polished-floor gym it is the cricket nets bunched up to the side of your pitch which catch above-head-high balls in a web of folded rigging. On the street it is the ball going beneath parked cars. In both cases, because you can actually see the ball, it seems to suspend any other basic intelligence around it.

In the cricket nets, usually held together by a large cotton bag chained to the wall above head height, the ball will fly in one direction and just hang there while players all gather to try and pull it out from another direction with seemingly no understanding of how nets work. It's the same thought process that allows fish to be caught and then struggle until caught fast. It can take ages until someone comes along and jumps and punches the ball back out the way it went in.

The ball under the car was equally frustrating. I spent half my childhood lying next to parked cars, swinging my legs under the chassis to try and boot a plastic ball back out the way it went in. Often while someone was on the other side, trying to drag it out by their hands but prevented from doing so by the height of the kerb. To clear a ball from under the middle section of the car you had to lie behind the wheel and aim a swinging kick at where you thought the ball was to release it.

This could take up minutes of vital playing time, while everyone waited with baited breath for the resumption of play. It felt great when the ball started to give and eventually burst out from under the car and shot back into action. Then it was a mad scramble to return to the fray. There was always the thought at the back of your mind, as you lay prone halfway under a car, with your upper body and head in the middle of the street, that another car would come along and squash you, but miraculously one never did. Nowadays we play street football in gyms and purpose-built centres and pitches, where no one has yet thought to drop in a car as a nostalgic obstacle. Sadly.

The Never-ending Search for Socks

Big fans of poor preparation won't be disappointed by this chapter. Given how much time we amateur footballers spend playing and talking about football, in particular recounting in detail great goals we've scored, it's a surprise that more of us don't approach it with at least some semblance of semi-professional preparation. I certainly don't. My preparation takes about twenty minutes and that includes travelling time.

If you'd asked me a few months ago if I had a regular pre-match preparation ritual I would have replied, 'No.' However, while thinking about it for the book I now realize I do. It's just not a very good one. In fact it's a recurring cul-de-sac of frustration.

Many of us wear pro kits, pro boots, pro shin pads, pro goalkeeping gloves and we drink protein shakes, but there are many of us who also show up and change seconds before kick-off. Later even. This attitude is so British that Eric Cantona sees it as a national trait and believes the English national team shouldn't do any proper prep for international tournaments at all. Speaking to the *Guardian* before Euro 2016 he said England should just show up before kick-off like the Danes did for the Euros in 1992. He's obviously been tracking my style of warm-up.

I think I've only ever once deliberately set out to affect my mood pre-match. A big believer in the influence of music, I once tried a Stuart Pearce-style playlist of Ramones for the drive over to Kentish Town on a Sunday morning, but, despite sounding great, it had no impact on my performance whatsoever and I realized, after a lacklustre game, that better sleep and a good breakfast would have been better than just singing along to 'Blitzkrieg Bop'. 'Sheena Is a Punk Rocker', not a fitness coach.

I have not pursued a wilfully ignorant path to preparation. I used to have a column in the men's fitness bible, *Men's Health* magazine, which was a gold mine of warm-up information: graphs, charts, lists, numbers and diagrams all designed to get the best out of you. There were hundreds of pages of the stuff that appeared eleven times a year. *Men's Health* is a very engaging read, especially if you have little desire to do any hard training and are on the lookout for short cuts.

All the helpful articles were in the rest of the magazine, not my column, which was mainly about my uncanny reluctance to train properly and my subsequent inability to get fit. It really was a true commitment to laziness.

Every month I would manage to avoid focusing on improving my health, preferring to document such abstract tangents as the music Fred Kindle played at his gym or why it was good for your mental well-being to keep in touch with old friends. One time I just submitted a Gratitude List.

Apart from the Haribo – yes, Haribo. I once read in *Men's Health* that the England Rugby Union team ate loads of sweets just before they went out for a match. I managed to remember and incorporate this bit, funnily enough. It wasn't the only evidence I uncovered that sweets might actually be good for an aspiring athlete.

One time when Leeds played away at Yeovil I went and stood by our dugout after the game to watch manager Gary McAllister do his post-match interview. Never mind the media call, I couldn't believe what I was looking at in and around the dugout, where the subs and trainers had been sitting. It looked like the back of a school bus. There were loads of empty sweet wrappers and drinks bottles glinting in the glare of the TV crew's portable light, like someone had tipped a bin out.

I was so stunned I missed Gary Mac's interview while I checked the discarded wrappers to see if there were any Starmix left.

Another time, with Leeds away at Leyton Orient, I was in the dressing room just before kick-off and was shocked to see the massage table was a brightly coloured picnic of Gummy Bears. If they hadn't stunk of Ralgex I'd have probably grabbed a few.

This sweets secret was a total revelation and the opposite of everything you're told as a kid. I looked all over that dressing room, behind Robert Snodgrass, between Fabian Delph and Andy Robinson, and nowhere could I see a player's mum shouting, 'Don't eat all those sweets! You'll make yourself sick.' It felt like I'd rumbled a great parental lie. So for many years that was basically my pre-match or pre-training meal: Haribo.

In contrast to the meticulous approach professional players go through in the twenty-four-hour pre-match build-up – staying in hotels, having a group walk, a light meal, a nap, stretching, tactical reminders – nowadays my own preparations start about twenty-three minutes before kick-off. This also has to include travelling time to various pitches up to twenty minutes away.

My pre-match routine or warm-up usually begins with my girlfriend, Lisa, trying to get me to leave the house. 'Aren't you going to play football?' she asks, desperately hoping I will leave as promised, so she can spend more time without me. To which I reply, 'Yes, I'm just looking for my boots,' even though I am clearly looking at something funny or pointless on Twitter.

Saying this does, however, prompt me to get my boots. They're in a cupboard in the downstairs toilet, next to boxing gloves, tools and a big knot of audio-visual extension cords and wires. My boots are pimple-soled adidas ones that are so old and cracked the pimples are wearing away underneath. The design style name has rubbed off. They're probably named after someone who cheated Leeds out of the European Cup in 1975.

As I pull them down, a load of sand or tiny black rubber pellets fall out of them, an indicator of where I last played. Given it was probably within the last ninety-six hours I don't need a reminder, but that's what this gritty shower of boot droppings serves as and I instinctively think about the pains in my body and wince a bit.

I make sure the insoles that support my fucked-up arches are inside the boots and haven't been transferred to some other trainers, then chuck them on the hall floor by the bottom of the stairs. The boots look good cast down like that, one facing up the right way, the other tilted over on its side. Beaten up, lived in. The architect and executioner of many a great goal and many a shot from distance that's missed the crossbar by miles.

I then make my way up a floor, to where my clothes are kept in the entrance between the bathroom and our bedroom. This is not so much a walk-in wardrobe as a corridor of uncertainty, spewing out sweat-shirts and trackie bottoms from drawers.

Before I get there I remember glimpsing a bit of the yellow inner lining of my best black adidas shorts in the washing pile earlier in the day, so I stop off and go into the laundry room and search through the towels, sheets, baby clothes, school uniforms and tangle of single socks that sit on top of the washing machine and dryer.

I find the shorts and drag them out by the yellow-netted lining. I then glimpse some six-year-old ironed knee-length cotton Aubin & Wills casual shorts looking all smart and inviting. There's a grey pair and a blue pair. I wonder very briefly whether they will make me play any better. The grey ones are tatty around the elastic waistband, the blue ones are smarter because I had the waistband sewn back in so they'd last another summer. They sit ironed in a small pile of my clothes, the pile itself beneath a pile of sheets fresh out of the tumble dryer. Disorder on top of order.

For a moment I weigh up the suitability of each pair of shorts for the weather. It's rare that all three are there at the same time, so I often just go with whatever I find first. I play football two, three, sometimes four times a week and every time I'm confronted by the confusion of looking for missing kit and trying to find stuff that is clean or fits me. I fleetingly wonder if it's true that some blokes' better halves sort their kit for them.

In my mind the Aubin & Wills cotton knee-length shorts make me look relaxed, like those Adrian Boot pictures of Bob Marley which always made him look relaxed, no matter how intensely he was playing. I like to look like I don't take the game too seriously and have just walked in from the park for a kick around, but maybe that's a flashback to childhood. In reality they probably make me look complacent and stumpy. They do, however, have big pockets and they're made of cotton, which means if I'm playing outdoors and it's raining I can wipe my glasses on them before giving up and stuffing them into said pockets. They also mean I can carry my inhaler, my subs and my house keys to the game, which means I don't have to take a sweatshirt or jacket with a pocket or a bag.

These are the pointless dilemmas rolling through my mind with just minutes to go before kick-off and a world away from the warm-up of professional footballers. Outside someone is waiting patiently in their car, wishing they'd never offered to give me a lift.

I know where this idea the casual kit will improve my performance came from. One time I was playing the Wednesday night game in the gym on Falkirk Street, Hoxton, and there were so many players we'd divided into multiple teams of five and had some sort of knockout. Rare in itself to adopt an interesting formula, but my team had been knocked out with twenty-five minutes to go so I'd got changed and was watching in my jeans and some old paint-splattered red leather adidas trainers when a player was injured. I agreed to step in and had a total blinder. To this day I can only assume it was the attire, the jeans and trainers. I was a one-man equivalent of Denmark being called off their holiday beaches to replace Yugoslavia in the 1992 European Championships and winning it. But anyway I'll park that flashback, as I know you're keen to hear more about me being almost naked in the laundry room.

When I finally just go for the adidas nylon shorts, I realize this shorts deliberation has taken a good couple of minutes and it's now less than twenty minutes to kick-off and, if they're really unlucky, someone is still downstairs waiting to give me a lift. I change into these shorts on the stairs and leave my normal clothes on the floor somewhere between the laundry room and the bedroom. Then I imagine my girlfriend carrying the baby down unsighted and tripping over them, so I ball them up and throw them into the bedroom. Their landing place will of course annoy her later, despite the move essentially coming from a caring place. How often are we castigated for doing something sensible and loving because it contravenes some other basic household expectation?

Anyway, a professional footballer would now be thinking about the game immediately ahead and might even be looking into the eyes of the opposition in the tunnel, not thinking about child safety in the home.

I then look at my naked feet and my boots and go back into the laundry room to see if there are any socks. As usual, there is one nylon football sock that I have no affiliation with. When I was a kid I would have an affiliation with my football socks, because they would be white for Leeds, end of story. It disappoints me now that I don't have a better relationship with my football socks. That I don't in fact have better football socks. The situation is this: I can't find good ones, as there are few decent sports shops around any more where the owner cares about his stock, so I buy cheap ones, and after I buy them they disappear into my eldest son's bedroom.

I bought the latest white pair at my local Sports Direct. They're as big as they've got, but they soon shrink down so they're pretty tight for my legs and way too tight for shin pads. I then wonder if I'm wearing my fifteen-year-old son's socks, but then remember that actually we are probably now the same size.

Like everyone ever confronted by the sock pile, I wonder where the other one is. If you think you're crap at staying in relationships don't worry, socks split up quicker.

I look at what's available and wonder whether I should just forget the football socks and go for some ankle tennis socks or trainer socks. Whichever I choose, I slump against a wall, awkwardly lift my legs and pull them on. It is now about eighteen minutes to kick-off. If it's Mikey waiting to give me a lift, he's by now shouting, 'C'mon, Jimbo!' He works at a leading sportswear company, so he can choose a new kit every day from the office.

Shirt selection has some degree of preordained boundary, because we must bring both a colour and a white. All my shirts are too tight. I ignore my stomach wok and look accusingly at the washing room. The best I have to offer are simple white T-shirts and a plain Gap blue one. If it's freezing I might stretch to a long-sleeve red nylon shirt I had in a works team years ago or a thick yellow cotton Leeds shirt from TOFFS I was given last century. Again I tell myself to buy some new kit. A shirt at least.

If you want to know how anyone should arrange their clothes watch Chas the Gangster (played by James Fox) get dressed near the start of the great bohemian crime film *Performance*. His drawers are perfectly arranged. When we moved into this new house I designated a whole drawer for my kit. At first this hopeful attempt at organization was fine, but within four months it was an assortment of trackie bottoms and tops, odd sports socks, T-shirts, old polo shirts, swimming trunks, snoods, bandages, headbands and more. As it faithfully reflected anything I'd wear to play, it quickly became a huge holding bay for pretty much everything but smart shirts, jeans, cashmere jumpers, coats and suits.

I put the coloured T-shirt over the white, grab a sweatshirt or track-suit top and go downstairs to stick my boots or some trainers on. If it's wet I'll put my boots on at the game – I know from recent experience that portly middle-aged men, slimy sloping pavements and pimply studded AstroTurf boots don't mix well. In fact you slip quick and are left lying on the floor helpless, the first glimpse of the vulnerability of old age. And no one helps you up. You lie there for a minute, hoping to be rescued, hobble through the park to the pitch, stupidly play with an injury and subsequently can't walk properly for two weeks. That's why I don't wear my boots to the game if it's raining. Safety first.

That's a very detailed breakdown of how clothes impact on my warm-up. The second major factor is food and despite my previous comments about sweets I do actually have good information here. For those of you who have misguidedly received this book from a friend who thinks it will help you with your game, there is one of maybe just four genuine tips coming up, so pay attention.

Beetroot. Disclaimer: I wrote this before the *Daily Mail* revealed that Leicester City were on the beetroot shots when they won the Premier League last season. Anyone who has read *The Secret Race*, Tyler Hamilton and Daniel Coyle's book about the Tour de France doping scene, will understand how important your blood is to your sporting perform-ance and why Lance Armstrong and co. were having illicit blood transfusions. It had such a big impact on the cyclists I actually decided I'd quite like to have a go at it, get the PCP, the lot, but without the uphill cycling obviously.

So you can imagine how my interest was piqued when, shortly after I had read this book, I saw in *The Week* magazine that scientists believe drinking raw beetroot juice is the natural equivalent of blood doping. The short article went on to say it would give you a 16 per cent uplift in energy and performance. Bearing in mind that I didn't have the contacts or resources to set up a complicated Armstrong-style secret blood-doping system in Kentish Town, I leapt on this stat with some enthusiasm.

I went to the local greengrocers and bought a big bunch of organic beetroot with their coats still muddy and their stems held together with an elastic band. I hadn't seen many healthy, natural-looking vegetables since reading a book at primary school about a giant turnip. I stuck them in the juicer, mixed them up with assorted fruit we had in the fridge and drank the frothy red brew like a vampire.

I did this a couple of hours before my Tuesday night game and genuinely felt the difference. After two weeks of it people were commenting about my good form. My running was better, my shooting more controlled; it felt like someone had just switched my performance up a level. Believe me, believe the scientists, drink it a couple of hours before you play. It works. You look like you're pissing blood later and you have to remember to wipe your mouth properly, and definitely get fruit to mix it with and don't used boiled beetroot, but you'll thank me for this genuine bit of warm-up advice.

With clothes on, beetroot juice drunk, subs and inhaler picked up, I then head to the door and open it. Much to the relief of whoever is giving me a lift. By now they're asleep in their car or settled down in my living room, talking to whoever else is in there. Then just as they scramble to finally get going, I drop whatever I have in my hands and go and start rooting around under the sink, looking for any type of used mineral water or fruit juice bottle. I fill this up from the tap and at last I am ready to go.

Then I remember my football glasses. At this point Lisa is saying, 'I'm sorry about this, Mikey/Gary, but he's impossible to get out of the house, always coming back to check things. We have to factor in extra time for him to enter and exit the house four or five times when we leave to go on holiday.'

They don't look surprised. I get the glasses I use to play football in. They're an old 'normal pair' with a drawstring on the back. And with that we're off to the Sunday morning eight-a-side game.

My understanding of an actual physical pre-match warm-up is this: 'Just do what you're going to do in the game.'

North Sea Ferry Rockabilly Schoolboy Incident: The Joys of Playing Away

One of the strengths of weekly five-a-side is that you never have an away fixture. You never really have to wonder how you'll get to the next match, what the parking is like or how you'll get the team down there.

The location, like a lot of the players I play with, doesn't move. This is what makes it a weekly pillar of life. It removes any confusion or suspicion. You arrive at the gym knowing the toilets have been flooded and the locks broken again. You get the regular nod from the bloke on reception. You sit in the same place to get changed. You borrow the same bloke's shower gel after the game. It fits perfectly into your weekly schedule. It's relatively near to where you live or work, it only takes an hour to play and for a few of the keener players it can actually be labelled exercise.

It's all regular, regular, regular. It's part of what makes it good. It does, however, rob you of the chance to undertake the away trip. Away days are a key part of all football-playing folklore and they are something you hope to get yourself on throughout your playing lifetime.

At school, away games involved either taking a minibus round the corner to St Michael's, Foxwood or Cardinal Heenan schools or getting on a massive old coach early on a Saturday morning at Lawnswood roundabout and driving west towards the Pennines.

It's hard to believe that the old Wallace Arnold coaches managed to get to places like Batley Grammar or Brighouse, but they did and they never spilled over the cliff like the one in *The Italian Job*. If you've not been up into the hills towards Lancashire you'll have to just use *Last of the Summer Wine* as a visual guide, only without the predictable pensioner in the tatty woollen hat bobsleighing in a pram. All there seemed to be on these Saturday morning adventures were hills, hills and more hills.

They had a different approach to pitch preparation from down in the sophisticated lowlands around Leeds. One team we played had cow shit all over the pitch, and they were still moving the cow off as we ran out. Another had solid blocks of iced snow the size of Second World War defensive pillboxes rolled just clear of the touchline. They'd reward us for showing up with post-match tea and biscuits. We'd thank them in return by pouring the tea through the holes where an inkwell should have been into the books in the desks below. At our school no one in their right mind would have left their books in a desk. They'd have returned to find them covered in ballpoint friezes of swastikas, stick fighter jets spitting fire, LUFC smiley logos, sexual gossip, shark fins and cocks.

Saturday mornings was just a long round coach trip with kids fucking about on the way there and throwing bags at each other on the way back. With a football match in freezing or windy conditions in between. You don't get any of this at the cushy floodlit Powerleague.

Strangely, we were allowed to behave on that coach in all the ways we weren't allowed to behave in class: shouting, throwing kit around, swearing. Especially if we'd won. It was probably the closest many of us came to the lifestyle of professional footballers.

Something that quickly became apparent when I started meeting and getting to know professional footballers during my *loaded* years is that they basically have a four-hour PE lesson every day, get the afternoon off and then have a school trip every other week.

These Lawnswood School away games weren't too different from what I know of when Alan Shearer, David Batty, Jason Wilcox and Mike Newell arrived at newly rich Blackburn Rovers to play for Kenny Dalglish in the early 1990s. When I did interviews with David Batty for his autobiography, the stories about his time at Jack Walker's Blackburn Rovers were great. From the moment Kenny Dalglish signed internationals from bigger clubs, the Blackburn Rovers story began to feel like an episode of *Dallas* set in 1970s *Corrie*. It is possibly the closest a professional team who won the league has come to replicating the lives of us less gifted amateurs.

When Batty and Shearer arrived at Blackburn the match-day dressing rooms were Portakabins and the training pitch was the lawn of a crematorium where players would bet each other to see who could hit a passing hearse. Travelling to away fixtures, the team, who would go on to win the Premier League, were fed old-fashioned pies, which they'd scoop the 'meat' out of and turn into mud bombs and throw down the coach at the driver.

On one occasion they gaffer-taped the same pie-splattered driver into his seat while driving and on another they took it in turns to hit the back-seat emergency-door window with the little steel escape hammer until it smashed.

Basically, the worst school trip behaviour imaginable. What a life. If I tried smashing my mate Gary's rear window in with a hammer on the way to Kentish Town on a Sunday morning he'd throw me out of the car or report me to the innuendo police.

The finale of Blackburn's English away trips involved attacking the locked Travel Tavern bedroom of a much-maligned teammate with fire extinguishers squirted under the door, through the keyhole and down through the asphalt roof one of them had climbed onto and kicked a hole in.

Once they were together again in Europe, at Newcastle, Shearer and

Batty amused themselves by gluing together Rob Lee's designer wash-bag and all its contents. In Monaco Batty's agent, Hayden Evans, was chatting to him in the hotel bar when he kept getting distracted by glints of lights flashing outside behind him. When he asked what they were, Batts replied, 'Oh, that's just Al, he's throwing ashtrays into the sea.'

If I'd taken the names out of this anecdote you'd just think it was a load of unruly amateurs from a Sunday league team. Which is exactly what they are, only they're better at football than the rest of us, they get paid better and they get more free Haribo than you can imagine. The spawny bastards. Never mind the WAGs, mansions and cars, what about the endless supply of pre-match Starmix?

Such stories are, of course, equally rife among us amateurs, but the Powerleague generation won't have experienced them.

A photographer I worked with on the *NME* and *loaded*, Derek Ridgers, told me about a team he played for that went on an exchange visit to another amateur club in Europe. It was suggested that each player buy a gift for their hosts. At Victoria Station all the chaps were ready with their kit bags and gifts, waiting for their last team member, who arrived just in time for the departure. Derek said the bloke only had the T-shirt, jeans and pumps he was stood up in, a six-pack of lager in one hand and a hammer in the other.

When I asked Derek what they were for, he replied, 'Well, he said the hammer was the only thing he could lay his hands on for a gift and he'd bought the six-pack for the journey over there. There was a slight delay in departure and before we'd even got to Clapham he'd drunk them all and was pulling himself up and down the carriage underneath the old-fashioned seats they had then. When we asked him where his kit was, he said he planned to borrow shorts and would play in his pumps.'

This story still makes me laugh today, twenty odd years after he first told me it.

The nearest I've come to an away trip like Blackburn storming the Premier League or Derek's hammer man was on a school football trip to Holland and Belgium when I was thirteen.

The football trip to Holland and Belgium was announced to the school football teams and then opened up to the rest of the school. The squad who signed up to go included a lovable six-foot rockabilly from the fifth form called Cos and a tubby lad called Terry, who had previously shown no sporting interest at all and presumably wanted to broaden his horizons. He was immediately given the green jumper and some gloves. The only sixth-formers who actually played in the first XI were a lanky giraffe of a bloke and his tiny mate, who was adept at overhead flicks. They were both good players and it must have really pissed them off that every week they'd be playing against blokes their own age with a team made up of kids from the years below.

From the younger years there were a few good players, including my mate Cathal Dolan and a tousle-haired Gypsy looking kid called Rocky O'Rourke. Rather than have one good team and one made up of lefto-vers, the PE department split us into two teams of mixed ability to play in the tournaments. To give us some sort of civic pride, a teacher called Mr Earnshaw, who had connections at Elland Road, managed to get us some real Leeds United kit to wear on the condition they all came back.

Before we'd even got to Holland Cos, the rockabilly, had managed to get served at the bar and was the worse for wear, doing Elvis impres-sions with the little guy, Simon, from the sixth form. Cos's height was clearly a factor in getting served, but so was his attire. He was sixteen but looked much older in his brothel creepers and drape. I don't think the staff of North Sea Ferries had seen a teenage Teddy boy; maybe

Matchbox's 'Rockabilly Rebel' hadn't made it to Hull yet. I imagine they assumed all Teds were in their fifties and Cos just had really good skin for a Bill Haley fan. So they thought nothing of serving him whatever he paid for. Which appeared to be quite a lot.

As would become apparent on the trip, any time Cos had a few drinks he'd decide to hang from something dangerous, and he started with the biggest stunt possible. While three of us thirteen-year-olds looked on in amazement, he set about preparing for his 'death duff'. He double-knotted his Leeds United scarf to his wrist, as was the fashion of the day, and then tied it to the top bar of the ship's railings, which prevented normal people from falling overboard. Then he just climbed over and hung above the North Sea by his hands.

He must have had an extra strong grip, or maybe there was a hidden ledge he was standing on, but he was definitely sea-side of where he should have been and battling with gravity when the rugby teacher, Mr Davey, arrived, shouting, 'Costello, get back on the boat. Now!' That's not something you expect to hear halfway across the North Sea at night. And certainly not between a rugby player and a Teddy boy.

Cos's insane nautical stunt in the freezing dark sea air set his own tone for the whole trip. Every night in the pension we were staying in he'd have a few beers and then insist on hanging off the balcony at the top of the stairs. This was fine for a couple of nights and then, like some bored psychopathic magician, he started asking for volunteers to join him. He wasn't a bully, so there was no threat involved; he was just very good at talking all the younger kids into trying it. 'Don't worry. I'll grab you when your hands start slipping,' he'd reassure you.

There was no way out. Everyone had to have a go at hanging off a balcony with a steep staircase fifteen feet below. On a football trip. Had it gone wrong we could have had the whole squad on the injury list with sprained ankles and Chinese burns. It wasn't about who could dangle longest, although that was favourably rated; it was about finding someone who was too scared to do it. No one was, because Cos had raised the bar so high on the way over. As far as we were concerned, at least there weren't huge waves or ship propellers below, and Cos was as good as his word in overseeing each display of dangling with care and attention.

The first night in Belgium saw scenes I'll never forget. There was some sort of beer festival going on in the town and there were stalls with long packets of sweets, massive pretzels, hotdogs, that sort of thing. Mainly they were selling beer, though. Loads of grown men were walking round in drag, with wigs, flowery dresses and outsized bras, clutching huge glasses of frothy beer. It soon became apparent these stalls in the marketplace would serve anyone and, with a week's pocket money on them, all the boys got stuck into the beer regardless of whether they'd ever drunk before.

I don't know why I didn't join in: maybe I could sense what lay ahead, maybe I just didn't like the taste of beer. To this day, thirty-five years on, I've never had a pint. Later in life I just couldn't see the point in drinking something that would take so long to get you drunk when stronger drinks were available. This wasn't the case for our school party, though.

With clusters of teenage footballers from Leeds necking cheap, powerful Belgian ale, you can probably predict what was going to happen next. There were kids puking all over the streets and others just buying more and more drink for everyone. Back at the hotel we climbed up the stairs, negotiated a route round Costello's brothel creepers, which were dangling along with the rest of him from the top-landing banister, and piled into our beds.

Our room had three sets of bunk beds and a double bed in front of the large bay window, which was full of light from the fair outside. All night kids were moaning, rolling around in their beds, shouting in drunken sleep-addled delusion. Then those of us who were awake and laughing at it all saw the guy in the double bed kneel up in his sleep, piss through his pants into his pillow, then sink back down into it and fall back asleep.

In the morning there were ructions everywhere. One bloke woke up in the wardrobe after finding he'd pissed his own bed. He wasn't the only one. Everyone who had drunk had pissed themselves. Rocky O'Rourke accused Cathal of pissing his own upper-bunk mattress and then swapping it with Rocky's mattress in the bunk below while Rocky was asleep. When everyone pointed out how ridiculous this allegation was, as Cathal's mattress was pissed in too, Rock insisted Cathal must have pissed through his own bed and down onto Rocky's.

Worse was to come. On waking, the gifted fourth-year midfielder who'd pissed through his own pants and into his pillow discovered he'd actually shat them too.

We then all watched as he hoisted his shit-encrusted pants into the morning light of the bay window to show the results like a triumphant scientist. He pulled his suitcase from under the bed, assuring everyone he'd just get a fresh pair and chuck the soiled ones away. His suitcase looked like it was his mum and dad's: it had proper locks on it and everything. He tried to flip the latches open only to find them locked. Pulling his shitty pants back on, he started looking for his jeans, which were all twisted up and strangled on the floor. He checked his pockets, looked around the floor and asked, 'Has anyone see a small gold key?'

No one had. It was probably out in the street under a hardening patch of vomit. He gradually took on a look of dismal acceptance. He was faced with having to wear his own horrific pissed-up, shitted-up underpants all week, or at least down to breakfast until the teachers could jemmy his case open. Which, as far as I remember, they were reluctant to do as the case looked so expensive.

Breakfast itself turned out to be lunch because we'd all slept in too late and was actually a big chunk of silver eel, not a bowl of Frosties in sight. You can imagine how many of them were left on the plate.

Anyway, that shitted-up underpants kid is secretary of a prestigious Leeds golf club now and I know there'll be plenty of members who know him if I name him, so I'll spare him that. Wearing those caked pants thirty-five years ago in that hot weather must have been punishment enough and might still weigh heavy on his memory. Could well be the reason why he chose a career outdoors with handy access to facilities, fresh air and showers.

As you can see, so far this trip has had nothing to do with football. That's because I can remember less of the on-field action and loads of the off. I remember breaking our goalie Terry's finger in the warm-up, challenging for a ball he was collecting. I can remember training on a beach. And I can remember the Dutch using rolling subs. That's almost it, except for the Big Bet.

The other teams were proving to be very good, but the younger of our two teams fancied our chances and Rocky O'Rourke and I had a cash bet on who could score most goals. I went into the game thinking it was a pretty fair match between us, even though he was a year older than me. Then we kicked off and he refused to pass to me at any moment, even when I was totally unmarked and free to shoot and he had two defenders on him. When I screamed for the ball, he shouted back, without looking up, from behind a scrum of Dutch players, 'No chance. I'm not losing that bet.'

Even other players on our team were yelling for him to play the ball, but he seemed to think the best way to score was just holding on to the ball until he could work his way through the opposition. As a strategy it was madness. Eventually the teachers wondered what the hell was going on, someone told them and they yelled at Rocky to start passing. 'No chance, sir!' came the reply as he shielded himself and the ball by the corner flag. If the ref hadn't blown up for a corner, he'd probably still be huddled like that now, with members of both teams hurling themselves in to get the ball off him. In the end we both scored the same number of goals, so nobody won the bet anyway.

The trip wasn't without its cultural highlights, which involved looking at a load of old lace shops in a big square in Bruges and Rocky and I pressing the stop buttons on the escalators in the Atomium. Crossing the border into Holland, we watched one of the PE teachers go into a sex shop and buy a see-through negligee for his wife. At least we assumed it was for his wife. The trip ended back at home with a major crime investigation into a missing Leeds United kit, which turned out to be in the coach driver's bag. He probably thought he deserved it for having to drive back up the M62 and then the M1 with a six-foot-tall Teddy boy dangling off the back of the coach. Danger money.

Comprehensive Years

No five-a-side back story is complete without the influence of school: PE teachers, teammates, legends, nutters, bad kit and muddy games. By the time I went to secondary school in the late 1970s, long-haired sixth-formers outnumbered punks. Older kids could occasionally be seen walking round with a Led Zep album or *Never Mind the Bollocks* under their arm, but down in the ranks of the third-years, which was the year we started in Leeds after middle school, mass tribalism broke out.

A full-on mod revival, with loads of kids in parkas and Harringtons, exploded around the Jam, Secret Affair, The Chords, The Who and *Quadrophenia*. The mods were at odds with both the rockabillies, who loved Matchbox, Eddie Cochran and The Polecats, and rockers, who liked Steppenwolf, Hawkwind, Zeppelin and Sabbath. Then there was 2 Tone, which music- and fashion-wise was the perfect scene for schoolkids. The Specials, The Beat, The Selector, Madness and The Bodysnatchers all looked like they were wearing school uniform, none of them looked much older than us, and none of them looked like they'd come from outer space. Skinheads mutated into casuals, with school trousers replaced by Ronnie Corbett chic: chunky burgundy cords, Pringle jumpers, Kicker boots and flick-heads.

There were great-looking black girls who loved Bob Marley, new metal kids into UFO and Iron Maiden, with patches on their brand-new denim jackets, and the punk son of a science teacher who would eat his own vomit for cash. If you were lucky a fit girl would write your name on her bag, and if you weren't a really mad lass would scratch your initials and hers inside a love heart into an old wooden desktop with a compass point. Spelt wrong.

It was a world of football, fights, snogging, petty vandalism, detentions, distractable teachers, reports, school discos, teachers who'd give you the ruler, daily tedium, Winston Smith, *Macbeth* and that long wait for each lesson to end.

As a sign of the times, only four people in the sixth form were doing a new lesson called computer studies, more people were taking Urdu, and Michael Lawrence was yelled at by our infamous PE teacher, Mr McCreadie, for showing up for football practice in a Hitachi-sponsored Liverpool shirt. The first sponsored shirt in English football.

'Get that shirt off, Lawrence,' bellowed the Fulton Mackay lookalike. No reason was given. But the implication was it was new, crass and wrong.

I can remember clearly the exhilaration of my first football trials, aged thirteen. About forty kids showed up on the sloping pitch that ran down the slight hill parallel to the Otley Road, away from the sixth-form block and the prefab maths blocks. We kicked off at twenty-a-side and the three sports teachers wandered round, asking kids who could play their names and class numbers and telling others who couldn't to drop out. It was pretty brutal. By the end it was eleven-a-side and about fifteen of us had had our names taken.

The sense of excitement when Mr Davey wandered over in my direction and asked for my name and class was immense. Writing this is the first time I've thought about it in decades, but that thrill is still there. Aged thirteen, playing football was everything. Somewhere else a trumpet player was probably feeling the same about getting selected for the school band. Probably Baz Taylor, who quickly used his proficiency on the instrument to knock off school in December and go busking carols at Holt Park shopping centre.

But fuck them, leave them to their cacophony of noise, I was thirteen years old and bombing around a really massive muddy field next to the Otley Road and I was going to be in the school team.

Across the pitch other guys were getting picked. There was one with bright red hair –Storer – I stayed friends with him for life. On the opposite wing to me was a streak of greased lightning called Streakin Ian Deakin.

At the back was Michael 'Winnie' Winterburn, from Beckett Park. Everyone figured he was cock of the year, either him or Craig Howes, and both of them were already playing rugby against grown men. Up front was a tall skinhead called Stuart Walker, who lived a few streets away from me. In the first year Stuart and I would get over twenty goals between us. Primarily because the star of our team, Mick Whaley in goal, could boot it three-quarters of the length of the full-sized pitch, where Walker would nod it down to me and I'd pass it back through their defence for him to stride on to and hammer home.

Whaley was a proper schoolboy legend and the only player in our team to turn pro – with Lincoln and then Peterborough. He played for Leeds in his age group all the way through, only to be released a couple of years after he left school. I'm not sure how good a judge of a keeper they were at Leeds United at the time. As I was going into the fifth form they released a young keeper and Leeds fan by the name of David Seaman.

All the Leeds City Boys – as the LUFC youth academy was called then – worked as ballboys, but Mick did it for an England game. To this day he is still the best keeper I ever played with. Having him in the nets meant we played with total confidence. He genuinely was another line of defence.

He had a big upper body and he liked the odd cig, but he was an absolutely brilliant keeper. Most people playing five-a-side would use that description for a quick-reaction shot-stopper, but at thirteen on full-sized pitches Mick already had so much more. When the opposition went past our defence you knew Whaley would either take the ball off them or stop them scoring.

Think about how nervous you are when a striker goes through one on one against the keeper of the team you support. We didn't feel that; we knew there was more chance Whaley would save it than the striker would score. He would come charging out, arms spread wide, weaving his body and legs from side to side, accelerating like someone sprinting through a game of British bulldogs, and while the striker wondered what the hell was coming at him – most school goalies would just be stood still, hoping the ball hit them – Mick would swoop in and take the ball from the striker's feet with his hands. He'd keep running and roll it out to one of our fullbacks, Ashley or Geoff. If he did have to take a shot in the air he'd actually pause to let the ball get away from him so the stretched dive and resulting catch or tip-over would look even better. If the shot was low down to his left or right he'd just bat it away with his hands. For a fairly bulky bloke he could spring through the air quite magnificently, taking balls from crosses and then putting his foot through them to release us attackers to go off and score. Like his namesake, Whaley would breach the choppy waters of a packed goal-mouth at a corner and take the ball, knee up at waist height to make sure no opposition centre back or forward fancied having a go for it.

We weren't an all-conquering team, as there were plenty of strong teams in the city, especially from the Catholic schools, but we were good, we played across West Yorkshire and it was a great team to be in. The best outfield player was another Leeds City Boys player, Gary Burton, who was widely believed to be nuts because he'd throw his head in the way of any type of shot to stop it. Gary was skinny, agile and could just pick the opposition apart with his tackling, passing and chipped shots. He was thin but hard, a laugh and another great player. No one could understand why he'd been let go by City Boys aged just fourteen or fifteen, as he was a different class.

What you know when you've played five-a-side in enough different places is that lots of games have these anonymous players, respected by their mates and known locally, who, but for another kid being slightly better than them, or a scout or coach preferring a different-sized kid, could have had a professional career. The truth is there are too many good players to get into the academies and then go on to a professional contract. The difference between those who make it and those who don't is, as often stated, down to mentality or luck more than technique.

At the end of the year, having reached the final of the Leeds schools' cup, the teachers dropped Streakin Deakin and me and replaced us with Scampi, a really tall mod everyone liked, and my mate Waigy. They both played for the rugby team, weren't bad at football in PE and Mr McCreadie decided we needed some height and strength, so that was it. Binned, I was gutted. Streakin never played football for the school again, just packed it in, and the last thing I can remember about him was a rumour he'd dropped a desk from a third-floor window onto the drive below.

The only use I had was to give Mr McCreadie my list of the results and scorers I'd kept all season. A list that had included goals I'd scored in cup games that had helped us progress through the rounds. No one counted assists back then, but I found it piss easy to lay the ball nicely in for Walker's giant galloping steps and I'd set loads of his goals up. None of it counted. He knew Deakin and I were skinny wingers and he wanted some strength.

All that was left was to go along with the reserve goalie, my mate Johnny Martin, and sit in the dressing room on match day. It felt terrible. We won 1–0, Waigy banging one into the roof of their net, so I guess Mr McCreadie was vindicated. I was delighted we'd won, but it didn't change the way I felt about not playing. When the coaches announced the team would go to Bryan's fish and chip shop to celebrate, while everyone sat round looking at their winner's medals it took Whaley to say, 'Sir, we'd better take James and Johnny.'

Naturally, during this time we'd play five-a-side or three-a-side in the old-fashioned gym – all polished wooden wall-bars, beams and ropes – but we also booted balls around in there as hard as we could in an impromptu game of murder ball. The medicine balls around in the gym vastly outnumbered the kids who had any idea what to do with them, so they would just get hurled at each other and things went up a danger level when basketballs started getting booted around as hard as possible. Heads were the target, heads were hit, people were floored and everyone was laughing.

I remember Mr McCreadie coming in just as Sammy Martin took one full on the side of the head and went down like he'd taken a punch from Muhammad Ali. The PE teacher was all for a laugh but he arrived to see Sammy take off and land on the floor, only to get back up dazed and confused.

Not long after the new school year started, the rains set in and the sloping football pitch turned to a camouflage jacket spread of grass and mud. Good for sliding tackles, but bad for popular team captain Winnie when he was standing on a chair attaching the nets to the crossbar for a game. The metal legs of the school chair he was on slowly sank up to the seat, leaving the giant centre back dangling from the crossbar shouting for help. The rest of us stood around in tears and then headed back to the changing room to get our kit on. He entered the changing room five minutes later, covered in mud and muttering, 'You bastards!'

While the football and rugby pitches would be ploughed by constant use, Mr McCreadie's cricket pitch was a different matter altogether. Show kids you care about something and invariably some of them will try and fuck it up. Mr McCreadie would be out there day after day with his lawnmower, going up and down inside the roped-off area. That patch was untouchable and 'woe betide anyone who goes on there without my permission' were the words that decreed it so. 'Woe betide' was one of those phrases that accompanied us through school life, though no one ever knew what it meant.

The whippet-fast head of PE was rumoured to have played for Huddersfield Town before he was a teacher. This and his close resemblance to the strap-harsh prison officer Mr Mackay in *Porridge* meant he was not to be messed with.

One lunchtime I was walking down the fields and I heard his voice behind me bellow, 'Brown, come here.' He was carrying a spade and he made me walk with him down to the rugby posts, where he told me to shovel up some badly positioned dog shit. It was a tedious order, but I knew I couldn't get out of it, and I doubt I'd even remember it if it wasn't for another kid from the year above, whose character was 'interesting' to say the least. He was friendly with older mates of mine, but what I remember most about him was the array of weapons he would bring into school.

If you wanted a high-velocity long-handled air pistol with telescopic sights, he was the man to approach – he had his own and had brought it in to show people. He could probably get you one too. Remember the scene in *Taxi Driver* where Travis gets tooled up? It was probably like that every night round his bedroom. I was surprised, when his younger brother made it as a famous designer and retailer, that their shop didn't have a weapons section.

On this particular day the kid had brought in a proper wooden Australian boomerang, not some piece of plastic shit from the front of *Action!* comic, and was busy almost decapitating unsuspecting groups of kids in various clusters on all sides of the rugby pitch. Just as I had shovelled the shit up onto the spade, I heard this whooping sound and looked up to see a flashing curved blade angling down at the PE teacher and me. Whether it was a deliberate throw or not, and I'd like to think it was, the boomerang clattered into the spade, sending the dog shit everywhere except over me. Mr McCreadie was fuming. He turned round, scanned the stunned and now silent rugby field, identified the master of arms and screamed the kid's name! And just left me and the spade where I'd dropped it to dish out a bollocking. I don't think the kid gave much of a fuck, he was only weeks away from leaving and had probably already lined himself up an arms-dealing position at the Barnbow tank builders on the other side of the city.

Weapons weren't needed at school. The swivel-topped wooden pencil cases with perspex release buttons you crafted in woodwork made excellent coshes. One nutter from Meanwood went five steps further when he made himself a collection of deadly kung-fu fighting stars, which he announced to the world by throwing them into the exterior door of the metalwork studio.

Naturally the more McCreadie manicured and protected his precious pitch, the more it became a target. Kids with mopeds or even cars would go at night and do wheel spins on it. One year someone planted a Christmas tree on it. The kids in the year below me ended their fifth year with a full-arse moon towards the school from the middle of it. But mostly people who'd received a McCreadie bollocking would do it after hours and away from his hawk-like glare.

One bloke in his late teens – none of us had ever seen him before and he'd never even been to our school – decided to have a crack at some wheel spins on his moped during a PE lesson I was in. Maybe someone had bet him to do it, maybe the pristine cricket square's fame had gone beyond the school boundaries. Whoever he was, he clearly hadn't anticipated the forces of fate being against him.

Unfortunately for him, Winnie, our school-year football captain and the hardest kid in the year, was at the crease at the time of the intrusion. Despite being a nice guy, fifteen-year-old Michael Winterburn was a mountain of a man and you only had to see him go through the opposition in rugby matches to know not to mess with him. In the football team he was just a huge, solid centre back.

Those of us who were fielding winced when the guy on the moped interrupted Winnie's innings. The week before he'd had a ball bounce up at him off his gloves, onto his head and into the hands of the slip, and had had to suffer a decision of caught bat and head. When this guy showed up it was another unwelcome interruption to his batting and you could see he wasn't too pleased.

Us fielders stood around watching in disbelief and intense amusement as the bloke spun round on his moped, revving away while looking up at the school towards the gym door like a dog waiting to be chased. As misfortune would have it, as soon as Mr McCreadie came tearing out of his office in his blue with red stripes adidas tracksuit, across the tarmac drive that divided the school buildings from the playing fields, the guy's bike just puttered out. It was amazing. Instantly all the schoolboy cricketers knew something different was going to happen.

Despite repeatedly trying to kick-start it, the thing was totally dead. Which is what we all assumed the bloke would be if he didn't leg it. Halfway across the rugby pitch, Mr McCreadie yelled, 'Winterburn, grab that man!'

Checking that no one was in a position to run him out, Winnie advanced out of his crease, taking two enormous steps down the wicket, and just yanked the grown man off the bike by the scruff off his neck and then raised his heavy wooden Slazenger bat in one hand, like the rest of us would have raised a badminton racquet. Mr McCreadie yelled, 'Winterburn, don't hit that man!' and then arrived on the pitch at full tilt, arms straight up into the pitch invader's chest, propelling him back off the square.

The lad had no real front and as soon as Mr McCreadie started booting him off his cricket square he legged it, getting a good distance between himself and the furious PE teacher before giving him a load of mouth.

Having seen him off the ground, the irate Blue Flash returned, congratulated Winnie on his handling of the situation and wheeled the stalled moped away towards his lair. The game restarted and Winnie smacked a six off his next ball with the fury he'd clearly had boiling under. Most of us were relieved he hadn't cracked the bloke's head with the same clubbed hook shot.

The lower sixth form would be my last full year in school and as I jogged out for a first XI match one Wednesday afternoon Mr McCreadie's farewell to me came in brutally charming fashion. News had reached him that I had somehow managed to secure a job interview with *Sounds* music paper in London. Given that there were no jobs going in Leeds at all and I'd scraped through my roughly revision-free exams with five O-levels and a CSE, this must have been quite a surprise to the teachers. Most of the time they were just waving us off to the dole, an FE college or trying to keep us in the sixth form. When I'd told the careers teacher I wanted to be a music journalist, they said I couldn't be as I hadn't taken music.

Anyway I was running out for a match and Mr McCreadie came past me the other way and, with an amused grin, said, 'I hear you've got a job interview in London, Brown. Who the hell is going to employ you?' He was right. I can still hear that laugh to this day when I'm sitting round wondering what to do with myself.

What Are We Doing When We Play Five-a-side?

I regularly get asked, 'Why don't you play less?' Normally it's when I'm too fucked after a game to do all the other things I'd said I'd do that day, night or morning after.

Over the years a range of people, including my current girlfriend, my eldest son's mum and a personal trainer, have all asked me not to play football so much. I'm sure you've had the same. I know, it's madness to even think about it. You can be encouraged to cut down your record collection, your magazine collection, your trainer collection, your football shirt collection (or whatever your collection is) on the grounds that the space is needed for nurseries, children's bedrooms, home office (a home office, not *the* Home Office), playroom, kitchen, bathroom, downsizing etc., but you can't be expected to stop that hour a week that keeps you alive, in touch with your mates and your childhood dreams.

It's very hard to get non-players to understand what we're doing when we play football, but it's not just kicking a ball about. It's much deeper and greater than that. The other day, while I was pondering this, it actually dawned on me that playing five-a-side weekly over a number of years requires the same sort of commitment, drive and focus people spend perfecting an art or learning a language or an instrument. Only outwardly the results aren't quite so obvious.

And that's why I've never or rarely cut back. I assume they don't understand what is really going on, they only see the time spent or the physical toll taken. Or the stinking sports kit in the hall.

What we are actually doing when five guys in different-coloured tops take on five guys in five unevenly off-white tops or neon bibs is physical, mental, ritual and social. We might not be aware that all of this is going on, but I believe it is. No matter how much we might protest or even advertise it as such, it's not just 'a kick-around'.

For me it is the most constant thing in my life, a factor I only realized when I was thinking about and started listing all the things that had happened to me during the seventeen years I'd been playing football with James, Gary, the Geoffs, Mikey, Ish, the Alexes, Dickie, Roy, Frank, Chris, Joe, Abdul, the Daves, the Bens, the Simons, the Johns, and on and on.

In that time I've had two children twelve years apart from two different serious relationships and been divorced once. I've moved house three times, been to about fifteen funerals (of good friends, I don't gatecrash strangers' send-offs) and ten weddings, built up a company employing seventy people and then sold it. More importantly, I've helped some people deal with their own drug and alcohol problems, and I've been lucky enough to travel the world, including trips to Argentina, Canada, Cuba, India, Russia, Thailand and Tanzania, to name but a few.

I've deliberately done all sorts of well-paid different work so I don't have to have a proper full-time job. I've co-produced a lot of TV programmes, appeared on even more, I've sold masses of magazines, and worked with and for all sorts of people, from the famous and instantly recognizable, like Madonna and Jamie Oliver and Leeds United, to the infamous, like Paddy Power and Peaches Geldof. I've consulted and written for old-timer publications like *Reader's Digest* just to see what it was like and I've done things that have never seen the light of day, like a sitcom about my time 'adrift in a sea of women' at *GQ*, written by Mitchell and Webb and edited by the late, great Reggie Perrin creator, David Nobbs. If people ask me to give them some professional help and it isn't going to take too long, I say yes. All of this has been in the last seventeen years, but mostly it feels like I've just been doss-ing around waiting for another game. The time I've spent watching the ball go into the back of the net has been some of the best.

The nearest I've come to my perfect job since *loaded* was when I spent two years every Saturday morning making people laugh, talking utter rubbish with Johnny Vaughan and Gavin Woods on *The Warm Up* on talkSPORT. The relationship with the listeners and how they contrib-uted through Twitter was a delight, and so were the ex-players we tracked down on the River Niall. But like lots of these things, when you're in other people's hands it ends in a way you have no control over.

I've been hired, fired, earned lots some years and less others. And I've managed to do most of that quite thankfully out of the spotlight, after the scorching attention of the mad *loaded* and *GQ* years. Through all of this, the constant has been playing five-a-side and not drinking, the former being a reward for the latter. That's how I've explained it to people asking me to play less. What I've lacked in ambition this century, I've gained in game time. At one point I knew a game I could play in every day.

My only constant, apart from the mutual challenge of staying clean and sane while still supporting Leeds United, has been five-a-side mid-week, eight-a-side on a Sunday and lots of other games across the week in between. There have been competitive leagues and tournaments every summer, seasons of Friday and Monday morning games, in the last few years there's been new enjoyable Tuesday and Thursday night games, plus over the years the occasional Saturday morning games.

Five-a-side has been there all the time. Maybe because I missed playing regularly – I.e. weekly – so much in my heavy-drinking *NME* and *loaded* twenties.

I'm not alone. Men absolutely love five-a-side, and now women do too. It provides us with important social groups as well as physical stimulation. It gives us status, standing and team interaction when so many of us increasingly work alone at a keyboard. It provides regular moments of humour and acts as an outlet for anger and frustration. It generates the opportunity to experience satisfaction, exhilaration and delight.

For some it fulfils a need to organize, for others a desire to keep and analyse stats. Some find washing bibs and booking pitches a bind but still insist on doing them as it gives them a purpose. For many it's even a job, organizing the competitive leagues run by instantly recognizable brands like Goals and Powerleague, or matching players to teams to leagues via social media apps and websites. Few of us think about the people who sort the centre out for us: they just appear at the beginning or end of a session, take our money and make sure the equipment is ready. They are the invisible facilitators.

They can, however, have an impact on your game, for as one woman I know, Suzanne Moloney Wright, told me, 'I worked at a five-a-side clubhouse in the 1990s in Manchester. I'd print the team labels for the evening shifts and change Lancashire Dairies to Lancashire Fairies on the spreadsheet every week. They hated me.'

AstroTurf-laying has become such a big business that it's something people with kids increasingly turn to for back gardens. Official five-a-side centres need building, preserving, running, organizing, protecting, cleaning, lighting. The list goes on.

Even before you build your centres and lay your pitches some scientist somewhere is trying to improve on the current surface. There are those who worry that the little black bits might be cancerous, so there are scientists and medical people looking into that.

Hopefully, someone somewhere in a sports laboratory is trying work out a way to stop all the little black rubber seeds they have on 3G pitches from going home inside players' boots. And maybe they should be making sure they don't stick to the outside of boots too, if the story from a guy I know in Leeds, Chris Collier, is anything to go by: 'I was playing in a match with a ref who had bought these cheap canvas trainers and whatever it is they put in five-a-side pitches, some synthetic rubber things, started to stick to his trainers. Bit by bit, as the game went on, they started to attract and, like ants round a dropped ice cream, got more dense until you could barely see his trainers. By the end of the match he looked like he was wearing a pair of black rubber moon boots while trying to keep up an air of authority, giving players a dressing-down as they sniggered at his feet.'

Indeed. All of this activity and the myriad commercial and emotional tangents it creates stem from people wanting to play close-contact competitive five-a-side. In the social media age, there are people whose presence on Twitter, YouTube, Facebook and Instagram is built around five-a-side. #HashtagUnited isn't five-a-side but it's an amateur football team building an audience, following and business by using social media reach: a football team in its own league. When the article that prompted me to write this book went viral after appearing on *The Telegraph* online it was tweeted, retweeted and linked thousands and thousands of times across the UK, the States, Europe and the rest of the world.

We pump money into sports retailers for equipment, clothing and boots; sports centres where we play; nutritional powders companies whose products give us energy or burn fat; corner shops for soft drinks, bottles of water, bananas, oranges and sweets; chemists for bandages, leg braces, insteps, Dextrose, nose plasters, painkillers like Voltarol, creams like Deep Heat, Deep Freeze and Wintergreen, and sprays like Deep Ice; and supermarkets for shower gels and grooming products, plus we use their shopping bags for wet kit and towels. Half a million people are doing all this every week. And that's before we even get to the pub or the curry house for post-match drinks and food and the all-important goal analysis sessions. Five-a-side adds to local economies in a big way and the national economy in a consistent way.

Sport England have stated that since 2010 eleven-a-side games have been decreasing significantly, while between 2010 and 2013 alone organized leagues declined by 3,000 teams. At the same time small-sided games have been increasing significantly as the organized leagues and branded five-a-side centres have expanded into full-blown, trusted brands. In 2009 Patron Capital paid £42.5 million to take Powerleague off AIM and back into private ownership. In the year ending 2014, the turnover increased from £29.8 million year on year to £32.5 million. Annual accounts recently posted at Companies House show an underlying pre-tax profit of £505,000 a year, compared to a £520,000 loss in the previous period. It's a big business, that's a lot of subs. And they play an important part in communities beyond being just a business. One player in Birmingham said of Powerleague, during research conducted by leading market researcher Terry Watkins, 'They understand their communities, geographically they know what is around them. They know our area is an area of disadvantage. They know there is trouble and there are problems. They embrace that.' And they do it so effectively that the emergence of Powerleague and the like has acted as a pressure valve in areas that have historically felt rejected and undervalued and have turned that into social disorder.

Regular games of five-a-side, eight-a-side or whatever the size have more reason to exist in our lives than most people realize. They offer continuity in an era when we're no longer expected to have relationships or careers for life. The games carry on with an ever-changing cast of players around a hard core of originators, so you can work away for three years and come back to find some of the same people there. They offer you a release from everything else and create memories you can revisit again and again.

A case in point being five-a-side player Will Deans, who certainly made sure his team were up for it during a tournament in Bournemouth: 'When Viagra first hit the scene years ago, our whole five-a-side team had some the night before kick-off. The next day it was still going strong and once we got kitted up rumour spread quickly, as it was technically impossible to hide the erections. Every match was pun central . . . "Ohhh, you're hard", "You've got a hard shot." In the car on the way home our striker seriously said, "We'll all be stiff tomorrow."'

Another player, Pat Ming, felt even more embarrassed by his tournament fuck-up: 'I entered my college team into an FA "Ability Counts" tourney. I thought they meant different levels of ability, so I put us in the top division. It turned out to be a disability sports day. We spanked the first team 15–0 before I realized midway through the second massive victory and we were asked to leave. I was so embarrassed when I realized everyone else playing had a physical disability. I just wanted the earth to swallow me up.'

The naming of the team can use hours of pub time and can then stay with a group of players for life. There are numerous corny old favourites, but some less obvious puns slip through, as Twitter user Iain McCallister can testify: 'I once heard of a five-a-side team in the Paisley area of Glasgow called Exeter Gently.' Also, in a savage indictment of a school maths department, five-a-side player David France told me, 'In our school tournament in Chester there was a five-a-side team named The Magnificent Seven.'

Five-a-side can bestow all sorts of organizational responsibility, but only one person I spoke to while researching this book admitted to managing a five-a-side team. Marcus Noble from West Yorkshire did, and in some style: 'Sunday was drinking day for me, so I was always too smashed to play. One week I found an old sheepskin in the house, popped it on with a flat cap and went to watch my mates. Next thing my Yorkshire accent changes to that of a mad Jock as I am pretending to manage the team from the sidelines. We won and I was encouraged to carry on, despite people pelting things at me. We went on a really good run until we lost in a cup semi and they asked me to stop then.'

Perhaps one of the best five-a-side stories I've come across is one of the simplest. To me it reflects the importance five-a-side plays in our lives. Keen five-a-side player Corrie Renton explains: 'I once saw a kid turn up and stick a suitcase behind the goal – he was going on holiday straight after the game.' Priorities!

When this book was commissioned by the publishers, my editor informed me that two female colleagues had said, 'Oh, we weren't that interested when you said it was about football, but when we read the pitch we realized why our husbands do it every week.' Which in its own way made me think even more about why we do what we do. Often in the rain, probably to a standard we sometimes wish was much better.

Ask participants why we play five-a-side and the response will be something along the lines of 'Well, I like playing football, you see your mates, stay fit and have a laugh . . .'

It sounds a bit like being in a pub in sports kit with no alcohol and more running around. But it's much bigger than that. People outgrow or move away from pubs, or the pubs close down and are converted into flats, but five-a-side rolls on. With the opportunities and facilities improving all the time. One of the most important factors of five-a-side is the length some teams, leagues and games have lasted. They provide a focal point of social and physical stability at a time when things don't last long enough any more. Phones are upgraded annually, Leeds managers change every half-term, Tinder relationships last a night.

Before James Kyllo's death, I had played with him and Gary King for seventeen years. Their game existed way before I showed up. Both my midweek indoor fixtures have players who have been together for the best part of three decades. It's a sporting polygamy: you play with a large bunch of people, but you stay faithful to the core while others come and go.

Dan Thompson, five-a-side player from the Midlands, got in touch with me to say he'd been playing in a works game that had lasted longer than the company that started it and had quite possibly out-lasted the industry itself: 'It's been running for three generations now, over thirty years. It's in Stourbridge in our local high school's 1970s gym. It was originally booked by my dad's factory workshop. The factory no longer exists but the game carries on.'

Graham Wokes is a player from Armley in Leeds whose dad told him about playing five-a-side in the streets after the Second World War because they could only ever manage to scrape together about ten kids to play: 'In the 1960s he became manager of Upper Armley Old Boys, who would train and then finish with five-a-side in the church hall. Until Betty Best the caretaker dropped in one day to find players sat naked on the draining boards of the stainless-steel sinks where they prepared our school dinners.

'The first purpose-built sports complex he knew of was in Billing-ham, Teesside, which was built in 1967 for public use, although I believe there was one in Crystal Palace in 1964, but councils didn't move into building them in a big way till the 70s. With this came a chance to play out of season after the council had removed the goal-posts from the park pitches.'

The never-ending nature of five-a-side certainly appeals to the club mentality of men, the desire to form mini-societies with rules, history and characters. Take the Old Robsonians, a team of accountants from Battersea (stay with me, don't leave just yet), who have a Twitter account, a club video featuring player profiles made by a mate in TV and a book about themselves. They have over 650 match reports penned from the twenty years they've been playing together and this year they're going on a tour of America. One year they even managed to talk Iain Dowie into presenting their annual awards, simply because he was drinking in the same pub they were holding them in.

For these guys the five-a-side club is a whole culture that has sur-passed everything else they've done together, like stag dos, birthdays and works Christmas parties. For me, though, there's a much greater reason for waiting to be picked, pulling on the appropriate colour and going out there to try and score the first goal. The moment we start I am concentrating on what is in front of me, where the ball is, how the combination of players on the other team is going to work, their threats and weaknesses, and on the space that's naturally appeared in their formation. Before we've even kicked off I've already clocked the make-up of my own team and assessed very quickly what I'm going to have to do to complement them and outwit the opposition.

This is a form of quick, important mental assessment and response that I just don't get involved with anywhere else in life – other than the basics of making sure I don't put my hand in the fire or walk in front of an on-coming bus. And so far I've been pretty adept at that. The only other time I've had to think like this was when publishing CEOs would call me and say, 'Can you take a look at it for a while and then write to me about why our men's mag isn't working?' I rarely do any tactical analysis in life, so on a weekly basis playing football competitively among regular groups of friends stimulates my brain in a way it isn't stimulated for the rest of the week. Watching the team you support isn't the same, because you have no influence over them at all.

From the moment we kick off for five- or eight-a-side I am concentrating, though in everyday life this is something I struggle to do. I subtitled Sabotage Times, a website I set up, 'We Can't Concentrate Why Should You?' If I'm engrossed in something challenging that interests me I can focus, but it's far easier minute by minute, hour by hour, month by month just to be blown along by the howling gale of distraction that makes up my head. I'm not sure whether other people's heads are the same, but the face-to-screen relationship we see everywhere we go now suggests almost everyone would rather have their mind somewhere other than where they actually physically are.

I met a well-known former magazine editor turned agony aunt,

Sally Brampton, who sadly died while I was writing this book, for the first time at a party a few years back. She gave me such an accurate reading of my personality and behaviour, even though we had never met before, that I actually went away, looked up what she had said (roughly that I had the Bipolar Starter Pack Entry Level 1) and sat stunned reading these definitions that were like a guide to my mind and thoughts.

Inside my head there's an ill-fitting mixture of Willy Wonka's Chocolate Factory one minute and something really dark and desolate from Poland, like *A Short Film About Killing*, the next. Imagine a colourful blur of waltzers, fruit machines, bouncy balls and gyroscopes one moment and it freezing and getting stuck the next. Well, five-a-side helps me with that, massively.

Other players have equally engaging stuff going on in their minds. They are packed with the pressure of so many physical, financial, professional, emotional challenges and the impact of life-changing experiences – birth, death, illness, jobs, relationships, homes – that we all face and carry. Add to that the social media envy and internet addiction that are fucking people up nowadays and there's a lot to deal with.

In the olden days there just weren't so many choices or distractions or pressures, because everything was simpler: people knew their place and most people accepted it; you'd work real hard, then sit knackered in a big tin bath in front of a little fire to get all the coal dust off you. Or if you were born with a silver spoon in your mouth you'd spend the afternoon in a top hat riding on horseback with an attractive woman. Who called you by your full name, not your first name. And if you were lucky the woman would be Kate Beckinsale. This is what the television dramas would have us believe. Social mobility and social media have upped the pressure massively. Have I got enough money for a pension, have I got enough followers on Instagram? Worry, worry,

worry. Luxury problems. But things people want to escape from and get back to something more physical and intense. It's probably the same reason people do iron man races.

That's now, but five-a-side through the ages is an interesting thing to consider. If you'd drawn fans of Lazio in a European competition 2,000 years ago you'd be playing against ropes, nets, tridents and lions. During the Dark Ages games would have been slower due to the armoured bibs. Tudor times would have seen you playing in ruffs, jerkins and tights, and coughing your guts up from half-time-stimulant tobacco. Codpieces would have been sponsored.

There wouldn't have been time for five-a-side during the Industrial Revolution between inventing trains and invading the rest of the world. They had a crack at it one Christmas on the Western Front in 1914, but after that international mass murder kept getting in the way and prevented completion of the league fixtures.

It was only in the second half of the twentieth century, when everyone got a bit more relaxed about work and relationships, or a bit more unemployed and angry, that the new leisure era began, during which organized five-a-side could thrive. At roughly the same time as the government realized Wham! and co. were bringing in masses of money to the economy and dispatched old skull-features Norman Tebbit to bring some gloom and doom to the Brit Awards to give George Michael an award, some bright sparks started thinking about running dedicated five-a-side centres as businesses.

But that's a brief history. To come back to the modern challenges facing modern man and woman, whether you are a twenty-two-year-old lunchtime five-a-side nut trying to forge a career (like I see wandering round Old Street, central London, in their kit) or a fifty-year-old Sunday morning merchant like me wondering why you spent so much of your life living in a country where it pisses down so often, five-a-side offers an escape from everything else. You cannot be thinking about that rising damp or new school uniform for the kids if someone's about to take the ball off you.

Regular player Tom Findlay sees five-a-side as a key part of his life: 'I'd put it up there with family and work. They are the big things in my life: family, work, five-a-side, music. It's that important, it's part of what keeps me ticking over. If I don't play for about a month because I'm injured or away working or something, it starts to affect my psyche. I can feel the difference. Given what I do for work [DJ/musician], I want to stay fit too, so it helps with that.'

So we carry all this irritating, distracting stuff around in our heads like a car boot full of a bad brown HMRC envelopes, but competitive five-a-side allows you to discard it and concentrate. It's lads' yoga and meditation combined.

Nothing else I've done wipes the mind like playing football. In yoga (if you want a laugh, I'm selling tickets to watch my next class) my mind wanders; swimming is great for thinking about things; skydiving you basically think you're going to die, then you jump and experience the immense rush of free fall, then you stop and wonder what the fuck you're doing stood up in the sky, like Wylie Coyote's moment of clarity. Meditation? A lot of people suggest I should try that, but where's the social side, where's the chance to think you're Tony Yeboah?

Fast cars and bikes fill you with fear and excitement, but for just wiping your mental screen like a brand-new Etch-a-Sketch, five-a-side football does that. And it's for a very simple reason. Not only are we playing, but we're also watching constantly because we know within seconds the ball will be with us again. There aren't long periods of time, as there can be with eleven-a-side games or rugby, when the ball is miles away in the other half and you can stand around at left back wondering if that's your car alarm that's going off in the car park. It's instant, it's competitive and it's fun.

In short: we play five-a-side because we like it.

Cooking with Gas

The last indoor football I played at school was a four-a-side tournament open to all years and the teachers. On our way to the final, I clattered into a maths teacher to get the ball as he shielded it in an alcove that led into the weight-training room. He whipped round and head-butted me. Thankfully he was wearing one of those skull-hugging cycling helmets, a bit like what Petr Čech wears, so it didn't hurt, but it was still a pretty violent assault. That would have been a sacking nowadays.

Amazingly I was sent off, the teacher was left on and two of his colleagues watching the match walked out of the gym in disgust at the decision. Mine was a fair but hard tackle, nothing Reaney hadn't done to Best. 'What the fuck was that?' the teacher screamed. 'A tackle,' I replied. He probably just hadn't expected it when he'd been showing off dribbling round thirteen-year-olds in the previous game. By the end of the day word had spread round the school that the teacher and I were going to have a fight down the playing fields. Which was amusing – and inaccurate.

My team with my mates Johnny, Geoff and Hemmy made it to the final, but unfortunately I wasn't there. I'd spent the night in Hull after hitching to see the Newtown Neurotics in Cleethorpes. I didn't make it back in time for the lunchtime fixture. By this point my school attendance had started to take second place to my gig attendance. There were more motorways than good gigs passing through Leeds, so I would just stick my thumb out and set off for Hull, Manchester, Liverpool, Sheffield or Nottingham if there were bands on I wanted to see. I spent a week travelling round Ireland with one of John Peel's favourite bands, Serious Drinking, who were like a punky student Madness, with songs like 'Love on the Terraces', 'Hangover' and 'Bobby Moore Was Innocent'.

On a typical Wednesday school night in the winter I'd be walking in the orange lamp-lit snow down Stanningley Road at 11 p.m., after seeing The Three Johns at the 1in12 Club, because the last bus home stopped halfway between Bradford and Leeds.

School had just become somewhere I cycled to during the day and I'd spend hours trying to distract the teachers with semi-pertinent questions during lessons. More distraction meant less work; I was just there for the football matches and the company.

When the mock A-level results came in I'd almost burned my last bridge – many of the papers just had song lyrics I'd written out to kill time in the exam. One teacher suggested they were 'the worst in the history of the school sixth form'. Another, our head of sixth form, David Frost, suggested I give it one last go and get into university. I was already going to universities every week to gigs or to sell my fanzine. There were some cool students, but they often seemed to be idiots with traffic cones on their heads, pissing in your back garden, quaffing plastic glasses of cheap beer and nicking your bike. At that point in life, where I grew up, 'student' was an insult, not something you aspired to be.

I told him the only reason to go to university would be to meet girls and play football and I figured I could probably manage both without wasting an education. Fair enough, he said, and he told me I should get out into the world because I could 'do anything, become a rock star or go picking tea in India'. It was a great speech, but a total lack of cash saw me going as far as my thumb and my fanzine could carry me. I spent most of my dole time a mile or two away from school back in a Kirkstall terraced house, the boredom and lack of opportunities crushing the life out me but not the ambition.

In about 1984, when I was eighteen, I read a book called *The New*

Journalism, edited by Tom Wolfe, and after that my life took a new direction. I knew there had to be more on offer out there somewhere. I'd sit in my attic bedroom, unemployed, in a dull under-populated part of the city my dad had moved to after he'd split up from my mum. I'd be reading the New Journalism classics my dad had, *The Great Shark Hunt*, *Hell's Angels* and *Fear and Loathing in Las Vegas*, and buying and throwing the *NME* away in frustration, and doing my fanzine. So there wasn't much in the way of local stimulus, Kirkstall not being the most inspiring place.

It seems mad to think about how little there was to do. There was no Powerleague or Goals where you could go down and pick up a game. To hear a new album or a classic old one you'd have to borrow it. There were the moors north of the city and I had a good bike to cycle up there, but then that was nicked and I didn't have the money to replace it. There was no sense of excitement about the prospect of work because there wasn't any work. At all. Something that was so blatant it was screaming in your face every time the evening news showed yet more reports about the decrepit state of the North.

There were no local media jobs like there are now. There was no social media or internet to dive off into and stay entertained, educated and entrapped by. No FIFA Football Manager game. Reading and listening to records, that was it. Or maybe a weird Friday night 'red triangle' film, *Brookside*, *Whatever You Want*, *Hill Street Blues* or *St Elsewhere* on the newly launched Channel 4. Video shops were appearing but didn't have much in the way of decent stock. Mainly just films that had flopped or you'd never heard of. It felt like there was nothing to do, nowhere to go, except I wanted to do everything and go everywhere.

In Kirkstall there wasn't even anyone my age to have a kickabout with. So I started playing in a weekly five-a-side match with our adult neighbour Alan and his mate Jonathan over on Scott Hall Road, by the playing fields where I'd played my second ever school match against Blenheim.

There was Alan, Jonathan (known as the Gent) and another guy who looked like a miniature David Bedford, with a lot of thick black facial hair. We'd had a teacher for a while at school who looked just like this guy, who inevitably got named the Ripper.

In these games I was able to zip past the older guys in much the same way seventeen-year-old Saul, Louis, Wiel and co. go past me now during our Thursday night games in Stoke Newington. Back then the fully grown men clapped my pace and said I was great. Nowadays I just look at these speed merchants tearing past me and, instead of thinking, 'Ah, the natural ability and joy of youth,' I think, 'Bastards! Is it too late to shed my midriff and get some sprint training to regain my pace, or should I just play with people my own age?'

So at a time when most professional footballers were breaking into their careers, playing organized football was in danger of becoming something I left behind at school And then someone I knew mentioned a local team who needed some new players.

With no school team to play for any more, my equally jobless mate Cathal and I joined this local Sunday league team called Kirkstall Eddies. People would often ask who and where Eddie was, but he didn't exist. It was an abbreviation of Educational, which was the name of the cricket club we played football for, Kirkstall Educational, on Queenswood Drive, just up from the bottom of the woods where I'd spent most of my earlier life playing football.

We were a football team representing a cricket club and we trained on a rugby pitch. Our pitch was on a slope next to the new housing estate where they filmed James Bolam in *The Beiderbecke Affair*. When the estate had opened a few years before I'd gone down with my dad to meet Barry Hines, who was the celebrity opening the showroom and co-promoting his book *The Gamekeeper*. They took our picture for the *Yorkshire Evening Post*.

An England Grammar Schools international, Hines is responsible for one of the best books on football ever, *The Blinder*, a novel about a teenager who signs for his local team. Largely autobiographical, it addresses the challenges that face a seventeen-year-old kid lighting up his town's pro club with his pace and skill, then having to face up to still being at school and trying to get an education. I read it when I was about fourteen and, as with all Hines's writing, it had pure realism running through it. Hines, Roddy Doyle in *Paddy Clarke Ha Ha Ha* and Hunter Davies in his collection of columns are the three authors who have captured football the way I feel it, see it, remember it and live it, more than anyone else.

I've only met about five people who've got *The Blinder*, which just seems mad as it's a classic. One of them was the popular author and radio presenter Stuart Maconie, someone I hired for the *NME*, and this made me like him even more than just for his writing skills. As well as *The Blinder*, Barry Hines more famously wrote the book from which the best football scene ever filmed was taken, *A Kestrel for a Knave*. Or, as it's known in the film version, Brian Glover's school PE match from Ken Loach's *Kes*. There's no analysis needed of that scene, just watch it, breathe it, quote it, live it: 'Who do you think you are? Bremner?' It was so important for a whole generation that Jon Wilde wrote it up as our first ever 'Great Moments in Life' in the launch issue of *loaded*.

Like that school football scene in *Kes*, most of the Kirkstall Eddies team were in our teens, albeit our late teens. The goalkeeper was a Dead Kennedys fan, which was unusual in that you didn't hear 'California Über Alles' too often around the social club scene. The full back was Chilli, who had a massive *Starsky and Hutch* knitted cardigan, which was pretty superfly for the time and location.

Another first-teamer was a lad from the year below me at school called Joe. One sunny Sunday about ten minutes before kick-off, Joe poured himself out of a car full of lads in jumbo cords, flick-heads and T-shirts, stinking of booze, with bruises, marks and grins all over their faces. One of them threw a cosh out of the car after him and then they sped off, laughing. When we asked where he'd been, he replied, 'In Blackpool fighting Scousers. Had a great time. Where's the kit?'

Despite Joe's swashbuckling seaside adventures with the Leeds lads, we were more boys than men. We could all play a bit with pace and skill, but we weren't very physical. This was a problem some weekends when you came up against pub teams full of gnarly old blokes still pissed from the night before. Like in most cities, there were infamous teams. My pal John Lee, who played for Dynamo Tetleyski, told me about a ruthless team of Catholics from before my time called Whinmoor Knives. I'm not sure whether that name related to a company they worked for or their choice of weapon, but John's memories suggest the latter.

The worst team we had to play was called the Plasterers. For the whole game they'd be kicking off everywhere, starting fights and intimidating the ref. Your marker would spend every minute telling you he was going to break your legs if you went round him. It was really horrible. You didn't know if he would actually try and break your legs, and mine at the time were like Twiglets, so the only thing to do when you did get the ball was run past him as fast as possible, which would result in more threats and late lunges. You couldn't be seen to be bottling it, but no one looked forward to playing the Plasterers.

The Plasterers managed to come first or second in the league by kicking everyone off the park, but I remember some dispute about who had finished where. At the league awards evening there was a massive fight between them and the other team that had come first or second. Both teams were banned and the third-placed team was awarded the league. This wasn't handbags at dawn, it was a full-on cowboy-film-style bar brawl, much to the delight of our coach, Peter, who was a glazier by trade and probably picked up enough work there to buy us a new kit.

Peter was very handy to know if you'd got pissed while your parents were out and accidentally smashed a window. Anyway, after this brawl he decided enough was enough and told us he'd be bringing in a couple of new lads he knew to give us a bit of steel. There were already about fifteen of us, so no one wanted to lose their place.

'Who have they played for before?' we asked.

'Well, they've not been around for a while,' he said, 'but they're great lads and just what we need. You'll meet them next week.'

The first time we saw Mark and Terry was running out in our kit for the start of the next match. Mark was a tall, well-built guy who looked like he could play a bit. His mate, Terry, ran on looking like a massive clenched fist. Small in height but immensely powerful, he ran with a very high rugby step, like his arms were karate-chopping people and his legs were stomping on them at the same time. They both looked rock hard.

Mark called everyone into him and just made this announcement: 'All right, lads. I'm Mark and this is Terry. I'm at the back and he's in midfield. Heard you've had a bit of trouble with some of these old cunts. Don't worry about that any more. Let's win this game and we'll get to know each other afterwards.'

That was it. No one doubted the commitment. They'd clearly assumed command on the pitch, we all just wanted to know whether they could play. We could see from their build and the hardness of their faces they weren't fucking about. And with good reason. It was rumoured they were just back from active service in the army! It wasn't that long since the end of the Falklands War. They had the moustaches, the fringes, the scars and the 'Don't ask us about it and we'll all get on fine' glints in their eyes. Mark did have the air of a tough family man, and he genuinely wanted to make the team better and look out for us. Terry went along with everything Mark said, but you couldn't help wondering whether one week he might show up with a necklace made of ears or something.

They looked like the sorts of blokes who wouldn't tolerate any nonsense on the street in town at night, but it was great because they were on our side. Suddenly the opposition knew things had changed and we could get on and play football. In our return fixture against the Plasterers we drew 5-5. If there were any issues with the other side, Terry would just run through their hardest player like a tank and leave him lying totally fucked in the mud. He'd make it look firm but accidental and apologize profusely to the ref and the other player. He'd get a yellow card, the opposition would get the message and everyone kept it to football after that. In many ways he was helping the ref, but not all of them saw it that way.

In one game Mark was sent off after a booking for a hard tackle and an immediate second yellow for dissent. The referee's report came back and Peter, the coach, read it out aloud to all of us in amused disbelief: 'I booked the player for a dangerous tackle and he then used hand signals to suggest I masturbated a lot. This continued as I ordered him from the field of play.' It's the only referee's report I've ever seen, and totally memorable for the hysterics it caused.

Worse than just missing the rest of the match and the next match on a ban, getting sent off meant Mark had to go and stand on the touchline next to Malcolm.

If Peter was the coach, then Malcolm was the general manager. Peter took us for training, organized transport to the away matches and spoke to us before and after the games, but Malcolm seemed to have a lot of input into picking the team, which we found bizarre. He seemed to know fuck all and Peter did everything anyway, so maybe he secretly owned the club or had been the previous coach or something. Malcolm was an old squat bloke with a gruff exterior who you wouldn't even notice but for his catchphrase: 'You're cooking with gas!'

He'd spend the whole game next to Peter barking out instructions, but when we scored and were in control of a game he'd start yelling, 'That's it, Kirkstall. You're cooking with gas now. Keep going, you're cooking with gas.' For us it was just embarrassing, but the opposition found it hilarious. They'd be giggling while trying to tackle you and when you weren't on the ball the marker would be just going, 'Who's that mad old get? Cooking with gas?' Some of them would just start shouting it back.

As far as I know no one else in football has ever used that phrase to encourage a team. He'd clearly appropriated it from an advert.

Years later, when I was coaching the Recreativo kids, we were winning a game in Camden and I couldn't help shouting out, 'C'mon, Recreativo. You're cooking with gas now,' just for a laugh to amuse myself. A very private joke but it got a response.

My eleven-year-old son, Marlais, who was playing, looked over his shoulder at me with an embarrassed scowl, mouthing, 'What?' and shaking his head in disbelief. This was after one shout, so imagine hearing that ten times a match.

The other thing about Kirkstall Eddies was by the time you got back to the clubhouse after the game, it would be Sunday lunchtime and the place would be packed. You'd be absolutely fucked and looking forward to a pint of orange juice and lemonade, but as you pushed the doors open with your cheap leather Head bags down by your knees, old ladies would be ramming the place out, going, 'SHHHHH!' A whole sea of blue and pink rinses and white blow-waves clinking pens and spoons on to their glasses in the middle of a meat raffle or bingo. It was the weirdest conditions for a warm-down ever.

You'd be dying for a drink and wanting to discuss the game while someone's grandma would be giving you a death stare. They were like the Plasterers in wigs. It was impossible to reach the bar without getting a load of abuse for interrupting whatever arcane form of entertainment they were enjoying in the hope of winning a pork chop or a side of beef.

There was one significant thing I learned about five-a-side during this time with Kirkstall Eddies and that was how to score good fast goals in a gym over and over again. When the weather got too bad and the nights too dark to train outside on the Queenswood Drive rugby pitch, we'd go across the Kirkstall Valley and the River Aire to a school gym. All we did was play four-a-side for ninety minutes. First-to-three winner stays on. It was a superb game of rolling football. You'd be on and off, competing against all the other four-a-side teams, with a mix of really fast, dynamic exercise and combative football. If you were fucked you could be on and off again in the matter of three kick-offs.

If the game was really well matched you could battle it out for a five-goal 3–2 victory, then stay on for the next game, which could end in a 3–0 defeat in two minutes. These were some of the best games I ever played in. Four-a-side meant one on the right, one on the left and one in the middle and you moved up and down the pitch pretty much in a line like that, doing one-twos. With roughly sixteen players, you'd only be sitting it out for a couple of games before you'd be back on. If a game was lasting too long Peter would just blow up and both teams would be off and a new winner would stay on.

As any sports psychologist will tell you, constant repetition of a successful action will make you better and better, and it was in that gym that I started to properly understand the runs into space you should make when on and off the ball. How to hold back until a called-for pass has been released or be ahead of the call to gain ground. How to overlap loud enough to receive the ball without even asking for it. How to cushion a pass into a shooting position for a sprinting teammate to hit. How to dash back in time to block a shot while an opposition team member steadies himself to let fly. It was a standard new school gym, but tight enough for fast balls to be controlled and players to improve distribution. Football not pinball.

I only stopped playing for Eddies when I moved to Manchester for sex and drink and rock and roll, and picked up a five-a-side game with former Fall musician and now 6 Music DJ Marc Riley. Then, aged twenty-one, to London for a job on the *NME*, for my first ever full-time job. On the downside, that was the end of regular Sunday league football for the best part of a decade. On the upside, I swapped playing against the psychopathic Plasterers for occasional matches against beatable pop stars like Spandau Ballet and The Blow Monkeys. More importantly, I was no longer cooking with gas but, like Dylan before me, had finally gone electric.

Who I Play with Indoors

Throughout this book I constantly feel guilty when referring to the eight-a-side games I play, like I'm being unfaithful to five-a-side, so I think I should probably shed some light on the Heroes of Hoxton Wednesday five-a-side game I have played with James Kyllo and co. for so long. Even if I lapse for lengthy periods of time, it has been for many years what I would call my five-a-side home group.

Originally most of these guys played on Sunday too, but slowly they just slipped back to it being a midweek fixture. I guess it's easier to escape the home in darkness than on a bright Sunday morning, when the lawn needs walking or the dog needs a mow. Or maybe the smaller pitch suits their skills better as they get a little older.

In doing this, I also hope you'll get some feel for the playing archetypes you may or may not recognize. There are so many different types of players: the battler, the bruiser, the thunderball shooter, the lazy bastard, the keeper who always wants to play out, the bad dresser, the great finisher, the young, the elderly, the dribbler, Mr All Elbows, Captain Dangerous, the talker, the moaner, the confused, the patient. That covers about three of them.

The significant thing about this game is that despite playing with these guys for almost two decades I hardly know what any of them do, where they live or what their surnames are. I only really thought about this after James died. I think that Dan or his brother had a clothing line, that Little Pete and Teddy Bear Peter are journalists and that Alex is a music agent, but that's it. There's no email asking who's playing each week, so there's no insight into people's jobs via their email addresses. James never felt the need to bring in such modern forms of communication, preferring a more holistic approach to team numbers. Being a mathematician and stats guy, he knew that even if there were seven of us one week and thirteen the next it would average out at five-a-side over the year. Good for his brain but bad for consistency.

To populate the cast I'll give you a few of the regulars names, old and new, from the Wednesday/Sunday crossover squad and then I'm going to highlight some of them to define archetypal players. And once you've read this list I'm going to tell you something about my mate Gary, who sort of organizes the game since James left us and has given the regular players some of these nicknames in the absence of surnames.

Here we go: Old Geoff, Big Geoff, Geoff Nutter, Beardie Dave, Derby Dave, Derby Dave's Brother Andy, Sunderland Graham, Tokyo Tim, Arsenal Paul, Charlton Dan, Young Danny, Big Ben, Little Ben, Blind Ben, Big Chris, Little Pete, Lofty, Marquel, Mad Alex, Frank, Ish, Pete, Peter, Mikey, Spike, Kelner, Pooley, Gary, News of the World Matt, Harvey, Roy, Keith and of course our organizer the late James Kyllo.

You want to know something about Gary? He's shit at nicknames. These nicknames are so bad because, beyond the hour on the pitch, the wider group of people here have little off-pitch familiarity. There's a core of Wednesday players who have a drink afterwards, but given that I don't drink and for many years was a single dad with a babysitter to take over from at 10.30 p.m., I've never been to the pub on a Wednesday with them. Nor have I ever joined them on their occasional eleven-a-side trips to tournaments in Margate, Brighton or Otley.

I know so little about them that, like Superman, away from the gym in Falkirk Street they just slip back into the invisibility of everyday life when they change out of their kit. I could hazard a guess at what they do, but I'll undoubtedly be wrong. OK, I'll give it one go. Given the noisy panic and haste with which he rushes into a tackle, I'd guess

Geoff Nutter might be a paranoid safety inspector in the really dangerous bit of a steelworks. The others? No, I won't even bother.

The only time I've seen more than three of them together in one place in clothes not kit was at James's funeral. I didn't even recognize one of them, Paul. He looked much thinner and more professional in his black suit than in his tight old blue Arsenal away shirt.

I've tried to think of a professional team I could compare these guys to but I can't. They aren't full of underdog violent endeavour like Vinnie Jones and Dave Bassett's Wimbledon. Nor do they have the skills and showboating ability of a part-time Barcelona. They don't pass their way from end to end with skill and precision. Nor do they get overexcited and wade into physical fights. They don't sit anywhere in between these examples either.

The only team I can really compare them to would have Pike, Jones, Walker and Wilson on the back of their shirts. And I don't mean Geoff, Mick, Des or Bob. The fellas I'm thinking of were managed by a bloke called Mainwaring and played their home matches in Walmington-on-Sea.

Anyway, on to the type of players they are. I think we all have some players like these in our games: the goal machine, the hotshot, the liability, the unstoppable force, the moaner, the shouter, the angry one, the placid one. We know who we are.

These are the player types that make up the mix. In a game like ours that doesn't revolve around a social or work group, you get to know the types of players they are before anything else about them. You might even get some advanced information about what types of players they are as the teams are being picked: 'This new bloke's supposed to be quite good.' That's Gary's idea of a scouting report. If he was asked to introduce each new £50 million signing at Old Trafford he'd say, 'This Anthony Martial is supposed to be quite good.'

But back to our player types. You'll have your own guys who might be physically different, but some of them will fulfil the same function. Let's start with the goals. I believe everyone must have a player like Sunderland Graham (so called because . . . you can work it out). Graham looks and shoots like one of those stubby powerful cannons they have on cartoons for firing men in helmets out of. Imagine a solid beer barrel in the cellar of a European castle and then give it the finishing skills of Kevin Phillips. That's Graham. Robust. Deadly.

On our basketball-court-sized five-a-side pitch his goalscoring stats are unmatched. He'll get the ball within a foot or two of the edge of the D and – BANG! – it cannons away from his foot, past you and into the net. The only way to stop him scoring is to say goodbye to a pain-free rest of the week and hurl yourself into the ball's projected route to goal. He's like the white Tony Yeboah with a range of thirty centimetres not yards. Lethal.

His physique gives Graham a neat turning circle and he uses it to twist past defenders with ease and just leather it. He's a nice friendly guy, so there was never anything malicious about his play, but his finishing is quite violent in its execution. The moment you see he isn't on your side you know you'll be conceding a lot of goals, so you'll have to score more yourselves to win.

Our second semi-unstoppable player and frequent goalscorer is Charlton Dan, a tall skinny bloke who attacks, all elbows and knees in a chicken-dancing rush, like he's got to get this move out of the way quickly and dash home to take some beans off the hob.

Imagine a basketball player with deckchairs for arms. He drives down the left wing, accelerating from a shuffle to a stride, one-twos off the wall, cuts inside and powers it across the low goal into the far side of the net.

I have watched Dan score hundreds of those goals over the years. Hundreds. Four or five a week. Over 200 a year since the late 1990s. That's thousands of identical goals. The only hope you've got of stopping him is to try and jockey him into the corner of the pitch and cul-de-sac him. Even then he can spin out like a ballerina made of planks into a shooting position and you're another goal down.

He can be frustrating to play with as passing isn't a key part of his game, but if you're on the opposite team he's very difficult to get the ball off once he's got it. And he's at his most dangerous with his back to goal – defenders drop their attention a millisecond and he swivels and scores. Again. Then hurries back to his half to get the beans off the hob.

Every game must surely have these unplayable players. They're too big for the basketball-court-sized game, but that's the opposition's problem, not theirs.

I've played with two slight variations of the Dan type, both more stylish in their play, but that might have been because we were playing on marginally bigger pitches. One was a Leeds fan called Pete, who designs magazines, and the other is a picture editor called Mike, who also works on a very nice magazine. Pete was lean, Mike was strong, both tall masters of the ability to cut in, spin and fire low and hard across the keeper into the net. Speed, power and precision, just like Dan only without the unintentional elbow attack. This type of player's goals invariably look fantastic. The moment the ball is dispatched it has a 95 per cent likelihood of reaching its desired destination, the back of the net.

Strangely the professional footballers these guys are most like aren't tall and strong at all but jinky-dinky players like Everton's Aaron Lennon or former Arsenal winger Anders Limpar.

These professional Speedy Gonzales types have used their size and mobility to make an impact in the top leagues, but in our games all three of the swivel and shoot players I've described are over six feet and good with it. I say 'are', but the latter two, Mike and Pete, have fallen in with the fashion and luxury travel world at Vogue House, so have long since traded in their football shirts for cashmere jumpers and scarves.

On the subject of fashion we move on to Frank, a long-standing regular in the Wednesday game. Every game must have a Frank, a player for whom sportswear holds no appeal, who dresses as if from a PE teacher's lost property box, who lets his play rather than his kit do the talking. And that's a language no one understands.

Frank's dress sense on and off the pitch is so unintentionally perverse it makes punk star Fall singer Mark E. Smith look like Sir Paul Smith. Like many of us, he's working on the incorrect assumption that something that fitted him half a decade ago still fits him now. However, for Frank it's cycling not overeating that has tightened them.

His coloured and white T-shirts both tend to have the same grey hue. Give him anything with the last vestiges of clothing dye in and he'll snap it up. Admirably, I have never seen Frank dressed in a corporate brand or sponsorship logo. He's the Naomi Klein of amateur football. It's as if he watched the football match in *Kes*, said, 'That's my look,' and has stuck to it ever since.

In decades of playing with him I've never received a clue from his football kit who he supports, if indeed he does support any team. To put it simply, Frank often wears sports kit that looks like he found it on the street. But 200 words later, let's not dwell on the negatives.

When I think of Frank's football playing, I normally think of him controlling the ball at thigh height and running diagonally across the pitch, then back again before heading up the wing that was originally in front of him and turning back to pass it into the space he has created – a bit like a drunk man trying to draw a letter S for Spaghetti, which if he wore a tracking device is what his possession would look like.

All the time he's dribbling an impatient teammate is screaming, 'FRANK, FRANK, FRANK, FRANK!' for him to pass it, when Frank knows full well there must be a way through the opposition's midfield and defence if only he can dribble into it. He's a strong tackler and has a distinctive shot that looks like a mallet banging a wooden stake, and he is very understated when he scores. He enjoys just a slight skip as he jogs back to his half, his T-shirt tucked tightly into his pulled-up shorts.

When it comes to player types I think many of you will be putting your own mates' names to the preceding players – the hotshot, the unstoppable runner, the scruffy bastard. If you can match the next one I'll buy you a unicorn. When I call the next player unbalanced, I don't mean mentally so much as physically. I've never ever seen a player like Alex Hardee.

Most of us have some semblance of upright posture. Basic walking and running have been mastered many years ago and incorporated into everyday and sporting life. To picture Alex, I want you to imagine your great-grandad in a state of total concentrated alarm as he slides about on an ice rink in shiny-soled slippers.

During which time he manages to keep a ball close to his feet, while pirouetting and jerking through the opposing team. The path to the opposition's goal is a bit like that early phone game Snake. Now imagine at the end of this bizarre clumsy dance he actually scores. That's Alex. Unpredictable, unique, entertaining, arse about tit. He manages to combine skill with lack of coordination and this can startle and surprise both his own teammates and the opposition.

When he runs it looks like a speeded-up walk – a tiptoe on hot coals, robo shuffle. And he only really runs when he's scored and is moving back into his own half. It's the only time happiness overpowers focus and lets his gait work properly.

Normally he just sort of scuffs his way into an attack. If he's on your side it's precarious to watch him go, and if you're playing against him it's utterly bizarre and often just funny. He's very easy to tackle, the slightest nudge will knock him over and his all-round shenanigans will make it appear he's simply lost his footing rather than been impeded. Maybe it's something in the blood, the ability to entertain.

Alex's brother, Malcolm, was an infamous comedy club host and comedian in Greenwich, London, in the late twentieth century. He ran the club that Vic Reeves and Bob Mortimer emerged from and for a while he managed Jerry Sadowitz, so there's clear evidence of 'personality' in Alex's genes.

I once walked past Malcolm Hardee at the Gilded Balloon Theatre in Edinburgh at a big party there and he was pissing down the stairs. When I asked him what he was doing, he replied, 'Someone was using the sink.' Alex plays his football with the same approach: his route to goal is the third choice anyone else would take. When Malcolm got married, in some impressive religious ceremony sorted out by his in-laws, he knelt down in front of the congregation and revealed the words 'Help' and 'Me' on the soles of his shoes. Genius.

I know Alex hasn't written anything on the soles of his boots because I've seen them frequently reaching for the sky when his tippy-tappy dribbling and lack of balance have seen him end up rolling back onto his arse. That is when he's brought his boots. In a recent survey, nine out of ten housewives we asked identified Alex as the player least likely to remember his trainers.

Strangely, given his corkscrew style, Alex prefers to play out of goal, when his natural disposition to fall over actually makes him a very good keeper. He's a true one-off. Years ago I bumped into him at Bestival, where the theme was Pirates and 10,000 people were dressed as Jack Sparrow or Long John Silver. Alex had shunned the trend and was wearing a dirty old grey mac with clear vinyl DVD envelopes stapled all over him. 'I've come as pirate videos,' he explained, as he tripped and stumbled off into the crowds. Never to be seen vertical again.

If Alex is your wild card, the next guy is your indispensable man. You must have a guy you want on your team every week, not specifically for his scoring or defending but just for the effect his performance has on linking the two.

In our game his name is Pete and as far as I'm concerned if you don't have him in your team your engine doesn't run. For the simple reason he doesn't stop running. Ever. He's small, which helps on a tight pitch, and he constantly makes good runs when he's giving or receiving the ball. He reminds me of Leon Britton of Swansea. When I find myself talking about people I play with, I always refer to Pete as being like the oil in an engine. He just keeps everything moving along.

He doesn't have the poise to shoot powerfully, but in terms of keeping possession and attacking he's vital. In an ideal five-a-side team everyone runs, but in an ageing one that's not always the case, so if you're lucky you have a Pete who'll do your running for you. In my case just allowing me to move into the space he's created or push the ball into the space he's moving into is a big help. He makes your passes look better, because a moving man is always easier to feed. Pete constantly keeps the tempo up for your team when you or the opposition is flagging. Nobby Stiles and Alan Ball were the Pete of the England 1966 World Cup-winning team.

Maybe it's because I can't run as well as I used to that I put so much stock in people who do. I really think it's vital. Obviously it helps, as is the case with Pete, if the player knows where to run to.

On the late Tuesday game I play in there used to be a quiet Scottish guy called Graham. Like Pete, he never stopped running up and down the wing of the huge two-basketball-court-sized pitch. He was impossible to mark if you fancied a rest when the ball went elsewhere on the large pitch, because he'd just keep running. A couple of times I thought, 'I'm just going to try and stay with Graham for a bit, make sure he doesn't sneak in at the far post and score,' but he would just run off to another part of the room. It wasn't a case of losing his marker so much as trying to kill them with stamina. For Graham, I think five-a-side was just short practice for marathons. Seriously.

I sat down with Gary King, or Football Gary as he appears in my phone, who has taken over the mantle of organizing our Wednesday and Sunday games now, and he gave me a bit of background as to how the Sunday game I'd joined had originated and who the original players were: 'I was thinking about what you said about bad nicknames. Well, two players before you were Cheesecloth Paul (he wore a cheesecloth shirt to play) and Blind Ben (he worked at the Royal National Institute for the Blind).

'The game started as Real Hackney with me and Old Geoff (who wasn't so old then, we called him Charlton Geoff then) playing eleven-a-side on Haggerston pitches with a few local kids making up the numbers regularly. One was Kevin Lisbie, who was already a Charlton first-team squad member and had made his professional debut. It was the summer holidays and his mate was playing with us, so he fancied joining in. Geoff was delighted. He played in a couple of competitive matches for us.

'Real Hackney also played in Spitalfields in the netted pitches and Frank of the crazy bad kit had a connection with James Kyllo, who would play after us on the same pitch. James was playing in a game with musicians and friends, Robert Lloyd from The Nightingales, Steven Wells from the *NME*, Ed Ball from Creation Records, who was a very good player . . .

'We ended up playing them on an eleven-a-side one time and then somehow the teams merged on a Sunday. When Spitalfields closed down, James found the Bishopsgate Goods Yard, which is where Shoreditch Station is now, and there's a five-a-side centre further along towards Brick Lane now. That's where you joined us under those arches. My main memory of that pitch was it was underground, dark, dripping water, sand and grit all over the pitch and expensive too, a tenner each.'

Coldwater Canyon

Billy Duffy had said, 'Just get a cab to the fire station at Coldwater Canyon and we'll be there.' It was a beautiful lush green circular space surrounded by evergreens and a sandy track which slim Californians in nursery pink, white and blue speed-walking outfits of ankle socks, shorts, T-shirts, towelling wristbands and sun visors were gently moving round. I looked up at an imposing house of angles and glass, frowned down onto the green from behind the fire station and wondered if it was where Axl Rose had got his piano stuck while trying to throw it out of the window.

Such madness isn't unusual in these hills and canyons, the playground of the insanely wealthy and those driven over the edge by fame. I was in Los Angeles to interview The Cult for the *NME* after guitarist Billy Duffy and vocalist Ian Astbury had become successful enough to move there. It was a long, long way from the northern English cities they had formed their first bands in, but knowing those same cities well it was hard to argue they'd made the wrong choice.

The Cult had dropped 'Death' and it's Goth implications from their name, made a great album, *Electric*, with man of the moment Rick Rubin and then an even heavier one called *Sonic Temple*, which they'd supported Metallica around the States to promote. They'd 'gone rock' and a lot of young Americans liked the almighty-sounding drums and the guitar levels, and the success had helped The Cult find their city.

LA was bright and warm, and the food could be either very good or very bad for you, whichever way you liked it, but either way it tasted better than what was on offer back home. Many of the best-looking women in America had congregated there to become famous and would happily go for a drink with you, based on the possibility you might be someone who could help them. After I'd first gone there to interview the Beastie Boys about their comeback album, *Paul's Boutique*, I'd started visiting Los Angeles a lot. I liked it there. So did Ian Astbury and Billy Duffy. The two English rockers even looked alarmingly healthy, like they'd been 'working out' with 'a fitness instructor' at 'a gym'. Such things were almost unheard of in the UK at the time.

'This is amazing,' I said to Duffy, looking around the pitch, as he climbed off his motorbike and started pulling a Man City shirt on. 'Yeah, whatever you do, don't fucking tell anyone back home or they'll all be over here.'

'Who are we playing with?'

'Just mates really. Some British and Irish lads who work here, carpenters from the movie industry, some City fans, a few musicians, that sort of thing. The Americans are all gym-toned giants and super-fit but not bad players. You'll be fine.'

And then a Sex Pistol arrived and even though I was the Features Editor of the *New Musical Express* I was really shocked.

When they'd first exploded in Britain in 1976, there were two sets of Sex Pistols fans. The first were the adults who clutched punk to their hearts and were inspired to start bands, fanzines and record labels, buy the records and go to punk gigs. And then there were schoolkids like me who loved noisy horrible adults being outrageous, flicking Vs, swearing, ripping their clothes, slouching and doing all the things we were always being told we weren't allowed to do. The fact they made startlingly abrupt and confrontational music too, and normal society seemed terrified of them, made it even better.

Aged eleven I'd seen the Sex Pistols on the local evening news in Leeds talking about a children's party they were going to host and play at locally. They looked great. Just the two of them, spiked hair, black bondage jacket and a straitjacket, filling the screen with their bored cocky sneers and a resolute confidence that they were doing a good thing putting a party on for kids. They both looked poisonously exciting. When their record 'God Save the Queen' was banned, some mates and I went into Woolworths and looked at the blank gap in the charts where their entry should have been.

When we visited London for a family holiday soon afterwards I really hoped I'd bump into the Sex Pistols. You know, taking a leisurely stroll around St James's Park or sitting on a grand black lion at the foot of Nelson's Column, taking a break from feeding the pigeons.

In the thirteen years between seeing them on TV and standing in front of Steve Jones, about to shake hands in our football kits, I'd done a bit more than just play football in the street. I wasn't a fawning superfan or anything – 'Take no heroes, only inspiration' was a line I liked – but I'd got their records, bought a mohair jumper from X Clothes in Leeds, dyed and shaved bits of my hair, seen lots of bands and bought loads of records by upstarts like The Undertones, The Specials, The Jam, The Dead Kennedys, The Redskins, Dexys. I had tapes of Lou Reed and The Clash, I'd worked in a record shop so I could buy more records. I'd created a fanzine, got a job as a music writer on *Sounds* and then by the age of twenty-one I was the Features Editor of the *NME*. And I had an unusually large amount of influence over the careers of many up-and-coming acts.

As part of my *NME* job I'd discovered and encouraged a few bands that made it massive, I was on first name terms with the Mondays and the Roses, I'd been to Germany with New Order, down the Old Kent Road with The Jesus and Mary Chain, looked at clotted pig's blood on a menu in California with The Pixies, smoked the government grass in Hollywood with the Beastie Boys, got stomped on by teenage girls in San Diego trying to get at Public Enemy, and I'd danced with Prince at his private party in Rio, and on and on for ever. I'd met a lot of famous musicians I admired and got used to it. And helped others I liked become famous, the younger bands in particular who were the same age as me and felt like my mates. The older ones were either amused or annoyed by this fifteen-year-old-looking skinny suede-head kid who could decide if they went on the cover of the *NME* or not.

But here was a Sex Pistol, Steve Jones, the man behind the guitars on those great punk hand grenades that had unnerved the establishment, the man who'd served up 'you dirty fucking rotter' live on teatime TV. Coming over to say hello and being introduced as The Pontiff. Right then music was the most important thing in my life and here was someone who'd jump-started rock and roll again after it had got satin-shirted Paper Lace showbizzy.

If you were a teenager in the 1960s you probably felt the same way about The Beatles, The Kinks and The Stones; ditto Oasis in the 1990s. Fifteen years after meeting Jonesy, his old band mate Paul Cook would sometimes come and play in our Sunday game and blokes older than me would look in amazement and disbelief and say, 'Is that Paul Cook from the Sex Pistols?'

But back in Coldwater Canyon we were playing eight-a-side football. I scored a goal and I totally missed an easy glancing header, which confirmed to me my eyesight was indeed going since the *NME* had given us computers. We had a great afternoon and hung out afterwards. They say never meet your heroes, but meeting them playing football is a very levelling way to do it.

As Gareth Senior, a five-a-sider I met on Twitter can explain: 'A very good mate of mine, Nick, was lecturing and studying for a PhD at Keele Uni. Top lad, loves his football, but not the best with "popular culture". We're going back a while into the 90s for this story, but a new lad was brought along to fill the gap for one of the weekly games and ended up on Nick's side. Rob, the new lad, was pretty decent, scored a few, lots of high-fives etc. Nick then starts chatting to the tattooed Rob in the showers, then they go for a pint, and it's not until Rob is getting a lot of interest from the locals that Nick asks Rob what he does for a living. Rob was better known as Robbie Williams. You can guess the rest.'

Years later I was in LA and called Jonesy to see if his weekly game was on and he said, 'Yes, come to Robbie Williams's house. He's not playing but he just lets us use his pitch. It looks down over the valley.' And he gave us his address. The pitch was fantastic, just like a Power-league set-up, only perched on the edge of a cliff with a net all round to stop the ball bouncing down from the Hollywood Hills into Sherman Oaks.

The British ex-pats of the Old Hollywood era played cricket and the current lot play five-a-side.

Unlike Gareth's mate Nick, if you *do* know your popular culture you can occasionally find yourself lining up alongside or against a household name or someone you've admired in film, book or song. Or even better, you've watched them play in the team you've supported all your life.

I wasn't sure whether to include this aspect of the games I've played in this book, because I wasn't sure whether it was just something I'd enjoyed because of the line of work I was in. Then when I started asking for general stories about five-a-side on Twitter and Facebook, people unexpectedly playing against famous people became a recurring theme. It might not happen to everyone but when it does, for obvious reasons, it's memorable and something people want to talk about.

The ways you find yourself face to face with an actor or former professional footballer vary. It may be someone has sneakily pulled in a famous ringer for an inter-works tournament. Or maybe someone else is a mate of a mate and they fancy a game. Or it may simply be because someone fancies a bacon sandwich. Really.

My favourite tale of famous people playing with everyday players is about Chris Waddle, the great Sheffield Wednesday, Marseille, Newcastle, Sunderland, Spurs and England player. He was a fantastic footballer, one of the best.

After he'd retired Chris Waddle was walking his dog on some playing fields in Sheffield and he came across a lady making bacon sandwiches. He went up to her and said, 'They smell fantastic. Any chance I can have one?' And she replied, 'Sorry, love, they're for my husband's football team after the game. You'd have to be playing for them to get one. If you come next week with your boots I'll make you one.'

Sure enough, the following Sunday he arrived with his dog and his boots and turned out for the team, and did indeed get his bacon sandwich. I love this story because it involves a footballer I really admired, a bacon sandwich made outdoors, and an amateur team who probably had their best Sunday ever. Well done, that lady.

Right, we'd better move on, as I really fancy a bacon sandwich now but am writing this on a train, so I know there's no chance of a decent one. Let me get a ginger biscuit and some tea and then I'll crack on with more football stories when I'm back.

Sitting comfortably still? Good. The first time I can remember playing against an ex-pro was in an advertising tournament when I was at *GQ* in a team with Captain Jamie Jouning and the ad boys. Jamie gave the best half-time team talk I've ever heard, clear, accurate, precise and encouraging. It was only afterwards that my workmate Geezer said, 'Yeah, that's because he was a captain in the army.'

The match with the unexpected ex-pro opponent was at the Powerleague pitches down in south-east London by the A21, and there was a little old bald fella absolutely creaming anyone he played against. When it came to our turn to play against his team, I went over to check him out and try and mark him and it was fucking Mickey Thomas! Ex Leeds, Arsenal, Man U, Wrexham, the lot. He'd shaved his long thick black curly hair off, or maybe he'd never got it back after his spell inside. I thought no wonder he was a class apart.

*   *   *

A guy I knew, Chris Payne, was a football agent who looked after Mark Viduka. I'd met him when he worked with Steve Kutner, who looked after Paul Merson, George Graham and Frank Lampard. Payney told me this story years ago but it's always stuck with me as an illustration of the huge physical gap between fans and players: 'I was playing five-a-side at Highbury, on the indoor five-a-side pitch they had there, and I was meeting Merse afterwards to discuss some business, but he came early and asked if he could join in our game. Obviously he's not supposed to, but there's no stopping him and everyone's well up for it.

'Right, I thought, I'm going to show him I can play, so I hit a chance as hard as I could and it caught the crossbar and flew off really high. Merse jogged over to me and said, "For fuck sake, Payney, don't try and place a shot like that, just hammer it!" And he meant it, he wasn't taking the piss.'

Of course it can be dangerous meeting your footballing heroes in a match. To you they've helped create some of the happiest moments in your life. To them you're just a bloke on the other team they intend to beat. As Leeds fan Jon Morrisroe discovered: 'In 1994 our rag-tag works team turned up in Derbyshire in our LUFC replica kits of different years to play a charity game. It was against our main supplier, who had recruited six players from Boston United, including the recent managerial appointment, Leeds legend Mel "Zico" Sterland! I was tasked with man-marking the roaming Mel whenever he came near our box, but the gulf in class was immense, and my poor marking was blamed for the cricket score and Mel's tally of ten-plus goals. When the final whistle blew I felt pretty dejected and completely leathered because he had kicked me everywhere. I had a shower and went to the bar to drown my sorrows, only to be greeted by Mel, who then paid for my beer. He still had it.'

Liverpool fan and *Awaydays* author Kevin Sampson had an experience playing against one of his heroes that was equally cruel: 'I played quite regularly in Liverpool with John Barnes for a period – this was JB's calorific years, post-Charlton. He's very competitive is John, *really* wants to win. He'll be talking and needling non-stop and, in this one game, he was on my case. Whenever I had the ball he'd be shouting, "Left foot, left foot, he's all left foot! Get him on his right . . ." I thought, "I'm not having that." Got played through on goal, decided I'd slot it with my right, shaped up and I completely missed the ball. Worst fresh-air kick ever, worse than Clare Grogan in *Gregory's Girl*, leaving me on my arse and John Barnes literally crying with laughter. I refused to share my crisps with him after.'

Leeds fan and five-a-side story goldmine Chris Collier had a slightly more life-affirming encounter with another Liverpool legend: 'We entered a big all-day corporate tournament and the trophy was to be presented by Liverpool's Alan Kennedy. We played some tough matches in baking heat and progressed to the final, watched by all the other teams. Won 3–2, last-minute goal, skilful young kid scored all three for us. Came off the pitch buzzing and into the bar for the presentation. Lad who'd scored was going berserk, still fizzing with adrenalin, and bumped into Alan Kennedy coming back from the bogs. "Whoaa there, mate, steady on," says Kennedy, nearly getting knocked over.

'Putting his hands on AK's shoulders and beaming at him, he said, "Sorry, been playing all day, mate. Just scored the fucking winner in the final! Do you know what that feels like?"

'Kennedy just laughed and patted the young lad's cheek. "Good lad."'

If you're too young to remember, Alan Kennedy scored an absolute beauty of a winning goal for Liverpool in the 1981 European Cup Final against Real Madrid. Three years later he scored the decisive final penalty for Liverpool to win it again, in a shootout versus Roma. There can't be too many left backs who've done that, so on balance he probably did share that feeling with Chris's teammate.

Games like this are a rare chance for fans to interact with their heroes in a way other disciplines don't allow. In later life Picasso didn't help out at an amateur life-drawing class in his local church hall. You don't often find Al Pacino doing am dram, and I'm not sure whether Ayrton Senna offered to drive back from a midweek away game.

On the subject of Brazilians, though, here's my mate Tom Findlay, who I play five-a-side with regularly: 'I've had two experiences of playing against famous players and there was a huge gulf between them. In my Friday morning game one of the regulars, Ross, turned up with Raí, the Brazilian midfielder who had won the World Cup in 1994. Raí showed up wearing black plimsolls like you had at school and I recognized him straight away. The reassuring thing was he wasn't that good. I don't know if he'd given up trying or deliberately wasn't that bothered, but you wouldn't have known he'd won the World Cup.'

Funnily enough us Leeds fans thought the same thing when another Brazilian international, Roque Júnior, played for us, and he hadn't even retired then. But I'll let Tom continue: 'At the other end of the scale I played with Frank Worthington, who was just off the scale. He must have been about sixty, long since retired, but I couldn't get the ball off him. Impossible. He was genuinely fantastic and it's only when you see that sort of player that you realize how big the difference is between us and the pros.'

And Tom's a good player. For those of us old enough to be kids during the era of the 1970s Fancy Dans (Worthington, Alan Hudson, Stan Bowles, George Best, Tony Currie etc.), the idea you could actually play with one of them and then have a drink with them afterwards is thrilling.

With celebrities now comes the media and not just the sports photographers, as my friend Jeremy Lascelles can testify: 'I was playing in a music business five-a-side charity tournament at Loftus Road for Deep Purple vocalist Ian Gillan's team, who was signed to our label at the time. We were called Gillan's Goal Getters. It was a great day.

Madness had a team, as did The Beat and Eddy Grant. They were all really big pop stars at the time, so they'd let fans in to watch. There were about 5,000 people there, with Jimmy Hill and Brian Moore as the commentators. That was great, when you scored a goal, hearing Moore's famous voice saying, "And that was a great goal from [pauses while he looks down for your name] Lascelles."

'Anyway, there was a sort of folky singer/entertainer called Richard Digance playing who had a show on Capital Radio at the time. I was a too bit physical for him in a tackle, nothing too bad, but you know it's a contact sport and if you're trying to win the ball you'll occasionally clash, and he spun round outraged and had a go at me. I didn't go as far as to call him a cunt, but it was almost as bad. It was only after I'd shouted that I noticed he had a microphone strapped to his throat and was broadcasting live from the game.'

When I was editor of *loaded* the music promoter Vince Power rang up and asked if we'd be interested in helping the playwright Mick Mahoney, who had been developing the idea of having a five-a-side tournament at the Phoenix Music Festival.

To one of my staff, Adam Black, this was like Christmas, birthday, barmitzvah and Man City winning the league all happening on the same day. Adam was absolutely fucking obsessed with organizing a five-a-side tournament. Any time an advertiser asked for some ideas about an event they could host with us, Adam would break out the metaphoric bibs and balls. It got to the point where he didn't need to come to the marketing ideas meetings because I'd just write 'five-a-side tournament' next to his name.

It was decided that each music industry/media team would have at least two celebs in it. Obviously if you were in a band like The Farm your own team were the celebs, but all the magazines set about asking friendly musicians and actors. I thought, 'Fuck that, we want to win this. We don't want someone off *Brookside*, our celebs need to be ex-professionals.' So we called Chelsea legend Alan Hudson and QPR legend Stan Bowles. This was generally seen as cheating, but it went down well with my staff and we won the tournament. I couldn't go to that Phoenix but the following year I was really up for it. This time we had our mate Billy Duffy from The Cult playing with us regularly anyway, and in goals we had Bob Wilson's son, Robert, who was a *loaded* photographer, but we also called in Stan Bowles and former Liverpool player and Predator boot inventor Craig Johnston. Craig arrived with nothing more than the clothes he stood up in and a pair of new Predators. Both players were very relaxed company and we had a cracking time. The five-a-side was exactly like you'd expect at a rock festival. Drugs and music everywhere.

I sat in a camper van with a well-known comedian friend who was playing in suede ankle boots. He pulled up his football shirt and there was just a massive snail trail of snot full of lumps of cocaine. It wasn't really a trail so much as a snail highway. He'd snorted so much he couldn't run and breathe at the same time, so was snorting it back out down the inside of his shirt during the match.

If you can't beat them join them and we both went out to our prospective next games like Maradona. I broke my toe against a security barrier during the match but couldn't feel any pain because of the amount of stimulants floating through my bloodstream. At one point I scored a beautiful goal and then had to remind myself it was against Frank Sidebottom, a man who was clutching his papier-mâché head as he dived to stop the shot. We hammered Frank's team about 6–0. They wouldn't be dancing in the streets of Timperley that night.

In the semi-final it was a tight 0–0 until Stan decided to step it up a gear. I fed the ball through to him near the edge of the D and he just did this little twist of his shoulders and the opposition keeper flung himself to the floor to stop a shot that wasn't there. Stan took another step to his right and passed it into the night. Given the opposition's special guest was from a Goth band, yes, it was cheating. Stan was England class.

We won the final, but when we were invited up onto the stage to receive our trophy I was off in the Manic Street Preachers' double-decker attending to other matters. Craig enjoyed the event so much he took the pro/celeb idea off to Sky and it became the Sky Soccer Sixes. Sky Soccer Sixes weren't the first television small-sided tournaments by any means. Film writer Richard Luck told me about going to the *Evening Standard* Thames Valley five-a-side tournaments, which you can still see footage of on the Football Attic blog. The clip I watched featured former Reading and Leeds manager Brian McDermott when he played for Arsenal, and a few others who went on to become first team players. The tournament was made up of Under-21s and squad players and seemed to be taken very seriously. The amazing thing is how the ball almost sticks to the ground, only veering above head height with a wayward shot or ricochet from a tackle. Richard told me the best player he saw in those tournaments was QPR's Stan Bowles, but he also saw Chelsea's David Speedie score a goal where he ran the full length of the pitch and went round everyone in a similar tournament at the NEC.

The year after I left *loaded*, the magazine was apparently drawn against a Factory Records team including unlikely footballer Bernard Sumner, from New Order, who told me this story: 'I had to play in a five-a-side team against your old mag *loaded* at the Phoenix and from the very kick-off, the very first kick, Bez broke a bloke from *loaded*'s leg!'

The Phoenix was a brilliant festival, easily one of the best I've ever been to, and a big part of it was the five-a-side. It had bleachers for the crowd, a celebrity host and commentator, sponsored shirts and a great atmosphere, all played out between the stages and the fairground.

Despite getting to play with true legends Stan and Craig, it isn't, however, my favourite experience of playing with unlikely teammates. As I mentioned earlier the Tuesday night game I play in has a few recognizable TV faces from places like *Have I Got News*. When they're not inflicting their own brand of footballing genius on each other they're making everyone laugh or worrying about the state of the Labour Party.

Last January I came back from holiday and my friend Gary said, 'You'll never guess who's been playing Tuesdays while you've been away?' Who? 'Woody Harrelson!' That obviously came as a surprise, because he's not a name you immediately associate with football. He was in London making another film about magicians.

Gary told me this as we were on our way to the game and sure enough, as we're booting the ball around in the massive double-basketball-court-sized gym, in comes Woody, looking a picture of health. We kicked off on the same side and it was like I'd borrowed 'Dead Shot' Keen's boots from *Tiger and Scorcher* character Billy Dane. After five minutes of 0–0 I hammered a shot over from the wing and it swerved in. Woody came bounding across and picked me up in a massive bear hug. It was great and like all deluded lunatics I now figured we would become best mates and I'd soon be sitting alongside him instead of Matthew McConnaughey in the next series of *True Detective*. I'd have been happy with that one goal and the hug, but from then on almost everything I hit went in. And every goal won me a hug and a massive grin. The next eight or nine shots ended up in the net and they weren't just a load of tap-ins. There were goalmouth scrambles, dribbles past players, short shots, long shots, chances from either wing. And this was a big pitch and the teams were fairly balanced. It was uncanny. I've never had a consistent run of so many goals like that.

All the time I was also trying to set Woody up. Every time I scored he'd give me a big hug, so I figured if it went on like this people would start gossiping. By the end of the game I'd scored twelve goals. This is true. No exaggeration. Every shit shot I could have had had been put on hold for future games. I spent the night laughing and shaking my head, a great way to spend 10.10 till 11.25 on a Tuesday night. And yes, in case you're wondering, Woody wasn't a bad player either.

So there you have it, your mates are your bread and butter, but occasionally someone brings you cake. And if you're playing John Barnes or Mel Sterland, they'll probably eat it.

The *loaded* magazine Phoenix Festival Champions. Back Row L-R: Craig Johnston, Grant Fleming, Madam Black, Billy Duffy. Bottom Row L-R Robert Wilson, Les Rowley, Rene Higuita, Stan Bowles.

'That Peter Reid needs a tackle'

On Sunday I played in a drizzling rainy 4–3 victory, ten-a-side on the Talacre eight-a-side pitch with a surface like a tennis ball meets plastic scouring Scrunchie. Great football weather but better suited to grass than an artificial surface. My grazed shins and ankles were still aching two days later. After the game I'd gone straight to bed with my laptop to watch the FA Cup matches and found myself thinking about that day's opposition, Dave Bassett, an amateur team in Barcelona and how good any of us really are.

I had arrived fifteen minutes late for the Sunday game to see a very flash-looking player I'd not encountered before running the show. He had box-fresh trainers, a hairband and a neon undershirt beneath his short-sleeved training shirt. Most significantly, he was moving around very quickly, giving and then regaining possession, passing well and shaping to shoot properly, and he had very clearly created an aura whereby none of my team or his own team would go anywhere near him. It was like the scene in *Catch Me If You Can* where Christopher Walken's character tells the story of how the New York Yankees' opponents are so dazzled by the Yankees' pinstripe baseball kits they forget about the game.

This guy, Darren, had appeared in our game like an exotic magical figure and people were just standing back in awe. No wonder he had all the space to move around – everyone was just admiring his look and movement.

He was agile rather than powerful, but as I pulled my boots on I soon recognized he was indeed a nice player to watch. After I'd joined in, he continued to boss the game unchallenged for a few minutes, then something Dave Bassett had mentioned on our talkSPORT show, *The Warm Up*, about telling Vinnie Jones 'that Peter Reid needs a tackle' came to mind. While play was elsewhere I went over and switched positions with his marker. The next time Darren received the ball he also received a tackle.

I won the ball, he ended up on his arse and won a free kick. In technical terms I went right through him. He got up and laughed good-naturedly at the audacity of it; it wasn't a dirty tackle, just a strong challenge. It was the impact of my body hitting his as my leg came round and took the ball he thought he was receiving that floored him, I hadn't out and out booted him or anything.

Still, it's a non-contact sport now and he took the free kick, from which they scored, so you could argue my intervention wasn't immediately ideal, but it did make a point to everyone on the pitch. Stop watching and start tackling this guy.

After that we started closing him down. My teammates stopped seeing the pinstripes and began to see the man with the ball shaping to shoot. We won the game, so I'm guessing in the long run the intervention was effective. Without it I think he'd have hammered us.

Anyway, my ankles are grazed, so are my shins. The greatest invention in the world would be a quick-hardening spray-on shin and ankle pad that would dissolve in a hot shower. If I'm going to start following Dave Bassett's mantra, I probably need some shin pads. Bassett had been an unexpectedly brilliant interviewee. He gave us a really funny, honest and frank interview, in which he explained he didn't spend much time with the players on match day itself because 'by then they're sick of the sight of me. I prefer to let them relax by themselves. If it was an away game I'd just go off for a run to relax myself.'

It suddenly struck me while listening to this that going for a run in a strange town in the pre-GPS-phone era might have its problems:

'Yes, that's correct. I did get lost once in Hereford. I went off jogging about 1 p.m. when the players were eating and pretty soon I'd left the city and was in the fields, and it was only when I found myself surrounded by cows that I realized I was lost and hadn't a clue where the hotel was. I stopped to think about it and the cows just came in closer and closer. I managed to ask someone directions and thankfully I got back OK and we won 1–0.'

The three of us in the studio were almost in tears. He went on to explain that the team were so self-motivated that he didn't really need to say much after the week's coaching other than something simple like '"That Peter Reid needs a tackle" and then, unfortunately for Reidy, Vinnie Jones would go out and give him one'.

This is what happens when you spend too much time on or listening to talkSPORT, you start upending blokes just because Dave Bassett suggested it might be a decent greeting.

The thing about Darren, and I've only played with him three or four times since then, was at our level he looked a little like the real thing. Plenty of blokes turn up looking the professional part with all the kit, but Darren had it and could play too. In the time I played games with him I never heard him make any claims to greatness.

But there are lots who do, and it is totally deluded, almost psychotic. In every passage of this book where I gleefully describe something good I did in a football game you have to remember, and I know full well, it is at a very normal everyday kickabout standard. Or a school game even. I knew I wasn't going to make it aged eight when I didn't get picked for Leeds City Boys trials, even though I thought I was a good enough player to. Admittedly not eating much until I was into my twenties didn't help, that's the simple truth, but so many people who make spurious claims to footballing greatness genuinely seem to believe them. I had a driver on Friday telling me he played for Palace sixty times under Malcolm Allison in the 1970s, but Wikipedia has no evidence of him. He was such a good liar because he seemed to believe it himself. I've a pretty good bullshit detector in real life, but I still had to go and check the validity of his claims.

It's true many of us think we're better than we are. I do, but I won't lie about past achievements on the pitch. When I came to work and live in the music business in London in the 1980s so many people would tell me, 'I had trials as a kid,' and then we'd have a game and they'd be shit. 'I had trials' was like Americans claiming, 'I was in Vietnam,' or Sex Pistols fans saying, 'I saw them at the 100 Club.'

Thinking about this I was reminded of two stories football writer Andy Mitten told me about a team he runs in Barcelona, in between bombing backwards and forwards to the UK to see Man U every week.

The first, Andy said, was typical of what happened when you run an amateur team in a foreign city. This English guy arrived in Barcelona confidently spouting his football credentials, and offered to help out Andy's team if he needed it. Initially, he claimed he'd played for Palace, but when Andy called him on that he said he'd been on Enfield's books. He was full of it. Little did he know that Andy had written about Enfield's two teams, so when he asked the bluffer if it was FC or Town his whole lie just fell apart. What was he like at training? 'Terrible! He'd put more effort into his story than he had into playing football. He might have been to Enfield on the bus or something, but I don't think he'd ever played for them.'

The other story Andy told me was the opposite of this. Pre-season one of his players mentioned seeing a guy who looked like he knew what he was doing, training with a ball in a park. So they went and met him and gave him a game. 'I put him in at left back because we were getting quite strong everywhere else and he ran the game from there, that's how good he was. He ran the whole game from left back.'

A couple of months into the season the guy's wife, 'who was a gorgeous Argentinian woman', went up to Andy and said, 'Can I just say thanks, because my husband's enjoying his football more than any time since the national team.'

Andy told me, 'I went, "What?" I was amazed. I went home and looked him up. Not only had he played for Belize, he was their captain, he'd played in World Cup qualifiers in front over 40,000. The good players don't have to make a big noise about how good they are because they can just show it.'

There's a simple message for all of us here. Don't over-claim. There's no need for bullshit, because all of us can do something brilliant on a five-a-side pitch at some point in our lives, that's the beauty of it.

You might have taken the bus to Enfield, but if so don't pretend you have played for them. And if you are a former international looking for a game, give me a bell and I'll build a Sunday league team around you.

Getting Fit

If you're young, lean and lethal but with self-destructive tendencies I suggest you skip this chapter, unless you want a really depressing glimpse into what might happen when you hit the wall around thirty to thirty-two. It's an absolute horror show of what a lazy man will go through to avoid the basics of getting fit. How his lacklustre, shoddy and downright pathetic battle for fitness stretches on and off across decades and is never won for more than a few months at a time. The tide of fat goes out and then it comes back in again. Believe me, if you're under thirty and fit, reading this will just fuck your day up. It will hijack whatever hope you've got for life. You're probably still at the age when you think you might still get a tap on the shoulder from a scout. This is about what you might go through to stop that dream fading. You fit young tigers go and run a half-marathon or check Tinder or order some Protein online. Maybe try all three at once. You're making me feel weak just reading this back right now. I don't need to peer out of these pages and see an image of what was once there naturally, what I assumed had been promised for life, and what has run off and got involved with someone else more disciplined than me. Lazy fat bastards who still think they have it? Step right in and enjoy my pain. Help yourself to biscuits and fizzy drinks and we'll get going . . .

The greatest irony of my playing life is that as a kid I didn't eat enough to be a stronger footballer and as a middle-aged man I've eaten too much to be a fit footballer. Fucking marvellous, isn't it? To quote a famous Luton Town fan, I've eaten all the right food in all the wrong order. And sadly even that isn't accurate, as you can't call chocolate, sweets, bread and crisps the right food.

If I drew up a team of the hardest sports-related opponents I've had to face for most of this century it would go something like this:

GK: Greed

RB: Gluttony

CB: Sugar dependency

CB: Fear of missing a meal

LB: Fake hunger

As you can see, in my defence I have no defence. I'm now too fat to keep up with the youngsters and not fit enough to dominate games any more. If you're slim you win, if your core controls you, you control the ball, you control the game. I know that because for quite a long time I could do it.

I've come to understand that what you gain in the dining room you lose on the pitch. Apart from darts, I can't think of another game where so many unfit people still give it a go so religiously as we do in five-a-side. Tug of war and rugby, I hear you cry, but have you seen those guys? Barrels of muscle.

It's a simple confession for me to make, and it's obvious to anyone who sees me, but like a million other Sunday morning Shearers or mid-week Maradonas – I'm out of shape. Twenty-five per cent of the personal ability I write about in this book is in my mind and probably the best thing that could happen to me, apart from slimming down and getting fit, would be getting a Prozone video of myself so I can actually see how little I run during a game.

I am, as a friend once observed, the Wok Smuggler. My XL T-shirts strain tight around the sides and XXL T-shirts bump out like a tarpaulin over a rock. I have photographs which, when I see them, prompt me to think, 'God, I hope one day I can look back at that and think, "How the fuck was I that massive?"' That day is yet to come.

Do you remember 'Belly's gonna get ya!' I shuddered when Reebok had that anti-doughboy TV ad campaign. In it a giant belly bounced around like the huge bubble that chased Number Six Patrick McGoohan around the 1960s cult TV series *The Prisoner*. Here Reebok's belly chased some blokes off the edge of a car park.

In the commercial the belly that was gonna get ya was like a big fat soft blob of uncooked dough. Mine doesn't look as bad as that horrible white floppy thing; it is what the experts in these matters call 'a hard belly'. Years ago, when I was still investing heavily in the South American economy, I read in a copy of American *Men's Health* that soft bellies are easier for men to ditch but more dangerous to have, whereas hard bellies aren't quite so dangerous but will stick around longer. You're fucked if you dough and you're fucked if you doughn't.

When that ad came out I could confidently shrug off the idea that belly was going to get me, because it already had. It was here like a sidecar from hell. The worst thing is that most people think blokes like me have beer bellies, but most of this has happened since I gave up drinking and took to consuming as much sugar in sweets, chocolates, drinks and everyday food as I used to consume in alcohol. I've basically got a Haribelly full of tiny gummy bears, crocodiles, footballs, fake teeth, bananas and everything else that dances out of Johannes 'Hans' Riegel's factory in Bonn (hence Haribo – Hans Riegel in Bonn – one for the pub there).

The general reaction to my stomach among friends is predictable. 'You're not pregnant as well, are you?' I heard that for nine months in 2013, but not exclusively then. I still get it three years on from my second son being born. Often from my first son: 'Have you got a ball up there?' That's a regular. 'What happened to the skinny little kid I used to know?' ask old friends, to which someone will reply, 'He ate him.'

The truth is I can't argue with any of these jokes because they are all well intentioned and accurate. If I could run as much as I can eat, Lewis Cook would be cleaning my boots.

Girlfriends and wives, if you are reading this out of curiosity, it's one of the main reasons we keep going out to play five-a-side, in the ill-conceived belief that it will get us fit. Obviously, physical evidence suggests otherwise. I play four times a week sometimes and I'm actually getting fatter as I get older.

I don't drink but I do eat. I have this thing where when I start doing something I enjoy my adrenalin kicks in and I feel like I need to feed it to stoke it up. I graze permanently. Not only do I like to eat massive meals, but I also usually eat a lot between meals. I eat nervously and habitually before watching Leeds or going on air at talkSPORT, I eat because the fridge is open, I eat because the cupboard has food in it, I eat because I'm going past a shop and I talk myself into seeing what they've got in there. I often eat red liquorice laces at petrol stations (in passing, not as a night out). I eat endlessly. Maybe it's because I talk so much my mouth is always open and inviting. Who knows why all of this is? Maybe it's because I didn't eat much as a kid.

Right now, I'm eating because the café I'm typing in has a massive array of croissants and cakes and seeing them triggered an impulse to order one. If only that trigger could zap the desire out of existence instead of prompting me to eat . . . Then I'd be back among the scissor-kick goals. In Leeds, the doctors have a name for this condition – Greedy Fat Fucking Bastard, or at least that's the diplomatic doctors you'll find addressing everyone's health in the bar when a problem rears up.

At certain restaurants I know the bread is delicious and it's very hard not to eat it. All. And then a second basket. In Rye there was until recently a sweet shop called Sweet Memories of Rye. I liked it so much in there that when the owner announced he was closing down (because the landlord had increased the rent) I offered to go into business with him. Old school harder jelly sweets like wine gums, sports mixture and fruit salad were my sweets of choice in there. Every trip to the seaside demands fish and chips, which is fine when it's a holiday, but when you spend half your time living by the seaside it gets a bit much. I once read in *Men's Health* that one portion of fish and chips equals a whole block of lard. That put me off for a few months, but then I negotiated myself back in with a plea bargain agreement of not eating the bread and butter. This could just go on.

Specialists would probably call this cross-addiction or an eating disorder. I'm certainly eating this order and eating that order. But whatever it is it doesn't help my game. For the simple reason that my body can't do what my brain tells it to. So you look and feel shit even though you're thinking, 'I used to be able to do that.'

My weight shouldn't come as a surprise. When I edited *Jack* magazine I used to eat so many sweets that the deputy editor, Paul, called me Haribo Lecter. I quite liked that actually, and I can still remember looking up across the small development office and saying, 'Do you think all these sweets are actually really bad for me?' Paul looked back at me in disbelief, replying, 'Erm, yes.' I am now fully aware of how this problem with food has hindered my ability to play football. My legs have been carrying excess upper body weight for a long time now, the knees and shins and ankles alerting me to it on a weekly basis.

So there we have it, I'm really unfit. I look like a snake that's swallowed a small elephant and been stood on its end. I'd like to say it hasn't always been this way, but in reality it has for a long time.

I do, however, know that I'm not alone. A problem shared is, like a packet of biscuits, a problem halved. On and off the pitch I have some hefty mates, most of whom have simply ballooned as their metabolism slowed down. Right now I'm fairly confident some of you are brushing crumbs and wrappers off the book to be able to read the next line. Tunnock's Tea Cakes? Choco Leibniz? Chocolate Malted Milk? I share your pain and your weight gain. Although, in truth, it's rarely been painful; it's just annoying when I'm too fucked to run. Also I've always got the asthma to blame for that. 'Sorry I can't chase back, lads, it's my asthma,' gets a more sympathetic response than, 'Sorry, guys, I've just started getting into Fry's Chocolate Cream again. They've reissued peppermint.'

Having been super-skinny throughout my childhood and slim throughout my twenties, I can remember clearly the first time I noticed I looked a bit fat round the midriff. The *loaded* day out to Hastings in about 1996, during which we actually had a really good game on the clifftops. Photographic evidence of the day captured a whole load of pasty-looking blokes eating, drinking, snorting and cavorting on the stony beach beyond Rock-a-Nore fishermen's huts. Topless. As I was going through the various prints in the office a few days after the trip (this was before phones had cameras and when everyone printed their holiday snaps to see them), I noticed a photo of our online editor, Adam Porter, crouching on the beach. Adam was a keen footballer himself who would much later join our Sunday morning game, but in this shot he was clearly sporting a spare tyre around the stomach. Then on the next print I thought, 'Jesus, I look as bad as Ad.'

Both of us were sitting on the beach leaning forward and just had these big creases of excess flesh wrapped round between our chests and shorts. Human Michelin men without the jaunty step, smile and cap, sat on a beach eating and drinking. This was a whole new world. My body had changed shape after a couple of years of publishing success and eating crisps and drinking for a living, and I hadn't noticed.

It's been pretty much downhill since then. Over the next ten years sugar replaced alcohol and lying on the sofa replaced dancing in clubs. Some of you are still with me on this point, I know. On the pitch I didn't think anything about it. I could still use my pace to go past players and step up or down a gear; it wasn't like I was falling over like someone in a fat suit on *It's a Knockout* or *Takeshi's Castle*.

The weird thing about the excessive football and food diet is your legs don't get fat. Where does this leave you? With the ability to quickly run into restaurants and takeaways, that's where.

My aim when I'd started playing five-a-side with James, Spike and Gary on a Sunday morning under the arches in Shoreditch, a few years after this *loaded* beach pic was taken, had been to get back to the standard where I could take the ball from my goal, go past everyone and score. As I'd been able to when I was eighteen. I did get back to that level – it's a quick sprint with invention and swerving and a good finish – but suddenly I was in my forties, not my thirties, and my metabolism was slowing and my scoffing wasn't.

One day I was chatting to Gary on the way home after a game and he laughed and said, 'Do you know what that Everton fan Ian said to me during the game today, just after you scored that goal against us?'

'No, what?' I asked.

'James is pretty fast for a fat guy, isn't he?'

I couldn't believe it. This was a double-edged compliment, the male equivalent of 'You're pretty sexy for a fat lass.' What's wrong with just saying I'm pretty fast or she's pretty sexy?

This was only the second time it had actually entered my head that I was no longer Slim Jim – first the beach photo and now this. Even just remembering and writing it down is making me want to eat less. The mad thing is that losing weight is simple but not easy. All you have to do is eat less and exercise more.

Needless to say, I've studiously avoided following this plan of action for a long time and, like the person who has researched but never established what they want to do in life professionally, I have undertaken all manner of attempts to get fit and never settled on any of them. I do know that the simplest way is just to eat less. Smaller portions, more often. Cut the grazing. Ditch the sweets, bread and crisps. I know this. I wrote for *Men's Health* for a number of years. It was staring me in the face every month. But knowing and doing are different things altogether.

My weight has never broken me. It's not quite as bad as I'm making out and I've never hit rock bottom. I'm about two stone overweight, it's not like they're taking the roof off and lowering me in or out of my bedroom by crane. But it has been tedious not being able to get back to a decent running weight in the last decade. As a teenager I could run for miles easily. I could get round the school cross-country course – which was mainly just round a bit of the ring road – in eight minutes ten seconds, which was fast.

Now I actually tell people I can't run because I think about what my shins feel like when I do actually run while playing, and I don't fancy it. What I mean is I can't run for a concerted time, but I can sprint if it's needed during a game.

So having given you a solid status report on my lack of fitness, the fats and figures, so to speak, I'm now going to recount my attempts to deal with this.

They fall into two different categories, which I'll name Regular and Spectacular. The Regular are obvious, anyone can do them and you, the reader, undoubtedly have done. They include gyms, personal trainers, cycling, swimming, diet, walking, chopping wood, yoga and pilates. I've attempted all of these, with varying degrees of enthusiasm and a consistent lack of serious staying power. And of course there's always playing more football. Which sharpens you up but doesn't really help you lose weight.

The Spectacular are things you are unlikely to have done, like colonic irrigation, drinking my own piss, yoga at altitude and kayaking near wolves. I'd fully understand if you read this list and say, 'What! Is the bloke insane as well as fat?'

Some of the Spectacular came about because I was open-minded and would do anything for a laugh, for a perceived health improvement or simply because someone suggested it. Others were done for money, in the pay of various media organizations. 'Give James a ring, he'll probably have a crack at that.'

Where shall we start, the Spectacular or the Regular? You have a think about this while I go and get another cup of tea and try not to open the cupboard doors.

Still here? OK, let's dive straight in with the tube up the arse. I'm hoping for all our sakes this comes under the Spectacular and not the Regular, because I like to think I did this for the good of mankind. I've done it so you don't have to. Just keep reminding yourself, 'There's a tenuous link to football fitness here.' Also if you *are* eating maybe put either the book or the sandwich down now. The sad thing about my experience with colonic irrigation is that it started because someone was killed. Really.

In the early 2000s, when I started my own publishing company, I rented the upper floors of a building above a restaurant in the City of London, midway between the diamond district and the banks. Our immediate neighbour was what was euphemistically called on their promotional material a gentlemen's club. You wouldn't find anyone like Mycroft Holmes in there – all white beards and high white collars and so on – because it wasn't the sort of gentlemen's club you find in Pall Mall, full of deep red leather armchairs, massive bookshelves and huge oil paintings of people who used to be in charge of India or Afghanistan for the British Empire. In those sorts of clubs they often don't let women in; in this sort of gentlemen's club they do let women in, but they don't let their clothes in.

This particular lap-dancing club was very popular with the local crime fraternity and most nights there were stretch limos parked up the road. One sunny morning I arrived at work to find my employees stood round outside the restaurant looking at a load of sawdust on the floor, and a cordon of police tape that was stopping them getting into the office. In the gutter was blood. For a moment it felt like *Farringdon Vice*.

A few hours before there'd been an incident outside the club and one of the punters wouldn't be coming back again. After milling around for a while my mate John Carver, whose company rented the top floor, arrived and we decided those who wanted to work could go home and do so, while those who wanted to go to the pub and talk about the sawdust and blood could do that too.

We headed up to the great Filthy McNasty's between King's Cross and Islington, and sat outside on the benches in the sun. It will give you an indication of what sort of start time media companies have when you hear that it wasn't long before Gerry opened the pub.

Noticing I was no longer drinking, and knowing what my consumption had been like before I stopped, John turned to me and said, 'With all that crap you put inside you, you should go and get colonic irrigation at this clinic in Regent's Park. That will sort it out.'

I looked at him like he was nuts. 'No chance. I wouldn't really want to see what's inside me. There's probably little plastic soldiers I chewed when I was a kid and God knows what else.'

'No, seriously,' he went on, 'you wash the outside of your body every day so why not the inside?'

'You lose weight doing it too,' added his wife, Anna.

At this I could suddenly see some benefit and started to slightly entertain the idea. Three weeks later I was stood naked but for a backless blue paper hospital gown with a very nice lady talking to me very gently about what was going to happen. I stood nervously, hardly hearing her, looking at a machine that resembled a cross between a petrol pump, a home brew kit and a massive spirit level. (If you're thinking, 'What the fuck has this got to do with five-a-side?' they used to say the same about yoga, but it helped Niall Quinn and Ryan Giggs, didn't it? One day all footballers might get their arses flushed for health reasons. How often do we listen to managers and think, 'God, they're full of shit.' Could work.)

I was looking at this machine, running things very quickly through my mind. I'd already had one life-changing treatment, called Metaform, in a thatched cottage in Dorset after I'd got clean, so I had that in mind. If I was healthier I'd play better football, surely?

So I lay on my back, looked at the crystals around the room and tried not to wince as the lady inserted the hosepipe. Yeah, I know, this doesn't read right at all. We should be discussing free kicks or something, but stay with me.

Anyway, she slowly pumped water into me, then seemed to swill it out, putting more in each time until it eventually hit the high-water mark and then the process was reversed. I only had a brief look at the glass tubes but it looked like there was Special K in there and all sorts of stuff. Imagine emptying a dirty goldfish bowl, that sort of set-up, without the weed and the plastic castle.

'Ah, a lot of heavy metals and candida,' she said.

You never want to hear you've got heavy metal coming out of your arse. This threw me a bit. Apparently you can get it from grinding your teeth and your fillings. Or in food. Either way, it's not good. The candida was some sort of infection that made me tired, which explained a lot. There were no marbles, little soldiers, bottle tops, number plates or anything else like that. I was relieved to find the clearance hadn't been like when Richard Dreyfuss and Roy Scheider cut open the first shark in *Jaws*.

This all lasted less than twenty minutes. Entry and exit were tricky, and the subsequent immediate visit to the toilet was something I'll sadly not forget in a hurry. I didn't pass any other five-a-side players on the way in or out.

Did pumping water up my backside help my football? No. The lady did notice a few other things that helped though.

'Do you drink a lot?'

'I used to, why?'

'Your liver is damaged. You're pretty run down all round.'

She got me some powder to help, but she noticed that by looking at my eyes. Not my arse. No, the colonic hosepipe up my arse had no direct effect on my game at all, but getting rid of the candida definitely helped my energy levels.

The second most spectacular attempt to improve my health and match fitness did actually lose me a lot of weight, made me more flexible and gave me one brilliant night of laughter with TV comic Rowland Rivron. It also prompted a woman who did the guest list at Brixton Academy to say it was the funniest thing she'd ever seen on television. So I'm guessing it actually worked. And I still have some muscle and mental memory to draw on to try and help myself ten years later.

Strange though it may seem to anyone who's seen me just dicking around on Twitter or labouring round a pitch, there was a time during and after the *loaded* years when I would get asked to do an awful lot of unusual things in the media. Appear on *Celebrity Big Brother*, edit national newspapers, host my own Channel 4 chat show, that sort of thing. Once I'd turned them all down for various reasons, including worrying what people thought of me, fear, being too young, drunk and stupid, and lack of interest, I was asked if I fancied going to the Himalayas to an 'extreme health' camp.

Given that I wanted to slim down, this actually appealed to me, and when they said Rowland Rivron was going too I agreed on two conditions: don't call it 'Celebrity Something' and nothing involving my arse on television. 'No, no, no, we won't do either of those,' promised the production company. So I signed on for some combat yoga up the mountains and a few months later I was in something called *Extreme Celebrity Detox*, shitting water up a mountain. There are still a few clips of it on YouTube if you want a laugh.

Spitalfields of Glory

At the very beginning of my rehab from drink and other ill-advised lifestyle choices, aged thirty-one, I would visit Clive Meindl the addiction counsellor in a room at the back of the company doctor's offices in Sloane Street, Knightsbridge. I was pretty suspicious of what was going on, and still drinking heavily, but knew I wanted to change how I felt at 3 a.m. most mornings and to do so I should listen to what he had to say. I needed help.

Early on in the process, Clive placed a chair five feet away from where I was sitting and told me to imagine there was a drink on it. 'Now I want you to place five things between you and that imaginary drink that you would rather have or be doing than getting pissed every night.'

I said the immediately obvious things about family and sanity, but significantly I also put in, 'I want to play football regularly again.' That was number 3. It wasn't so much the consumption that had stopped me playing regularly for over a decade but the total chaos and disorganization that came with it. Travelling around the UK and abroad with the *NME* on a fortnightly basis had initially stopped me finding a regular game, plus the fact there were so few visible five-a-side places in the mid-1980s.

It was the lifestyle that removed any consistency and reliability from my social life. In fact my work and social life had become totally blurred. Like most music writers I went to gigs every night and I'd be drinking at all of them; then there were long weekends away flying across the Atlantic discovering America. It was great.

By early 1992 I'd just left the *NME* and split up with the long-term girlfriend I lived with when my mum died. So after that there was no structure at all to my life. Naturally I was deeply disturbed and depressed by her death, but I was twenty-six, the Beastie Boys had introduced me to pure grass spliffs and were encouraging me to go and live in LA, and music publicists had introduced me to fine wine and cocaine. I was hanging around with a bunch of mates in a small-time band just doing fuck all really. When I needed cash I'd sell some of my records or write a piece for the *Sunday Times*. I had no structure, no deadlines, no relationship, no requirement to show up anywhere every day or week. There was nothing for five-a-side to be an escape from. Around this time I was developing a men's lifestyle magazine about football, music, comedy and clubbing and was wondering whether to go to LA or stay and see this development out.

Once I'd stayed and launched the hurricane that was *loaded* I'd washed up fucked on the exclusive tropical beach that was *GQ*, desperately in need of some structure and a rest. Even in the early *GQ* days I'd stay out all Friday, go to bed about 8 a.m. Saturday, wake up for *Final Score* and do the same Saturday into Sunday.

So when I was lucky enough to have the company offer me rehab on the insurance policy and Clive asked me what I wanted back in my life again I knew I wanted to play football every week. I had missed it. I wanted that kick of excitement, the adrenalin rushes and the competition that came with playing a lot. Throughout my childhood until the early years of secondary school I'd been playing three or four times a day. It was in my blood, my routine, it was linked to my adrenal glands, and all of this had been largely bombed out by a decade of music, travel, drinking and drugs. Not bad things to bomb it out for, but I wished I could have maintained some form, fitness and regularity. I could have done with the natural endorphin rush. Instead I'd been treating my body and mind like a dustbin lorry.

By my late twenties and early thirties I'd been using drink and drugs not just for fun, but also to blot out recent feelings about my mum's death and other experiences that had sat unwelcome and ingrained since my early childhood. When I finally had an opportunity to get professional help, I wanted to recapture those feelings I had as a kid playing in the streets in Headingley, to obliterate the ever-weakening cradle of excess that was both supporting and ruining me.

I wanted to feel like I did tussling for a ball on a concrete road and turning and hammering it against a terrace end or the garages next to our house. Not sitting up at 4 a.m., God knows where, with a storm of paranoia whirling through my head and my nose and sinuses totally clogged with baby laxative and some shitty fake British cocaine.

I also knew that as much as I'd like to be back on that wall at the corner of Headingley Avenue sucking ice pops all day long, I'd taken the grown-up dollar at *GQ* and the second childhood at *loaded* was over.

I did understand and remember that feeling, though. I knew I was good at football, especially enclosed-environment football, where invention and quick thinking worked in your favour. I knew I could hit the ball harder than I had ever done as a kid. That had come simply from reading about Ronald Koeman's amazing three-step free kick that knocked England out of the 1994 World Cup. How positioning your body right and hitting the ball at the correct pace and angle gave you all the power you'd need to hammer the ball with direction.

During the early sessions Clive also gave me a leaflet called 'The Cross-Addiction Questionnaire', a multiple-choice tick-box Q&A sheet that was designed to discover whether I might be addicted to anything else beyond the obvious drugs and drink. It's fair to say I performed better in this than I'd done in my mock A-levels. I got A grades in the two I was in for, and Cs for sex and food. I know what you're saying, these all sound great things to get addicted to. It's the repetitive bind that wears you out, the lack of control, the fear, the lies, the social and physical cost. The overpowering sense of not being in control over what you're going to do next. I still feel it today around the internet, which is why I dumped my smartphone.

Weirdly, there was a section about sport addiction. Yes, sport addiction. I read through the questions and just laughed. Clive looked at me enquiringly.

'People don't do this, do they? Sport addiction? Who's addicted to the gym?'

'You'd be surprised,' he said, before telling me how lots of people acted out in different ways, from bulimia and anorexia to overeating, gambling, sport and the obvious two I was in for, drugs and drink. He said he treated people with all of these problems. Bulimia and anorexia were becoming big issues in the media because of the controversies about super-skinny catwalk models, and Princess Diana had admitted suffering with bulimia. I had never heard of sport addiction, though, despite a massive boom in gym culture. The sport questions seemed really strange:

Do you hang around at gyms and sports centres hoping to join other people's games?

Do you keep spare kit in your desk or work bag in case the unplanned opportunity of a game or training comes up?

Do you have bags full of unwashed kit lying around at home? [Some of you are starting to nod 'yes' now aren't you.]

Do you ever drop and do press-ups or other exercises when no one else is looking at work?

I ticked the 'No' box on almost all the twenty questions and then just looked up at Clive with an amused look. Really?

'Yes,' he replied, 'as real as your problems are.'

I didn't like doing press-ups in a gym, never mind voluntarily dropping and doing the punishment scene from *An Officer and a Gentleman* for fun. The only time I'd seen anything like this was at a Billy Idol gig at the Astoria Theatre on Charing Cross Road. The Bromley Boy with the Platinum Quiff now had a head full of short blond dreadlocks and was singing a set of his hits, including 'White Wedding', 'Rebel Yell', 'King Rocker' and 'Dancing with Myself'. In the middle of delivering his first-generation MTV anthems he dropped and banged out twenty press-ups during a guitar solo. Maybe he'd swapped drugs for treadmills. Maybe it was just a way of helping keep himself clean. Hadn't Iggy Pop and Alice Cooper famously taken up golf when they'd kicked their drug habits?

Back with the sport section of the cross-addiction questionnaire, Clive said, 'These questions might seem weird to you, but the drug or sex ones can look utterly bizarre to others.'

Fair enough. And we moved on. None of my lesser questionnaire results had done enough to get him to move away from the issues of drink and drugs, but the reality is it's all the same addictive issue, as the questionnaire implied. It was just a case of how you let it manifest itself, in what area you acted it out.

It would be almost twenty years later, in 2015, before I could say my interest in five-a-side became obsessive, but I don't think it was ever addictive. Even then the desire to play more and more games was driven by wanting to get fit and enjoy myself, and also, as I hit fifty, there was the slow realization that I might not always be able to play.

Thankfully, Clive and I kept on seeing each other twice a week and after five months I actually stopped using and drinking, which my friend Paul, an Everton fan who had helped me, described as 'a total miracle given the state you were in'. It wasn't as simple as those sentences make it seem, but I guess that's for another book. It was very difficult, very emotional, and what came after, being clean and sober, was a whole new deal. A big massive sky of raw experience. But it did mean I had masses and masses of time that used to be taken up with drinking. The days and weekends seemed so long now.

To fill that time I did two specific things. I started an official football magazine with my club, Leeds United, called *Leeds Leeds Leeds*. And I started looking for five-a-side games to play.

When I told the boys back at *GQ* I wanted to play football regularly again, Tony, the Everton-supporting art director, said he knew a game every Sunday in Spitalfields Market. So he called Pete and Gary and Ersoi, who were his mates and former colleagues on the *Sunday Times* magazine and as fortune would have it, they needed a new team to play against every week. So that was that: we needed to get a team together from the staff at *GQ*.

People often asked what it was like working at the apparently strait-laced Condé Nast Publications (*Tatler, Vogue, World of Interiors*) after the chaos of *loaded* (Crisps World Cup, Platinum Rogues, Buy Us a Pint Tour) and I'd just give them the ratio of women to men at the company, around 400 to 60. It was a very comforting environment, especially after what had happened with my mum. It only took me to explain that stat for blokes to see the upside of the move.

Around this time I interviewed Rod Stewart in his local in Essex for the front of the *The Times* Saturday magazine, and while we had a good kickabout in the car park for the photo session he asked me the same question, 'Why did you leave *loaded*?' When I told him the ratio, he looked at me wolfishly and replied, 'James, my son, you work in Spunk Towers.' By the time this story made its way into a newspaper gossip column it had been toned down to Totty Towers. Which to me is a rugger bugger's word, the only known use of the word in football being when Leeds United played Roma in the UEFA Cup and young centre back Jonathan Woodgate said, 'I'm not sure how I'm going to tell my girlfriend I've just spent the night in Rome chasing Totti about.'

Much as the ratio created a lovely working and socializing environment, there weren't many men to select a team from. The prospects that lay before us weren't good.

On the subs' desk there were two redheads called Mike and Paul who supported Liverpool and Man U: Mike looked like a teddy bear and Paul a ginger version of the monster in *Carry On Screaming*. Despite being great at their job, these subs weren't going to make our five-a-side bench.

Likewise Tony's art department wasn't really boasting anyone who looked like they could play competitive sport for an hour. There was senior designer Ashie G, who was very laid-back and ran the Hampstead Hip Hop massive from his mum's house, but that was the only running he did.

Junior designer Jamie had been a child extra in *Grange Hill*. When I asked him what that had been like he replied, 'It was great. Whenever they stopped filming I could sneak away and get some sleep on the bamboo beds on the set of *Tenko.*' He was a big lad who obviously preferred being horizontal to vertical, so we tried him out as a possible goalie. But then it turned out he also had an array of really old school diseases, like gout, gangrene, botulism and ague cheek. Anything mentioned in Shakespeare, he'd have had it. It's hard to turn up regularly on a Sunday for five-a-side when you're in and out of the apothecary's.

Beyond the designers' and subs' area was the writers' room. There were more people in there, but they offered little in the way of potential world-beaters on the small green pitch. At the editorial meeting for my first issue I announced I'd secured a Roy Keane interview from an Irish TV producer. One of the section editors asked, 'Who's Roy Keane?' This was the season Man U would go on to win the Champions League.

What of the candidates? There was Morgan, who did boxing and training but claimed to be useless with his feet. There was Leeds fan Iestyn, who had communication issues – he only spoke native Welsh out of patriotic duty – and he preferred golf. There was Bill, who was a former *NME* colleague and Creation Records musician I'd signed from the check-shirted boys at *Q* magazine. Then there were Sanj, who'd be up for anything but wasn't very well coordinated, and Martin, who had the physique of a snowman.

Tony and I looked at each other and decided it might be better to form a women's team. We agreed that 'at least the after game drinks would be better'. I did, however, have a solution. Tony needed another designer for his art team at the time, so instead of interviewing anyone else for the job I suggested a good footballer called Miles on the *loaded* art desk. Once he'd seen so many women walking around, and the increased wage packet, Miles was in. He was really into fashion and could design magazines no problem, but essentially he was hired for the five-a-side team. We couldn't give him a signing-on fee, like the boss, Mr Newhouse, had given me to defect, but he was more than happy with the deal.

The most popular bloke who worked on the mag was David Gyseman, Geezer, who oversaw the production process between the editorial, advertising and printers. I'm not sure Geezer ever really liked his nickname but given he was from Hoxton (when it was horrible) and he was one of the few Condé Nast employees who hadn't been to public school, finishing school or owned a large part of Devon, it was perhaps inevitable he was painted as some sort of Arthur English in *Are You Being Served?*-style character. Which really was unwarranted. Anyway, Geezer was great at football too, having spent years playing at the Hoxton Young Ratters and Robbing Society under Coach Fagin. So that was four of our team.

Someone knew a goalie called Vince who fancied a game, so then we were five. I had to go to New York for a meeting with the American *GQ* publisher to discuss starting the *GQ* Man of the Year Awards in Britain. The publisher there was actually a Brit who'd played for Crystal Palace, and he told me I'd be able to get some kit from Nike Town, which turned out to be the sort of retail battleship we just didn't have in the UK back then. I bought five new burgundy and black football shirts and a keeper's top on expenses and back home I explained it would be 'good for morale and team bonding' to the MD, who'd queried it. They were good shirts and I still have mine.

So how did we figure fitness-wise? Miles and Geezer were in good nick. I was fresh from my early days of rehab, a bit shaky, couldn't sleep at night and had big detox swellings on my gums, plus I still had thick curly hair all over my face. On the upside I was still skinny and could run, so was raring to go.

Tony, meanwhile, was suffering from mild delusion of sporting grandeur. He was probably the fittest of us all because he cycled to work every day. This short sprint from the Barbican to the West End was, in his eyes, proof he was fitter than the England team of the time. Which seems mad thinking about it now, and even madder back then, because he genuinely believed it and would argue the toss about it. Anyway, such self-belief and fitness helped us. Although it was best not to get him talking about professional football or he'd just start muttering and growling about Liverpool being 'Red Shite' and singing the praises of the mighty Duncan Ferguson.

We arranged to play the *Sunday Times* mag lot the following Sunday and we were on our way to Wembley. Well, we were actually off to Spitalfields, situated between Liverpool Street and Brick Lane. The venue was unusual in that the pitches were smack bang in the middle of this huge East End market, which at the time was slowly starting to undergo the beginnings of gentrification.

When I'd first begun coming to London regularly in the mid-1980s, and stayed in Whitechapel, we would regularly walk home from parties and gigs in King's Cross and Camden through this dark, deserted warehouse area and see the flower lorries loading up at Spitalfields. It couldn't have been less like Shoreditch is now.

By the time we started playing football there in the late 1990s the

Chapman Brothers had their art studio, there was a good bar, and a wide variety of second-hand clothing, record and food stalls, not to mention the slight encroachment of really expensive pointless stuff like windmills made out of wire and painted wooden ties, which were a sure sign of things to come.

It was half Sunday shopping area and half market sports centre. The two five-a-side football pitches lay end to end across the breadth of the market and were surrounded by floor-to-ceiling nets and waist high boards. There were two tiny pitches for little kids next to them. The Spitalfields pitches were great to play on because you'd have the buzz and music of the market, and loads of light and fresh air coming in through the huge open gateways to the market itself. Plus there was the waft of all sorts of exotic food. It really was a superb atmosphere and many people I've spoken to in the course of researching this book mentioned they'd played there.

Geezer and Miles had both grown up in the heart of the East End in Hoxton and Bow and were already amazed by how the area was changing. It was better in many ways, but transforming into a trendy commercial hub they could never have imagined.

The opposition were designers Gary, Big Pete Winterbottom and Ersoi, and others. Ersoi was a brilliant keeper, one of the best I've played against, and that meant that while we could zip past them with pace and good passing we'd still have to get past Erse in the nets.

This was probably the best regular five-a-side game I'd played in since school. We really complemented each other and playing the same opposition every week meant a consistency grew up between both teams that made for very good games.

This wasn't lost on blokes who'd been dragged out to go shopping in the craft market. Whoever was playing on those pitches at weekends would regularly be performing in front of an interested audience. You knew you were playing well when people actually clapped a goal.

I can't remember whether we had a head-height rule, but both teams were good enough to keep it low, fast and moving, as classic five-a-side should be. We had excellent teamwork and could all score, but the opposition had Pete's cannon of a shot, which could puncture a hole in our defence any time.

I was healthy, I had Sundays free and it wasn't far from my house. I was living on Cheshire Street, off Brick Lane, which was like a ghost street, empty refurbished shops, a junkyard, an old café and Blackmans shoe shop, where I had bought black DM shoes in the late 1980s. All just a couple of minutes' walk from the pitches.

As in our school first XI, a great team with good mates gives you a second sense of where your teammates will be and allows you to play passes without looking up, knowing they'll have moved into that space. When you come to know a player's movements and runs, it becomes almost telepathic and simple. The great striking partnerships like Beardsley–Rush, Beardsley–Cole, McAvennie–Cottee and Snodgrass–Beckford all had it. So did we. That sounds arrogant, but all of you who have formed a great competitive five-a-side team with your mates know what I mean. It *is* instinctive. Turning out of a tackle and playing it to the wing without looking up, knowing your teammate is already running into that space, is one of the great rewards of five-a-side. You think you're just going to boot a ball around, but then you discover your sixth sense.

I have nothing but good memories of this game where, even if you hammered the ball and missed, it would bulge into the dividing netting and swirl around like it was actually in the back of a full-sized goal. Sadly, after a short while the owners announced their intention to knock half the market down and turn it into a proper retail area and that was it, the pitches were gone.

This meant we had to find somewhere else to play, as did the two other teams on the next pitch, who turned out to be the guys I'd spend the next seventeen years playing with. Then they were a strange mix of unlikely indie-music figures – my old colleague S. Wells of the *NME*, Robert Lloyd from The Nightingales, my really old mate Martin from The Redskins, Ed Ball from Creation Records and friend of a friend, James Kyllo, and his mates. I'd filled in for them every now and then, and when the *Sunday Times* boys didn't fancy a new pitch I started playing Sundays with James in the dripping dungeon of the arches by Brick Lane.

Normal Fitness

I said we'd get on to normal fitness, so relax, there's no more colonic. Five-a-side is one of the few games I can think of where, if you're not fit, you can get worse the more you play over the long term. With tennis, fishing, cricket and golf I'm sure patience, age and wisdom benefit you. But with five-a-side football as time passes your body gets older and the opposition gets younger and your teammates get older and creakier too. If you're not fit you're fucked. I speak from a lot of experience in this area, as my fellow players will testify.

If you think about it, someone offering five-a-side-specific training would probably rake it in. Technical tips on playing in a very small environment are available for little kids in the Brazilian Soccer Schools, but for us adults who remember Brazilians as runners and distance shooters there are fewer options. Ian Rush's Finishing School was a great idea, I'm just not sure why these things are always aimed at kids or pros. When I mentioned to a guy I play with that I was thinking of getting some tips from Rushy for this book, he looked at me like I was cheating. Which seems bizarre given how many people get professional fitness help. Why not spend money on improving your game?

Another potential successful entrant to this market would be the personal trainer who specializes in what will specifically help you over an hour of five-a-side. Short, sharp bursts of speed, constant running, directional change, intense use of stamina, the ability to turn quickly and shoot – these are the things you need. For the last ten years what meagre training I have done has revolved around hitting things and people quickly and powerfully, with my fists rather than my feet. I would gladly have spent more time training to play, not training to live. Once you get involved in working on your fitness, there are a lot of people you play with to match yourself against or be inspired by.

One specimen on the fitness index was the Lionel Jeffries lookalike who turned up alone one Sunday morning in white shorts, T-shirt, socks and pumps. This was about a decade ago and I'd say he was well into his sixties then. If you don't know who Lionel Jeffries was, he played the grandad in *Chitty Chitty Bang Bang*. Bald head, white moustache, clichéd British Empire dialogue.

This old boy looked the spitting image of him. Only he was deadly fit, like he'd been a PE instructor in the army. He was like a fucking time traveller, no one knew him, no one could fault him, he was a great teammate, and no one ever saw him again. He just ran the back four of the team he was on, talking quietly and confidently, intercepting dangerous balls and passing them on to his midfield. A total mystery, but he was fit and a lesson to us all. Stay fit and flexible and you can keep playing. Which is apt, because right now I feel like an old washing machine someone threw on a grass verge.

There are the fitness obsessives too to consider. One regular at our Wednesday and Sunday games for quite a few years was Lofty, who managed musicians for a living. He would cycle from Hackney to Camden and then run and run throughout the game without looking a bit knackered. He hadn't just crawled out of a car like most of us. The year I got fit and came top of James Kyllo's 6aside.net players' league the actual result came down to the last game. I wasn't aware of this and thought I'd already got enough winning points to have beaten the rest of the sixty-odd players who'd shown up on a Wednesday or a Sunday at least five times across the year. At half-time and with the game nicely balanced I said to Gary, 'Why's Lofty going for it so much?' He replied, 'Because if he wins this he overtakes you and wins the league.'

Blimey, I went out and bagged a couple and made sure our team was safe. It was a great second half, very competitive and tight. A one-on-one battle in the middle of an eight-a-side game. Later that week I was out with Lofty and his wife, Michelle, said to me, 'Lofty was taking your football league very seriously. At half-time during the Cup Final he was in the living room doing press-ups. When I asked him what he was doing he replied, "Must beat James." '

That's fitness nuts for you, they're mad. Fitness is natural to some, spoiled by lack of exercise and bad diet by others, but to play five-a-side regularly you definitely need a bit of it. That's where the challenge comes in.

We may live in an era when Generation Selfie thinks they can stay fit and body-conscious for life, but you've only got to go to a Leeds match to realize this isn't the case for those of us born in the 1960s and 1970s. We have lived through the fitness lifestyle boom and managed to avoid the lure of the doors of the high street gyms.

People take gyms for granted now, but there was a time when high streets and hotels weren't plastered in branded fitness offerings. The first time I saw wall-to-wall lines of running machines and step machines was in New York in the late 1980s. Nothing like that existed in the UK then, but now they're everywhere.

When they did arrive, they were closely followed by their evil counterpart, direct debit. People found themselves signing up to get fit, going for a month after Christmas, another month before the summer holiday, and the rest of the time not noticing the monthly fee slipping out of the account while they rarely went anywhere near the gym. This was the business model. If everyone who is a member of a gym actually showed up at the same time it would look like Glastonbury.

As you can obviously tell, I'm not a massive fan of corporate gyms, but on the other hand I have had the pleasure of knowing three independent trainers who've been of some use to me, while I presumably have been of some amusement and mild financial benefit to them.

The first was Ray Klerck, a six-foot-plus copper-headed South African who was sent round by *Men's Health* to give me eight weeks' intensive training for their 'Media Fitness Challenge' feature in 2006. The idea was to see how fit eight of us in the world of TV, radio and publishing with piss easy jobs and expense accounts could get in two months working with a trainer for five hours a week. The answer is: very fit. This was the fittest I've ever been as an adult and I was also disappointed that I hadn't got fitter. The eight weeks came either side of a week in Cornwall with my little boy and it was so hard not to get seduced by that lovely Cornish ice cream, so sadly I succumbed to seven days of very bad dietary behaviour. In layman's terms, I robbed the sweet shop. The impact of this break in my diet on my final results after the eight weeks depressed me, but the lack of self-control, though really disappointing, was hardly surprising.

Looking back, though, the upside of training far outweighed the downside. I actually enjoyed it, which made a difference. And it definitely improved my game.

Ray got my attention in the first session by making me lie down on my living-room floor with my arms up to catch a medicine ball and then throwing it straight through them into my face. It was unconventional and painful, but it was such a shock it made me laugh. He apologized profusely but months later told me he'd done it on purpose to make sure I was paying attention. Naturally, after that I was. Ray was an excellent trainer and a few weeks later I was well into it.

On shitty days we'd run to the park in the rain and do push-ups and dips on fallen trees. On hot days I'd be banging backwards and forwards on an amazing rowing machine, later used by Frank Underwood in *House of Cards*. *Turns to camera and quotes Shakespeare*

Ray brought in a pretty basic running machine, we fixed a boxing speed ball to the wall by the laundry room and pretty soon it was like *Rocky*. Seriously. OK, *Rocky* by Lidl. As I was running for twenty minutes at a time on the machine, then sprinting and running again, five-year-old Marlais would stand at the top of the stairs looking down and mimic me. He looked great. I kept going. I'd see his cherubic curls and cheeky big grin and he kept me going strong. Making your kids laugh is a good incentive to get fit and stay around.

The running machine might have been pretty basic but it was all I needed. It had two height settings and you could increase and decrease the speed. The running bit was like a wide strip of skateboard grip tape passing round two rolling pins, with a lectern at the front with the controls. The more I pounded it the more likely it seemed it would break. At the far end of the dark basement corridor was a small square window that looked out onto the garden. That was the view, a glimpse of bright green light at the end of the tunnel. That was also pretty inspiring. I felt like I had something to run towards.

The speed ball took some getting used to. It was suspended from a black square that we fixed to the wall with a heavy steel bracket. It looked a little like the 'How Hard Can You Punch?' machine at the fair. Once I'd worked out you hit the black leather ball once then let it swing back before hitting it on the second swing I was away. Luckily I had the corridor down the side of the kitchen towards the laundry room to put this stuff. No one wants a gym in the living room.

The fittest *Men's Health* cover-style washboard stomach I ever saw was on my cousin Simon, who has never been near a gym or a trainer in his life. He's an eighteen-hour-a-day farmer and does everything. He works for a living. Personal trainers and gyms are for those of us who faff about on computers and sit on our arses all day eating and tweeting.

The training with Ray worked, though. I started to see through my misconception that playing five-a-side three times a week alone would get me fit and I began thinking about what I ate. Also I got to the point where I wouldn't walk anywhere when I could run; walking or getting a cab seemed pointless when I could leg it there. I'd show up to meetings or lunches in shorts and T-shirts just to make use of the chance to run somewhere.

Ray wrote me a Do and Don't Eat list and I started keeping a Food Diary. There were six days of guided diet and then one day when I could eat what I wanted. This was the most pertinent part of losing my gut. Breakfast became a protein shake with fruit and porridge oats. The diet plan made a massive difference. It's a tough thing, changing how and what you eat. It comes down to what you know you should or shouldn't do and what you actually do. In that respect it's similar to shooting from the halfway line.

Early on Ray brought round some pads and showed me some basic boxing tips which I liked. It helped immensely at the time when I was dealing with divorce lawyers. It wasn't always easy doing it at home, simply because there were so many distractions and interruptions, some of them valid, others not so. I was pretty slack at times, but also so much fitter and more focused than I'd ever been. Ray was good company too, so that helped.

The impact on my game was massive. Mainly my improved core could control my ability to stop and start, so I could change direction with the ball much quicker. To be honest, I had never even heard of my core before. This control over my movement made me a better player, enhancing the other skills I already had.

My fitness was key to a great summer of five-a-side and Sunday eight-a-side. I could piss it. In the prime of my youth I could always do most people for pace, but now I found I could stop and start and change direction like a knight on as chessboard. Dragging the ball back, turning inside people and jinking side to side with the acceleration to move quickly away from a standing start felt fantastic.

Shots stayed low and went where I wanted them to, the return passes of a fast one-two were met without any problem and I could score from distance easily. When you think about it, getting properly fit is a no-brainer but if you have a tendency towards excess rather than fitness, then it can be so much easier to do the settee than the plank.

This training with Ray was a decade ago. I was just turning forty and just getting divorced, and both were good reasons to get in shape. At the time I was able to go to my Sunday morning 11 o'clock eight-a-side ninety-minute game and then join Keir for his game immediately afterwards, and just stay on. Keir and I had some mutual friends in Leeds when he was a student, and he would occassionally ask if people from our game could make up the numbers in theirs. No problem. I had the time and stamina. Three hours of football in the sun. Great times.

Not having to pay Ray also helped immensely. He donated about £1,800 worth of his time and effort. Or he would have if he'd been an independent trainer and not the *Men's Health* fitness editor. At the time the magazine was run by a few boys who'd worked for me at *loaded* and *GQ*, and I can just see them now saying, 'Let's send Ray to James,' and then laughing at what he was going to put me through. And he did put me through it – I'd say we worked at a level of 75 per cent intensity. It wasn't easy, but he got me there.

When it came to being photographed for the 'after' look I was disappointed the mag hadn't done a sideways 'before' shot, because from the side you could really see the improvement in shape. From the front I just looked a bit more toned and slightly better photographed, but from the side I'd clearly ditched the stomach wok and it almost looked flat. At the photo session the photographer kept offering me a glass of red wine, which I repeatedly declined in a polite fashion, until exasperated he said it does something to your veins to make you look more buff in the photo. I had to explain I was a recovering alcoholic, had been clean eight years and didn't want a fucking glass of red wine at 11 o'clock on a Thursday morning in Hampstead.

It's appropriate that that session ended in Hampstead, because naturally I failed to keep up Ray's routine and eventually ended up with the body condition of Mr Messy again. A year later a good mate, Tony, told me about his trainer, Fred, in Hampstead and insisted I come and meet him to try him out. I could do boxing training at the same time as Tony. It sounded like a good idea. The way he described Fred made it sound like I'd be going to Burgess Meredith's gym in *Rocky*: all creased-up old face, woollen hat, spitting into a bucket while the wooden walls dripped with faded glories and memorabilia. 'He's real old school, you'll love him,' said Tony.

When I met Fred at his gym above an optician's something had clearly been lost in translation, because the actual place was all clean, white and modern, but the personality recommendation was spot on. I loved going to see Fred, his mate Jakey and his wife, Abby. Imagine Paul Whitehouse playing Robert Redford, that's what Fred looks like: he's a greying, suntanned Cockney energy bomb. He bounces around everywhere in his Abercrombie & Fitch gear like he has springs in his trainers and then slaughters this nice-guy image with all sorts of brutal circuits and horrible encouragements.

We were there to box, but as usual with all these things it also involved circuit training and weights and planks and various other fucking contraptions that could easily be turned into medieval catapults or instruments of torture.

After I'd finished with Ray, my body clock slipped from stopwatch to grandfather clock. When I wasn't lying on the floor after a session with the heavy bag, Abby would have me running round Hampstead past Ricky Gervais and Robert Pirès and all sorts of people moseying in and out of the cafés and bookshops. Hampstead is not Philadelphia and I wasn't Rocky.

There are more therapists per square mile than anywhere else in the UK but no steps with a statue of Stallone at the top of them. The nearest they've got is Peter Cook's old house and he was an altogether different type of athlete.

Apart from going to the Everyman Cinema, with its plush seats, chair service, holders for wine glasses and out of the way location, and the nearby Holly Bush inn, which was equally suitable for going somewhere with someone you shouldn't have been with, I had rarely visited Hampstead village before.

I knew the Heath from walking the dog with my son, but I couldn't picture a beaten-up old boxing gym in the heart of the village. A yoga retreat or a book signing, yes. The Kronk, no. But Fred knew his stuff: he'd grown up in Kentish Town and had the CCTV evidence to prove it. He taught me how to stand, move forwards and backwards, keep on my toes, punch and avoid slaps with the pads; and that last bit was the most important: 'Keep your guard up.' If I lowered it he'd just fucking dig me with the pads, the bastard.

It was a weird clientele. There was a renowned cellist from a quartet who'd met in Auschwitz, a drummer from a world-famous 1980s New Romantic group, a smattering of lawyers, some blonde Hampstead wives, some nice older couples in perfect matching gym wear. I've no idea what they made of it when I was sweating and swearing and shouting as I staggered around.

One day I was struggling with the relationship between my body and gravity when Kevin Shields from My Bloody Valentine wandered in. I'd known Kevin since I met him in Berlin when I was nineteen with Serious Drinking. Another time I'd bumped into him in New York, where the band were sleeping in a padded cell. That didn't seemed weird at all, but he was the last person I'd have expected to see in a perfectly lit, super-clean, white gym. But that was the appeal Fred had, he could make anyone do things they don't want to. Especially Tony, the guy who'd introduced me to him.

A punk rock literary warlord who'd created his own market in male single-parent fiction, he'd be battering into Fred, wearing what looked like ancient Japanese battle flags for shorts and gloves the size of cauldrons. Meanwhile stick-thin Fred would be leaning into him in a confrontation that looked like a dragonfly holding back a bull terrier. Tony could keep that up for an hour and Fred would still be zinging around the gym.

It was good fun, but I had to drive halfway across north London to get there and eventually that was the excuse I used to slacken off. It would be a while before I bumped into my next trainer, Isaac Hayes lookalike Dominic, in my local park. This is where I am now: up and down steps, dips off benches, punches, squats. It's not as hard as Fred and Ray, but Dominic is well respected and known in our area, having grown up boxing at Repton Boys Club. Unfortunately, every time I show up with an ankle or thigh injury he tells me, 'The worst sport you can be doing at your age is football.'

It's almost as if he's seen me play.

Exiles on Maine Road

It may, at this point, come as a surprise if I mention I did actually play for another team on and off for a good fifteen years or so: the Exiles in the Camden Musicians League and the Coram's Fields eight-a-side league. You'd be perfectly within your rights to be saying, 'Hang on, how come no mention of this up to now?' Sometimes you forget things because they need forgetting. Loose lips sink ships. (As I wrote that sentence I could imagine some of them reading it and shifting uncomfortably in their seats.)

As you will see, very little of the discussion about the Exiles will actually be about playing football. But then again, the world of five-a-side can be as much about what happens off the pitch with your mates as on.

I met them through Paul 'Bucky' Buck, or Buckly as I now call him, who was the concert booking agent for a band I was managing in 1992. He said to me one day in his tiny Berwick Street office, 'Hey, you play football. Why not come and play with me and my mates at Regent's Park? We have a team called the Northern Exiles, we all support Man City, Man United, Leeds and Everton.' So I did and in the wider group of football fans this team was at the heart of, I found some of the funniest people I've ever known.

The core of the Exiles became very good mates. The ones I went and stood with in the bar when the *loaded* parties were jammed with celebrities. The ones I've been away on foreign jaunts to watch Leeds with. The ones whose motto is 'For fuck sake, no one tell – about this.' The ones I've crashed with when relationships have run aground. The ones I've got up early mornings and played competitive matches with despite being fucked up. The ones I figured the *loaded* audience would be.

They are my mates, but they are a terrible bunch, reprobates and maniacs to a man. Even the quiet ones. Their stories and behaviour have for many years had me in tears of laughter and disbelief. One of these stories accidentally ended up in a Paddy Power TV ad campaign recently when another mate of mine wrote it in, thinking it was an urban myth. Channel 4 even commissioned Irvine Welsh and Dean Cavanagh to write a comedy pilot about the Exiles as a cross between *The Likely Lads* and *Dad's Army*.

Most importantly, these people are my football mates: Johnny, Buckly, Kell, Tony, Oli, Olly, Terry, Tees, Simon, Barney, Nige, Ben, Neil, Roual and the rest are funny, good footballers and nice blokes. When sober.

When they're drunk and out of the house? Well, as I write I'm trying to think exactly how to balance what is and what isn't incriminating, who may be affected by certain stories, who was going out with someone at the time, who is still working for the same boss. The simplest way to ease us in here is perhaps to recount the first story Buckly told me when he, Kell, Johnny and I caught up at the Dog and Duck in London's Soho to try and get them to share some insights into playing football.

Thankfully it isn't about fights in bars, scaling up the sides of hotels, getting handcuffed to a tree, breaking back into nightclubs, spectacularly insulting people, starting cowboy fights in hotel receptions, getting picked up by a gay barman, 'prostitutes in a nunnery' or waking up in places we really shouldn't have been.

As I said, I tried to get them to discuss football, but instead the other stories poured out, with lots of shouting over each other, like kids eager to tell a joke, and lots of brief arguments while they attempted to clarify who did what. It seems the football was just the glue that kept us together.

Buckly: 'One time I was out with Johnny and Claire [Johnny's wife] and a few others and talk turned to the physical effects of playing, and I said, "You wanna try doing that for ninety minutes once a week at my age."

'Then Claire said, "Hang on, ninety minutes?"

'I replied, "Yes? Ninety minutes."

'She looked at Johnny and said, "You go out at 10 on a Sunday morning and don't come back till 7 at night and you've only played for ninety minutes?"

'She seemed to think it was an all-day affair, like a Test Match, when we'd obviously all been in the pub.'

My memories of playing for the Exiles in the early days are sketchy for this very reason.

'As I remember,' says Kell, the Man City-supporting former captain, 'when we were eleven-a-side you'd play the first two games of every season and then just disappear to America or somewhere for a couple of months. Then one year you said, "I'll be the manager." And then just disappeared again.'

The Camden Musicians League was naturally full of musicians from Camden, but by the time we'd hit the early 1990s a lot of the musicians had become DJs and were up all night in clubs. Or running them. Jonathan and Eko, who ran the popular student indie nights at Camden Palace, were good players and had a team. It being a musicians' league, everyone was living similar lifestyles. The only other team I socialized with in that league was the Hyde Park Cosmos, who ran the Wall of Sound record label, and were DJs at loads of good clubs and parties I'd go to. *NME* photographer Lawrence Watson introduced me to the captain, Mark Jones, and Nipper, Dean and co. They were space cadets, the lot of them.

Jonesy was a lovely player, but cursed with a flappy running style. He'd be moving through his own half, swerving round the opposition lunging in at him, and in his mind he knows he's playing like Gerry

Francis or Rodney Marsh, but he looked like Bernie Clifton when he was wearing that giant bird.

While the Exiles had the cheapest, worst-looking kit in the catalogue, the Cosmos always had immaculate all-white adidas Real Madrid kits. Obviously to me they looked like Leeds. Jonesy was going through his mum's Persil like nobody's business. One time he tried to recruit me for the Cosmos based purely on the speed I'd raced off the pitch to get a ball as it tore away going downhill. 'You've got so much energy.' He was right, but a lot of it wasn't of my own creating. This was the era when you'd open the door of a club toilet and two of the Cosmos would be in there and two Exiles would try and get in there with them. I'm sure it was the same for you and your mates.

The value of my time with the Exiles to this book is, however, not only anecdotal but also to show the camaraderie that can build up around small- or large-sided weekly amateur games. In this case, the team gave me a new social group at a time when I was leaving the *NME* and my mum passed away. As Irvine Welsh put it in *Trainspotting*, when the male and female pairs came back together in the nightclub: 'What are you talking about?' 'SHOPPING! What are YOU talking about?' 'FOOTBALL!'

Football can be an excuse/cover for a lot of things. I have known the Exiles so long now that I had indeed forgotten we all met playing football and still had a competitive eight-a-side team well into this century. This is primarily because I now think of them as great company rather than good footballers.

Buckly: 'Do you remember Tommy's cousin Ryan?'

Johnny: 'Ooh yes, a great player. Came down from Liverpool to do work experience with Tommy at the hotel and played a few games for us.'

Kell: 'He was a brilliant player. What happened to him?'

Buckly: 'Well, Tommy was showing him the ropes of the concierge game, and he'd been down from Liverpool for about three weeks and then he didn't show up for work one day. Tommy called him and there was no reply.

'The same thing happened the next day, and then on the third day Tommy was getting worried about him. So he went round his flat and banged on the door, going, "Ryan? Are you all right?"

'Ryan opened the door just a bit and peeped through the crack and said, "All right, Tommy" in his thick Scouse accent. "Sorry I've not been in, Tommy, I've been sick." Anyway, all the time they were talking Ryan was doing his best to keep Tommy out of his flat, so Tommy knew something was up and pushed his way in. Soon as he did he came to a dead halt. The whole flat was done up with furniture, curtains, paintings, carpet, everything nicked from the hotel. He'd been taking a bit home every day.'

Me: 'Like the Johnny Cash song!'

Buckly: 'Exactly. Once he'd got his whole flat furnished he hadn't bothered going back any more.'

Johnny: 'It wasn't even nice stuff. It was really cheap nylon curtains, stuff he'd got out of the storeroom, really bad old hotel stuff you don't get any more. Fuck knows where he'd found it. We all stayed in that hotel at one time or another and it was quite nice. But Ryan had clearly nicked as much as he could lay his hands on from the shittiest rooms that were rarely let out.'

Me: 'What happened?'

Johnny: 'Well, he never played for us again.'

Me: 'No, with all the stuff and Tommy?'

Buckly: 'Well, Tommy didn't shop him, but he was asked to leave town and told to not come back to the hotel. It turned out he'd pulled a few other scams like that too.'

Kell: 'Great player, though.'

Johnny: 'Ray Houghton's dad would come and watch his other son at Coram's Fields.'

Kell: 'Kenna Houghton.'

Buckly: 'Imagine going to see Ray Houghton at Villa Park on Saturday and then coming to see Kenna play us lot, aged forty, at Coram's Fields?'

Me: 'To be fair, that sounds like good parenting.'

Kell: 'What about that time with Alan the goalkeeper, when he went up to the sub?'

Buckly: 'No, the sub went up to him.'

Johnny: 'No, I know this story because I had to tell the police. We were playing this game, which we won 2-1, and Alan was in goal. He didn't have too much to do and this bloke came up and started chatting. Asking what the teams were, what the score was, who certain players were. He pointed out we didn't have a sub and did Alan want him to go and get changed and just fill in for us? Alan said, "Yes, good idea," and the bloke went off to the changing rooms, which did have security on them, an old boy who kept them locked up.

'Anyway, we knew nothing about this conversation. After the game we went back to the changing rooms and everyone's clothes are all hanging up from the hooks – Paul's, Terry's, Tony's – and then there's just a big gap where mine were. I had no clothes. At all. While I was looking for my clothes and saying, "All right, come on, where's me clothes?" Terry's gone, "Where's me towel?" Then he found his dripping-wet towel by the shower and he's gone, "Who's used my fucking towel?"'

Me: 'It's like *Goldilocks*!'

Buckly: 'Exactly. This fella Alan had been chatting to has gone to the security guard, said he's our sub, given a few players' names and the name of our team. Then he's got undressed and had a shower.'

Johnny: 'Then he's got dressed again in my clothes and just fucked off and kept his other clothes with him too.'

Kell: 'Then Alan's gone, "Ah, I wondered why he didn't come back," and we've all gone, "WHO?" and Alan's explained about the bloke asking to be sub.'

Johnny: 'Anyway, I had no clothes whatsoever. No one had any spares apart from Nick, who was a nice centre back but he was unemployed.'

Me: 'What's wrong with that?'

Johnny: 'Nothing wrong with it, I just mean he didn't have much money for good clothes or anything and he just had a spare pair of really ratty old trackie bottoms, and then someone a lot smaller than me lent me a T-shirt.

'I had to sit about in these until the police came, took statements and we left. Nick offered me a lift home because my Oyster card's gone, my wallet's gone, I've got nothing. We're halfway up Green Lanes and Nick's car runs out of petrol. He stays with it and I'm having to run down Green Lanes in this fucking tiny tight T-shirt, ratty old trackie bottoms, with a petrol can and a few quid change, which was all the money Nick had, looking for a garage. Apart from winning the game the whole day was a disaster.'

Me: 'You sound like you looked like one of those speciality petrol beggars.'

Buckly: 'I was on my way up Green Lanes once with this woman I'd got off with after a match. We were heading back to her flat up Crouch End/Muswell Hill way and all the way home she kept going on about how she couldn't believe how cheap the flat she'd just got was. When we got there, we were going in and I realized it was Dennis Nilsen's house!'

Me: 'What the actual flat?'

Buckly: 'Yes, the actual flat. That really spooked me out. She had no idea so many people had been murdered in her flat, she was just chuffed to get such a good deal.'

Johnny: 'Didn't you say the same pans were still there?'

Buckly: 'I might have done, but they weren't, she had her own stuff.

Later she was asleep and she had locked the doors so I had to climb out of the window.'

Johnny: 'No, that wasn't her, that was another woman, that was Mad . . .'

Buckly (changing the subject): 'Anyway, Neil's new diet. Every few weeks winger Neil would be on a new diet. We'd go and eat after a game and Neil would always order a salad and tell us all about his new diet. Then ten minutes after he'd finished the salad a burger and chips would arrive. We'd all be going, "What about the new diet?" and he'd just look up and say, "A man's got to eat."'

Johnny: 'Then you'd get in his car to go home and the seats would be covered in empty crisp packets and sweets wrappers.'

Me: 'Didn't Neil do wholesale vintage jeans? I remember interviewing him once for a story.'

Johnny: 'Yes. His car was always full of jeans. He could get you really cheap football socks too, but then you'd put them on just before a game and they'd be kids' socks, which only come halfway up your shin pads. He'd listen to the complaints and say, "It's OK, I'll only charge you a pound for them."'

Buckly: 'I remember one time Neil booted a kid up the arse. This kid, about seventeen, had been running him ragged all game. Every time Neil got the ball the kid would nick it off him and set off, and every time he had the ball Neil couldn't get near him. Eventually he just went up to him and booted him up the arse as hard as he could and just walked off.'

Kell: 'Didn't even look at the ref, just knew he'd be getting a card and went. Hey, Buckly, what about the time you left the kit on the train to Brighton and it ended up in Eastbourne?'

Buckly: 'Ah.'

Kell: 'Then he didn't even tell us until just before the next match, when we're all in the dressing rooms.'

Johnny: 'One time we were invited by someone's work to go and play a match in Ireland for the weekend, but the bloke in Ireland said, "I know what it's like with you English teams. You come over on Friday so you can get absolutely smashed in Dublin and then you're in no fit state to give us a decent game."'

Kell: 'So they got us plane tickets for Saturday morning, thinking we'd be sober and we'd go straight from the airport to the game.'

Johnny: 'So we just got absolutely smashed in London on the Friday night instead. Then drinking at the airport and on the plane. We were totally fucked by the time we got there. They were all in their late forties and fifties and we were in our late thirties and twenties, but they thrashed us.'

Buckly: 'Another story about Tommy's cousin Ryan. We went away somewhere to play a game and the fire alarm went off in the hotel very late at night. Everyone was outside freezing and wrapped in blankets. The whole hotel in the car park.'

Kell: 'And we looked up and there was Tommy's cousin Ryan grinning through a third-floor bedroom window, giving the thumbs up. Only we were all staying on the second floor.'

Johnny: 'He'd set the fire alarm off, so he could rob people's rooms.'

There were so many Leeds fans in the wider group of Exiles that the Man U and Man City supporters would regularly come with us for away-game weekends for a laugh. In amidst all this there were our own football matches, plus regular accusations of who was or wasn't past it or who had or hadn't been the worst behaved. It was the template for the *loaded* tone of voice.

The eleven-a-side team boiled down to the eight-a-side team and a new generation of younger players who'd joined and made the team stronger all round. Coram's is a charitable trust in Bloomsbury, just a few minutes' walk south of King's Cross. The pitches and grounds were well kept – apart from twigs, leaves and branches that would fall from the giant trees behind the King's Cross end goals – and a nice place to play. I've put in many questionable performances in the top division there and only two decent ones I can remember.

You get to a point when you've got to maintain a level to enjoy it and, with younger lads coming through, some of the old guard found ourselves on the bench or not even playing. Then you have your own kids and you hand your life over to them. Before you know it, you're not playing competitive league football any more.

I'll leave the Exiles with a story that really floored me, when Simon Leyton, the funniest of our bunch, told it upstairs in a pub in Bristol on the Leeds–Yeovil away weekend. Simon started it and then Paul Teesdale, the bloke it was actually about, took over when Simon couldn't talk any more for tears.

Tees: 'Years ago in the mid-80s, I was getting a wedge cut in a hairdresser's in Harrogate. I was a regular and it was around the time of the big wedges. I'm halfway through the cut and someone shouts to the girl cutting my hair, "Tracey, there's a call for you." This was before mobiles, so she's gone off to take the call in the back.

'She's taking her time and I'm sitting there under the big purple nylon gown, and I've just that week got glasses for the first time and I've taken them off for the haircut. So while she's away I've pulled them out of my pocket in front of me and started polishing them on the bottom of my shirt under the gown.'

Simon (in tears): 'She's come back and seen this polishing movement in his lap under the gown and she thinks he's having a wank. So she starts screaming.'

Tees: 'Then the next thing she does is pick up one of those really heavy fancy metal-backed hairbrushes they used to have and yells, "You dirty fucking bastard. You fucking perverted bastard!" and starts hitting me round the back of the head with this metal-backed hairbrush. It's absolutely killing me, really violent, and there's blood spurting out everywhere, but I can't get my hands through the gown to show her my glasses or even get them up to stop her hitting me. I'm stuck and getting beaten up with a heavy metal hairbrush.

'I've got blood running down my face and she's still screaming and whacking me. Then the manager, who knows me, runs over and manages to stop her. I've finally staggered up from the leaning-back position, opened the gown and managed to show her my glasses in my hand. I'm swearing at her and the manager's giving her a bollocking while telling her to calm down, and she's still screaming, "You fucking dirty bastard!"

'They wrap my head in a towel, my haircut's only half done, and as the manager is getting me into his Porsche to rush me to hospital, he turns and says, "I won't be charging you for this cut, Paul."'

On the Subject of Violence

I was sitting in the living room today, resting a fresh thigh injury, and found myself surrounded by my little boy Billy's *Fireman Sam* people, loads of these small blue firemen and women with yellow helmets – Sam, Penny, Elvis, Steele and Boyce – and their friends Trevor, Tom, Dilys, Norman, Mandy, Helen and the rest of the Pontypandy gang. Right now they're as important to him as the names Clarke, Bremner, Giles, Madeley, Cooper, Reaney, Harvey, Hunter, Bates, Lorimer, Gray, Jones etc. were to me when I was a kid.

Anyway there were fire engines everywhere. I was hoping they'd come to put out the pain in my right leg but they hadn't. If anything they were adding to it as they were looking for the Pontypandy Snoggle Monster, who was lost in the woods. The woods being some cushions that until recently had been propping my leg up on another chair. You try telling a two-year-old about ice packs on thighs, leg elevation and torn muscles. I've got to count myself lucky he's not still whacking my bad thigh or dangling over it.

So I'm sitting and pondering how long it's going to be until my leg gets better and I can play football again when the phone rings and it's my good mate Mikey on the other end.

'All right, Jimbo, how's your leg?' he asks, from somewhere that sounds like Siberia.

I can tell from the buoyancy in his question he's got something specific to ask or tell me. Mikey's a very good mate and we've played football together for well over a decade, but unlike most of the other five-a-side blokes, I see him fully clothed outside of the gym too. In fact I introduced him to the games we play together.

As a footballer Mikey's short, stocky and hard to knock off the ball. The previous month he'd scored a memorable header in our Thursday night eight-a-side match. The goal came from such a fantastic ball in from such an unlikely source I had to double-check with Rob, the crosser, to see if it had been him who'd got the assist. Rob's cross and Mikey's finish were so good – he leapt like salmon, a smoked salmon, and connected with it at such a perfect angle and with such perfect timing that the ball sprang off his head and back across the goal into the far inside netting. We were still talking about it the following week. That's Mikey as a player; physically, he looks a bit like a curly-haired sawn-off shotgun, but he's a very good mate, he regularly gives me lifts to games and he's recently had a training shoe named after him.

Sure enough he was keen to tell me something: 'Listen to what happened to me at the weekend and maybe you can stick it in your book. Last summer in the Monday game I play in with Des and Cathal, under the Westway, I had a bit of a face-off with this local kid. There's always these teenagers hanging around for a game if you're short of a player and they're a different class. This one slammed into me when I was in the corner, though, and I spun round and asked him what the fuck he was doing.

'There was a lot of scowling and a few sparks until someone got in the way and that was it. We got on with the game, but it left a bad taste in my mouth because I thought maybe he had gone in a bit hard but I'd probably overreacted. The following week I saw him by the changing rooms when I arrived so I went over and apologized. We both admitted we were probably a bit at fault and we sorted it out and everything was left on good terms.

'Anyway, this Sunday I had to take Art, my son, to hospital in Cambridge, when we were over visiting the in-laws, and I saw this young black bloke in A&E reception with a smashed-up, bloodied face. He was wearing prison greys – the sweatshirts they get given – he was handcuffed to a seat in the waiting area and there was a prison officer near him at the counter. I was sure I knew him from somewhere but I didn't know if it was from work or wherever.

'So then he clocked me and we both let on and I suddenly realized it was the kid I'd had the flare-up with last summer. So I went over and said, "How are you? I can see it's obviously not that good at the moment. What's up?" And he told me he'd just started a twelve-year sentence for a second offence of discharging a firearm. I thought, "Fucking hell! Thank God I'd made it up with him!"'

'What did you say next?'

'I just went, "Can I get you anything? A Mars bar, some water?" I was thinking, "Fuck, that might have been a close call."'

I guess Mikey was right to be retrospectively anxious and relieved nothing worse had happened. In five-a-side people are flying about pumped up with testosterone and these ructions can certainly get out of hand.

A reluctant footballer, Geoff Glendenning, told me on Facebook about a baptism of fire when he was secretary for the Rio Spartans in the West London Sunday League: 'At my first league meeting as sec-retary, a team got thrown out of the league because one of their players had stabbed the ref after a game.'

I've yet to see anyone pull a knife or a gun at a five-a-side game, but then again I don't mix with gangsters. I play with teachers, actors, cab-bies, writers, marketing men, music agents, comedians, bike messengers, blokes who put ad posters in bus shelters, students, musicians, magis-trates, photographers, lawyers, social workers, plumbers, rehab workers, dads, decorators, drivers, chefs and the magnificently unemployed. So there might be a paintbrush or a staple gun kicking around, and a bit of pushing and shoving, but that's about it for experiencing five-a-side violence for me.

Mikey's call got me thinking about player-on-player violence and I was reminded of a story the writer Chris Collier told me. I'll simply call it 'Goalkeeper Has Breakdown'. Leeds fan Chris once counted and quoted every instance of swearing in every episode of *Curb Your Enthusiasm* for my Sabotage Times website, so he's attuned to confrontational behaviour.

'This keeper with a screw loose took goals scored against him personally and threatened the scorer most times. We spent a lot of the match calming him down. Oppositions used to play on this and really celebrate ecstatically to wind him up. He usually ended up chasing the offender with us in pursuit, which should have been set to the Benny Hill theme.

'One time he let a goal in and ran off the pitch like he was going to explode. We thought he'd gone home and we carried on without him, but five minutes later he reappeared with a tyre iron, still furious, and started chasing the goalscorer round the pitch, brandishing the weapon. After a while he stopped, knelt down and, to the bewilderment of onlookers, started crying, blubbing, "I can't take this any more," and then trudged away. As he was going off, the ref booked him, not for violent conduct but for re-entering the pitch without his permission. He's a copper now as well. The keeper, not the ref.'

Not having played in a rough competitive league since my late teens with Kirkstall Eddies, I had a think about where I could go to find out more about the occurrence of violence in five-a-side. Naturally there are the pitches I play on round various parts of London, but even there I couldn't imagine encountering much full-on confrontation. It always seems quite good-natured, with gangs of mates rolling on and off as each hour ends.

Eventually I looked at my bad leg with the blue ice pack on it and realized I couldn't go anywhere anyway due to physical limitations and parental responsibilities. So instead I reached for the laptop and the internet.

Twitter and Facebook are wonderful things for most people but especially for sofa-bound authors who are supposed to be bouncing about researching a book by playing football. A lot of the people I interact with on Twitter date from when I was on *The Warm Up* on talkSPORT. They'd never let me down when I was asking for tweets answering things like 'What are the weirdest clothes you've ever been to football in?' (The best answer to that one was roughly: 'A mate didn't get home from drinking after work till very late and missed his anniversary meal so his Mrs cut ALL of his clothes up including the ones he'd been out in. All of them. He only had his trainers left. Anyway he showed up a few hours later at Elland Road, just before kick-off, in his girlfriend's culottes and her tank-top. He looked pretty good actually.')

The replies to the call for five-a-side stories were staggering. Eight thousand words' worth once they'd all come in via tweets, Facebook messages, emails and direct messages. That's almost 8 per cent of this book! My big challenge now is to smuggle them all in here and there as if I've gone out and actually interviewed people.

In terms of full-on controlled violence Keith Ames, who works for the Musicians' Union, had perhaps the most obvious anecdote. He was playing in a five-a-side team in Chelmsford in the early 1990s 'alongside a work colleague who was an amateur boxer. He had fought at international level. He would wear bin liners under his shirt to try and keep his weight down. This made him somewhat hot and always on a short fuse. Once, when challenged by an over-eager opponent, he proceeded to beat up the entire opposition – by himself!'

Which sounds funny but it probably wasn't if you were on the other team. That was a normal match, but even charity games can become too aggressive. Johnny 'Two Rs' Lorrimer, a bloke I go to Elland Road with sometimes, has evidence of this: 'I played in a charity game once where we all had to play in nightwear. There was a bit of a scuffle after a bad tackle and two blokes had to be dragged apart, swinging fists and spitting at each other. Violence between two fully grown men just looks so wrong when one is wearing powder-blue silk pyjamas and the other a pink baby-doll nightie.'

Ed Needham, who edits *Coach* health and fitness magazine, told me, 'There was a time when we played in a little football tournament against the other teams – hockey, cricket – from the Brondesbury Sports Club. Suggs was in our team and brought some of the other Madness people and their road manager, who was called Chalky. We were playing football against the cricket team, who all had names like Gaston, and one of them made the mistake of going in a bit hard on this Chalky chap, which he didn't take too kindly to. So while the other bloke was lying on the ground after his crunching tackle, Chalky stood up, leaned over him, and said, "If you do that again I'm going to stab you right through the fucking heart." A little strong for the occasion, I thought.'

I asked Suggs if this was the same ever-friendly Chalky I knew when he worked with The Farm? Suggs replied, 'Correct. My oldest friend, Andrew Chalk. He gave up the booze and now lives in Eastbourne working with troubled kids, much to my admiration. I have little doubt it's true.'

I got in touch with Chalky and he emailed me: 'All true, mostly, and I'm afraid what is completely correct is my response to the tackle/harassment. However to put it in context (if one can put stabbing someone in the heart into the context of a five-a-side game) it was a simple Sunday kickabout and every time we had the ball I felt the physical presence of the opposition player constantly jostling me from behind. It was as if he thought he was in a serious game and had watched a video on "how to defend like a pro". In the end it was not the one-off brutality of a crunching tackle that did for my tolerance – I played in too many Hackney Marshes games for that to be a problem – but his strange attempt at "fruttocking" during a Sunday morning kickabout, and the constant invasion of my personal space (which was already fully occupied with a hangover).'

Thank fuck he calmed down or there'd have been skewered hearts everywhere. The strange thing is, in the years I knew him, Chalky was a friendly, happy-go-lucky bloke and I couldn't imagine him threatening to stab anyone. Clearly either some people are different on the pitch from off it, or maybe he'd already calmed down a bit by the time I knew him. I was just pondering this when Suggs sent me another message saying, 'You could write a whole book on Chalky's adventures,' and suggesting I track down an anecdote about a five-a-side match between Madness and Danny Baker's *NME* team.

There are of course many different reasons why violence erupts in five-a-side. Issues as simple and childish as another player annoying you or your team losing and your inability to change this can really piss you off. Chris Collier told me about a bloke who had a special goal celebration: 'He used to drum the opening bars to "Eye of the Tiger" on the boards at the side when he scored. Without fail.' I imagine the first few times that would make you laugh. If he's walloping them in, though, it could start to get on your tits.

Playing when carrying an injury and knowing you can't give your all can prompt you to lose it, which happened to me the other day. Just hating someone because they're a fucking knob is another reason that violence flares up. And then after hate there's love, sex and relationships. If you think about how complicated they can be elsewhere, it's probably best they're not allowed to influence what goes on in a five-a-side match.

Aaron Pearson, a Leeds fan based in Liverpool, told me about this well planned piece of provocation: 'At the work five-a-side the organizer (Jon, a miserable sod) and one of the lads (Ricky) used to have a bit of "bantz". Jon's (fit) sister also worked in the same office. Anyway, one week, while playing, Ricky scores, pulls his top over his head to celebrate à la Luis Enrique, to reveal a T-shirt underneath with a pic of Jon's sister, with the slogan "BEST F*CK EVER". The fact Ricky is an otherwise placid six foot five Welshman with a big nose and little round specs probably made it funnier.' So, 1–0 Ricky.

If you bring a resentment into the game, fail to park it in the changing rooms and leave it simmering away during the match, you'll be playing with a hairline trigger. The temperature inside hot gyms can also lower tolerance levels.

Thankfully in most cases it's easy to read and with so many players to hand people tend to intervene before any clashes get out of hand. In my experience most blow-ups in five-a-side tend to fizzle out and rarely carry on after the game. I'm a big believer of leaving it on the pitch.

Clashes are perhaps more likely in eleven-a-side amateur competitive football, where you're less likely to encounter the same opposition week in, week out.

One simple reason for inter-team tension is rival team support. However, Peter Hooton, singer with The Farm and long-standing Liverpool fan, found himself in the opposite situation, taking part in an impromptu five-a-side match to diffuse a tense fans' stand-off: 'I played in a five-a-side peace match once between Liverpool and Roma fans. It was the 1984 European Cup Final – we went on Mono tours, fifty or so of Liverpool's away-match finest, including the Huyton Baddies and the Halewood Chains. We left on the Friday night on a St Trinian's-style bus to Manchester airport and were promised a stay in Ostia for a week – that's the seaside playground for Rome's rich and famous a few miles outside the city – but we ended up in Ladispoli, miles away from Rome. Some years later Yugoslav refugees rioted against being "dumped" there.

'There'd been a lot of trouble already between Roma and Liverpool fans and they all hated us. On the Saturday night, while having a quiet drink, about fifteen of us were attacked by scooter boys with chains. We took refuge in a bar ironically called the Internationale.

'Within an hour or so the whole town appeared to turn up outside, including nuns, priests, mothers with prams etc., to stare at the "invaders" barricaded into the bar.

'A local plain-clothes policeman restored order by firing a gun into the air and then over the next few days "Angelo", as the copper was known, hastily arranged a "peace match" between the locals and our contingent. It was a great idea and everyone was immediately up for it and the atmosphere just changed. A crowd turned out to watch and suddenly everyone was friendly.

'I declared myself captain of our team but soon realized during the first half their superior skill/technique and better kits were going to be our downfall. At half-time my team talk went something like this: "Listen, this isn't working, we're not used to the pitch conditions, it's too hot and we can't match them for skill, so we're going to have to do a Leeds United and kick them off the park" – which we did and they still won.

'After the match some of our contingent were even invited for bowls of spaghetti in the homes of our adversaries, where the truce was officially confirmed by handshakes all round!'

This from a man who spent most of 1990 in a 'No alla Violenza' T-shirt.

Stress released through noise and body language is very easy to assess in such a close-quarters game. Pay attention to it and you've a clear advantage over your opposition. Andy Murray's former tennis coach Amélie Mauresmo, from whom he split in 2016, didn't like the way the Scot shouted and showed his frustration during a game. She seemed to feel it gave too much away. Murray, on the other hand, didn't want to play in total silence, and given his subsequent second Championship win at Wimbledon, either he or Ivan Lendl understands how far the volume/anger controls can go. I think Mauresmo has a point to a degree. Frustration is one thing but inter-teammate bitching can suggest weakness.

This is certainly the case when I play football. When you see the opposition rowing with each other, niggling, shouting in frustration, these are all clear signs they're losing it, and if the noise is being directed at one player in particular or going on between two players, the obvious thing for the opposition to do is to target them in terms of who to go round before you score. Or even start agreeing with one of them and wading into the opposition's dispute. That really pisses them off, 'Oh, you can fuck off too,' being a common reply.

Accentuate their weakness and it winds the opposition up. If you're on the receiving end, there's nothing worse than the same player making the same preventable error. A clever goalkeeper will switch who he distributes the ball to from kick-off, but some just can't read what is going wrong and keep setting the same fuck-up again and again. Especially on the indoor pitch or small outdoor pitch, where the same ball out to the same bloke showing for it sees him guided down into the same cul-de-sac by the opposition, where he loses possession yet again. These are factors in the incremental build-up of tension that can eventually erupt into a smothered stand-off that passes for a fight, a slanging match or even a storming off.

People often look to animals for comfort and five-a-side Twitter source Will Deans may have evidence of their influence on our game: 'A mate was playing when a fight kicked off and someone ran on the pitch with an Alsatian that started biting people . . . I asked my mate "how did it end" and he said, "Like all fights, everyone mates and patting the dog."'

Perhaps it's obvious that with competition, ego, adrenalin and physical interaction inevitably comes violence. Sports bags at dawn, choose your seconds and no clashing kit! When older fans of the professional game continue to cherish and glorify the memory of early 1970s hard men and the 1980s Wimbledon Crazy Gang, when modern high-kicks, punch-ups and on-pitch chases from around the world go viral on YouTube, it's obvious that things are going to erupt occasionally in our own games. I've thought about why tensions can explode into violence in five-a-side and I've come to the possibly previously overlooked conclusion that one factor is how little space there is. If you weren't allowed to leave a designated area like the goalkeeper or netball players there might be fewer flare-ups.

We like our space and in five-a-side people tend to hold on to the ball far too long. Anyone's free to come and invade your space and remove the ball from it.

The range of offences varies, of course. A blind shunt from behind can prompt an outswinging retaliatory arm. A dirty, dangerous hacking will provoke a full stand-up face-off. There's the inexplicable eruption in response to the irritating counterclaim for a throw-in. There are often too many people around for a clean punch to be thrown and to land. None of the games I play in regularly are in competitive leagues, so we know we'll all see each other next week, and this keeps some semblance of order. Not knowing the opposition might prompt you to keep some level of respect – or not, whichever the case may be.

Here's Chris Collier again: 'Fixture congestion meant we had to play arch five-a-side rivals two weeks running, both going for the title. First game, heated affair, loads of fouls, two lads kicking each other all match. Final whistle they square up, hands twisting each other's collars, Bremner–Mackay-style, screaming and swearing at each other eyeball to eyeball.

'Ours: "YOU FAT FUCKER!"

'Theirs: "YOU LITTLE CUNT!"

'Ours: "YOU'RE FUCKING DEAD, MAN!"

'Theirs: "I'LL KILL YOU, Y'BASTARD!"

'Ours: "FUCK OFF!"

'Theirs: "RIGHT, NEXT WEEK, BE READY! I'LL RIP YOUR FUCK-ING HEAD OFF!"

'Ours: "WILL YOU FUCK ... AND ... AND ... I'LL TELL YOU FOR FUCKING WHY!"

'Theirs: "GO ON, THEN, YOU LITTLE SHIT!"

'Ours (still screaming): "COS NEXT WEEK I'LL BE ON FUCKING NIGHTS, THAT'S WHY!"

'Turns to the rest of us sniggering, in a normal voice, 'What? I am on nights. What?'

For me, narrowly avoiding dangerous tackles or receiving hospital balls from a teammate is much more likely to wind me up than a fair but heavy challenge or a losing scoreline. Whatever the factors, certain people just let it all store up until they go into meltdown.

If some five-a-siders go to their game to release tension, lose the stresses of everyday life, there are others for whom such close-contact sporting combat tips them the opposite way. I've played against mouthy, over-competitive people but they're forgettable. Really.

One of the most niggly games I ever played in as an adult was supposed to be a friendly for the *Independent* newspaper against a load of waiters from a posh café in St James's Park, not far from Buckingham Palace. They might have had T-shirts from that café but I'd be surprised if they dealt with the public for a living, because their manners and timing were terrible.

Before we'd even kicked off at Market Road, Islington, the bloke I was lined up against along the halfway line spat at my boots and asked me what I 'was fucking looking at'. I just laughed in disbelief and told the bloke to fuck off. He seemed a bit unsure what to do next. I don't suppose he expected the curly-haired bloke in glasses just to give it him straight back. I was in my mid-thirties, confident, and I was fit.

Compared to the terror of the Plasterers' verbal abuse I received as a skinny eighteen-year-old, his insult was like getting dissed by Peppa Pig.

Once we started there was nothing physical to match the bloke's spitting and swearing, either in the tackle or on or off the ball. Just all piss and wind. I waited for a late tackle but it never came. He wasn't a very good player either. In my experience, a true hard man usually doesn't advertise the fact, you just feel it in the tackle. When I volleyed Simon Poole's corner into the back of the net from the edge of the area before it had even bounced, the fella just looked beaten. Imagine how embarrassed you must feel to get trounced by a bloke in glasses you thought you could spit at forty minutes before.

The opposition's big centre forward, on the other hand, decided he was going to use our centre backs, Matt and Danny, for headbutting practice. When he had the ball he played with his head down and arms out, like he was used to people just getting out of his way. Maybe he'd always been the big kid in the playground. He was like a drunk MMA fighter, very slow on the ball, almost willing people to come near him so he could smash them. Thank fuck he wasn't that good a player.

From adversity comes greatness and, as blatant and hard as the headbutt was, the response from our tall, rangy centre back, news reporter Matt Beard, was immaculate. He didn't even flinch, he just got up, wiped the blood from his face, looked briefly in disbelief that the ref has missed it and got straight back into the action like it happened every week. That really confused the bald bear, who had clearly been hoping for a fight. He was stood there like a cartoon ogre, fists clenched, and Matt just put the ball down for the free kick, played it and got on. Genuinely didn't even blink in the bloke's direction. I guess he knew if he caved in or whined that would be it.

The game continued in this sort of fractious vein and would have been a free-for-all but for the referee, who was an *Indie* office junior called Oly. Despite being only about twenty-one years old, he didn't take any shit at all. He stood up to these idiots who seemed to want to have a kicking match not kickabout. Even the cartoon ogre couldn't ruffle Oly and eventually he just sent him off. Oly is the editor of the *i* newspaper now and last time I saw the headbutting nutjob he was walking through Victoria Park in a sunhat, Kickers and flares, all happy and smiling and friendly looking like one of the Hair Bear Bunch. He seemed a totally different character altogether off the pitch.

Even your friends can be dirty bastards. The most violent tackle from behind I've received must have looked savage. I suffered it at the hands, or feet, of The Cult's Ian Astbury, who would sometimes go by the name of Wolfchild. For quite a while Ian's fellow Cult member, Billy Duffy, was a member of our Exiles eight-a-side team. Any Sunday they were in London they'd drop by Talacre in Kentish Town for a game. On the day in question I was through on goal early in the game, about to slide it past the keeper when, *whhoooomph*, I was felled and lying in a heap with someone else's legs wrapped round mine.

It felt like I'd been hit by a buffalo and I looked round laughing in total disbelief as Ian said, 'Morning!' in a fake Home Counties stock-broker English accent, then he tried to pick us both up from the tangle of legs. Luckily he hadn't brought his tomahawk. It was such a blatant chopping down I couldn't help but laugh. Quite like being back in the park as a kid. I'd always had the blatantly laughable foul on mates in my repertoire, but I'd never dished out or received one quite so severe before.

In five-a-side I think the violence can sometimes manifest itself in a form of mental torment as well as physical aggro. You can get really wound up simply because of the ongoing nature of a punishing defeat. You claw one back and they immediately score two more. It can build up the sort of frustration where some people just topple over the edge of what's acceptable. And there's certainly a sadistic pleasure if you're trouncing a team that have got on your nerves for some reason.

For a long period during our Sunday indoors and Wednesday mid-week games, when I was fit and fast, I knew if I accelerated across the front of the D, drifting away from the outstretched leg of a defender or keeper, I could bury the ball, again and again and again. It felt great seeing them go in, but it really fucked the opposition off. The worst thing you can do is tell your opposition you've a good new player, because straight away any team worth their salt will target them to work out their weakness or put them under pressure when they're on the ball.

If we want a masterclass in goalscoring abuse, then we must head to the North-West, to a land of pies, rugby league, inflammatory football chants and men who stare at coats (see p. 221). To Wigan.

'Orrible Ives, a popular but frequently inappropriate member of the infamous Wigan Athletic Twitter fraternity, tells a story of how his five-a-side Dream Team of some of the best amateur footballers in the city deliberately set out to dominate a newly formed league. Because of the nature of his Twitter personality, 'Orrible Ives (named after a charmless little nurk in *Porridge*) feels it's best he keeps his real name obscured during these anecdotes but you can detect his love of the game seeping through.

'I played for a couple of teams in the five-a-side leagues in Wigan. The first year it opened we put together a team of some of the best amateur players in Wigan and called ourselves the Dream Team. We played three seasons and never conceded a goal. Never. Last match we scored twenty own goals against PSV Hangover to give them a start. We beat them 38–20. Then we quit straight after. Never played another game. We were some outfit.

'One of the Dream Team matches we were 15–0 up with five minutes to go. They got a free kick. Just as they were going to take it their centre forward shouted, "Ref! He's nipping me." I turned and saw our centre half Ste Marsh nipping him. He had a hand full of his skin and was giving him a right nip. I asked him why . . . "I was bored, Ives. He's fucking shit."

'I signed for the Wigan Athletic Fanzine team, Cockney Latic, who were a very good side. We won a couple of league titles. At the end of one season we got challenged to a game against Wish FM, a local radio station. They promised us a hobnailing for weeks, they were even mentioning it on air. So much so that we thought maybe they were a decent side. It was a close game in the end, but we won 36–0.

'Absolutely battered them. They had Ralph the Fireman in goal and he had a knee brace on, like one of those fibreglass children that you used to put your change in outside a shop. He needed a back brace after he finished picking the ball out the net. They were still in the game at half-time. Just 16–0 down.

'We had a chat during the interval and decided to step it up. We defended as tight as we could, a bit like when you don't want to concede an away goal in Europe. Someone gave our keeper a newspaper to read.

'After the game one of their players was heard saying to the lad who had organized it: "I thought you said they weren't that good. They were like the fucking Harlem Globetrotters." On the radio the next day a couple of the presenters spoke about the game and when they admitted the score they'd lost by one of the girls asked, "Was it rugby?" They never asked us for another game.

'The referee that day was fat Alan Greenhalgh. He refereed both five-a-side and eleven-a-side. During eleven-a-side matches he'd stand in the centre circle eating midget gems; during the five-a-side games he'd lean on the fence eating them. Think he kept score against Wish FM with the number he ate. A bit like an umpire with stones or coins in his pocket.'

'Orrible Ives's fellow Wiganite and fanzine editor, Jimmy Mudhutter, had to resort to grovelling and bribery to make up for one violent episode: 'I got sent off for punching someone once. They'd been kicking me all game. On the way off I gave the ref a right mouthful. I had a Sunday league cup semi-final that weekend and it was only when I got home that I realized the red card would mean I was banned from that. I managed to get hold of the ref's phone number and rang up to apologize, but he wasn't having it and was still sending the red card in. I ended up begging him on the phone, asking what could I do for him to rescind it. He made me go round his house and deliver him a handwritten letter of apology for swearing at him. I'd also said, "Is there anything I can get you to say sorry," and he said, "Twenty Embassy Number Ones," so I did. We lost the cup tie 4–1.'

To say 'Orrible Ives loves amateur football as much as anyone is an understatement. After a week of endless running anecdotes on Twitter that had been pushed his way by a variety of Wigan fans, he used a day off work to get them all down in an email to me. This is the sort of enthusiasm, passion and self-belief that grips those of us for whom playing football is everything. His tweets contained a thousand references to players and pitches and clubs and opposition I have never heard of, nor will ever meet or visit, and yet they were truly engrossing.

'First season I played for Newtown we played Hindley Victoria away. That doesn't sound too bad, does it? Well, Hindley Victoria was actually Hindley Borstal. They weren't allowed to play away games any more after four of their players went to collect the ball over a fence and haven't been seen since. We played the borstal on Christmas Eve 1988. Freezing cold day.

'On the way there some of our lads were telling me not to drink the tea after the game as it stops you getting a hard-on. When we got inside, one of the screws said to Billy, our Scottish centre forward, "I said you'd be back." We played on a pitch inside the borstal surrounded by fences and barbed wire. It was obvious straight away that their captain was also the daddy of the borstal. Although he was shit, he took all the free kicks, all the corners, all the throw-ins. He also missed a penalty in injury time to scrape a draw against us.

'On the way back to the showers the prisoners were calling us all sorts, F'ing C this, F'ing T that. Billy told them he was going to shag their girlfriends that night while they were banged up. They weren't happy about that one bit. In the changing rooms two of their team came in with cups of tea. I was having a cig with Billy. The lads came over to us and asked for a cig. Well, it was Christmas so what could you do? I took a couple of cigs out the box, then handed him the whole box with the rest in. "Merry Christmas, pal." His face lit up like a fucking beacon. He almost cried. Billy did the same to his mate. A few years later a lad came up to me with a pint in a town centre pub: "That's for you, mate. You gave me a box of cigs in borstal on Christmas Eve. Thanks again."'

When they arrived written out in an email, the quality of Ives's anecdotes was good enough to build a stand-up routine around. 'Ladies and gentleman, may I present 'Orrible Ives from Wigan, Britain's first five-a-side stand-up.' Here's his 'Playing against a violent ex-player' anecdote in full: 'My claim to fame was playing in a cup game for Golborne. We were drawn against a team from Billinge called The Smithy. Imagine being a nineteen-year-old lad, captaining your team, but you had to shake hands with former Liverpool left back and Smithy player-manager Tommy Smith. Not only a former player but he'd also been given the MBE a short while earlier. The ref that day was Ray Fletcher, a great character. Ray was only a small bloke but he was the fairest ref in the town. As I put my hand out to Tommy, he shook it and said, "Good luck, Wool." I sensed then he wasn't in the best of moods. Within five minutes I'd hit Tommy with one the best tackles I've ever done, and he glared at me and said, "You're dead, son." I just stood over him and said, "You won't catch me, you doddering old cunt." Not a wise move, I know. A few minutes later our centre half clattered him and I started laughing at him. He just winked at me.

'Just before half-time I was put through on goal, one on one with the keeper, picked my spot, pulled the trigger and, *bang*, Tommy hit me from behind on the penalty spot. I went so high in the air I had time to think how I was going to land. I ended up in the back of the net, feet tangled up. Tommy stood over me and said, "Who won't fucking catch you?" I heard Ray Fletcher whistling like mad, then he shouted, "Number three, come here." As Tommy walked towards him Ray said, "Name please." Tommy looked puzzled, as if Ray didn't know him. "Tommy Smith, MBE." Ray just looked at him and said, "Ray Fletcher, unemployed, take a bath," then showed him the red card. The whole of the pitch, both teams, were rolling around in laughter, fans on the side in hysterics. Tommy trudging off. I tucked the penalty away and we went on to win. After the game one of their lads came in the changing rooms and said, "All back to The Smithy, lads. Tommy has put food on." My reply was, "No thanks." The lad said, "He said you had better come. Seriously, he wants to see you." So I went, I walked in behind my centre halves, Tommy stood behind the bar. He shouted me over. I thought, "This is where I die." He said, "You drink lager?" "Yes, Tommy." He put a pint on the bar and said, "On me. You were outstanding today, son. Don't ever change anything about you. I gave you the man of the match."

'You could have knocked me over with a feather. Then he said, "You can tell your mates you played against a European Cup winner." I replied, "Nah, I played against someone who scored in a European Final." I chatted with him for hours. A true gent and a right fucking hard case.'

Does football violence get any better than that?

My 'Intorelant' Self

Five- or eight-a-side football tells us a lot about ourselves. I know I'm impatient and judgemental and critical and shoot too often and too early. Can I do anything about it? Hopefully, but distribute earplugs to my teammates and put a guy outside the court behind the goals I'm shooting into just in case I can't.

Someone I used to work with and played five-a-side with regularly, Chris Jenkin, once said to me, 'You're the hardest player to play against because you're just so niggly in the tackle and chasing down.' When I reminded him of this recently, he replied, 'I think you can learn more from playing football with someone for an hour than by talking to them or working with them for years. I don't know who said that originally but I think it's true.'

I have played eleven- and five-a-side with Riz and Steve Ball, founders of the successful Columbo Group, which owns bars and pubs in London, and when I ran into Steve recently at his place the Old Queen's Head in Islington, he told me something quite interesting I hadn't heard of anyone doing before: 'Riz and I think five-a-side is a really good insight into people's personalities. If they're a selfish player they're probably a selfish person, not a good team player etc. Sometimes when we've hired people on the strength of their professional experience we take them for a game to get a sense of how their behaviour might be on the job. And that helps us manage them.'

The idea that five-a-side can be used as a personality gauge makes sense. Then again, some people are totally different on the pitch. Crossing that line onto the AstroTurf can either transform a man or give a total insight into them. A player called Matt Morgan told me two stories about the same bloke who was so upset about being sent off by a teenager during a tournament he'd organized that he dismantled his goals and took them home in a strop. A grown man. On another occasion the same bloke, who worked for a water company, flooded a pitch overnight to force a match to be abandoned as he couldn't get all his best players together for the tie. This is someone who seriously needs to calm down and have a think about life.

Thankfully, I'm not that bad, but I do know I need to be a lot more tolerant, or as we call it at home 'torelant', of what's going on around me in a game.

Torelance is a big word in our house. Everyone needs to be more torelant of the people they play football with. Sometimes there's too much anxiety, frustration and anger going on in a five-a-side game, as you can see from the previous chapter.

One Saturday morning my girlfriend and I were driving to Brighton from Rye to watch Leeds United play. Rye Bay is where Kent meets East Sussex. It's an amazingly barren landscape that includes Derek Jarman's famous house and Dungeness Power Station at its tip, and just along is Camber Sands with its invasion-sized beaches, dunes, holiday camps, kite-surfing and retro music festivals. Brighton is about an hour westwards.

Given that I was nervous about what the result might be and wanted to get there quickly, I said I'd drive. Wrong decision, as this meant Lisa had to do the directions. I guess I should have rolled the metaphorical roof down, packed some sandwiches, put on the radio and made a lovely drive of it. A normal person might have, but I'm not normal, I support Leeds United. Also I felt I was probably going to see Leeds lose and I didn't want to be stuck in traffic before doing so. Among many other things, I'm a bit obsessive about routes and the time it takes to get somewhere.

We were going down country lanes directed by signposts made of wood, so pretty soon the map ceased to be of use and you couldn't tell people's private drives from lanes and we were lost and tension was rising and then a full-blown row ensued.

This lasted for about five minutes of really horrible mutual frustration and anger and then, as we left a bushy lane that had probably only seen sheep on it since 1066, we re-emerged onto the correct main road and Lisa, exasperated, said, 'I'm not good at reading a map. You're just going to have to be more torelant of me.' I left it a beat to pull out safely into the main road and across onto the next side road we needed, and then said with a smile, 'Sorry, I have to be more what? *Torelant?*'

And that was that, her mispronunciation punctured the row and she laughed and said, 'I hoped you hadn't heard that.' I agreed I should be more torelant of her. Then we were happy again, with the row coming to a welcome end. We got to Brighton's temporary Withdean Stadium and saw a young Fabian Delph score an amazing solo goal, picking it up in the right midfield position in his own half and just running and running while Brighton backed off until he walloped it into the back of the net.

I jumped so high in celebration I fell backwards over the shit school chairs they had at their temporary stadium and landed in Theo Paphitis's lap. He didn't say, 'I'm out,' but you know he could have done.

It was a great laugh in League One. Norwich, Leicester, Southampton and Leeds were all down there. The others sold out and got successful back in the Prem. In Brighton after his amazing goal I told Lisa that Delph would play for England one day, which was quite a call given that we were in the equivalent of the old Third Division. Roy Hodgson was sitting just along from us at that game with a view to signing Delph for Fulham. Thankfully he didn't, but he did give him his England debut and Lisa remembered my prediction. And I remember her request for me to be more torelant.

So I need to be more torelant of people I play football with and there is a reason why I'm thinking about this. I recently made up the numbers in an outdoor eight-a-side game for some guys who were a few men down. As we were playing I saw some behaviour I didn't like, especially as it seemed personally familiar.

At the back of the team I was on, a guy had taken it upon himself to ask people where they should be playing in a manner that was undermining them. He asked me if I had the energy to run centre midfield given that I'd just finished another game earlier. Sensing the way this was going, I replied, 'I'm not going to do any running at all, I'm just going to pass.' He nodded and moved on.

Out on the right was a guy who was keen to get up and down and had just scored the opening goal. I'd seen him play before and he wasn't Jamie Vardy or anything, but he worked hard, was a personable guy and obviously enjoyed the fact we were winning because of him.

For some reason the guy at the back, the team organizer, had decided to tell this right midfielder that he didn't have the legs to play that role either and he should swap with me. I couldn't get my head round what he was saying, as I'd told him I wouldn't be running too much. He just seemed to keep undermining this guy, who'd given his team the lead. Meanwhile the opposition striker was strolling past the vocal centre back and scoring regularly. He'd have been better concentrating on his own game, but every time he lost his man and a goal occurred he'd look everywhere but himself for the reason. You know the type of player, I'm sure.

It's strange when you play in someone else's game like this, because you don't know the relationships, the history, the social roles or the dynamic of the group. You don't know why people occupy certain positions, but it was clear this guy was available in other people's eyes to be shouted at despite what he contributed. The following week I asked the goalscorer why this happened and he replied, 'Oh, it's just what he does. You just have to live with it and not let it bother you.' I know I've behaved exactly like the mouthy defender in the workplace towards employees (belated apologies if you're reading this). It's not ideal.

So I did wonder, 'Am I like that at football?' I know I'm mentally very critical of what's going on around me, but I'm unaware of how much of it is verbal and how much of it is just inner dialogue. I also know that for every goal scored as a result of someone else's mistake, 20 per cent of them wouldn't have gone in if I'd bothered to chase back and try to stop them properly. Are you part of the solution or the problem? I guess we can be both.

There are usually at least three dialogues going on in a game as far as I can tell. The conversation in a player's head, the opposition's dialogue (which can be a great gauge of how they are coping or not coping) and your own team's dialogue.

The conversation in my head covers how I'm playing, what I think of it and what I think of the rest of the players on the pitch. Ideally I'd be keeping any negative thoughts to myself, but you know, I'm not exactly known for keeping my mouth shut. Positive comments are far more productive, but negative ones seem to escape more easily. Five minutes later I'm thinking, 'What the fuck did I say that for?' and then after that I'll be oversupportive for as long as possible.

At school our Fulton Mackay lookalike Mr Macreadie once came over to me while reffing a first XI match and said, 'Brown, if you don't shut your mouth I'm subbing you.' That was the first time I was aware I talk too much at the expense of teammates.

What I try and tell myself now when I see a hesitant guy dribble the ball out for a corner under little pressure, when he could have just calmly passed it inside or hammered it up the field, is, 'James, you've been the poorest player in games, you've just had two weak passes intercepted, your shot flew well wide, so keep your thoughts to yourself.'

The old adage, 'Does it need saying? By me? Now?' is a good one to play football with. Then again, in the heat of the game, it's just as easy to forget that and shout, 'For fuck sake, keep it simple.'

Simon Kelner, a Man City-supporting mate, once told me he'd heard the following shout directed at a much-maligned player who'd come right up to the fans to collect a ball for a throw-in. 'Fucking hell, Edghill. Believe in yourself, you wanker.' That's the standard of emotional support pros can expect from the frustrated fan.

Every game has its temper spread, from the totally laid-back to the utterly irate. At that end are people who either lose it irrationally or annoy the fuck out of you. Recognize any of these or is it just our game?

'*Don't Panic! Panic!*' The sergeant-major who gets far too wound up when things are actually going well. You're winning, in control of the game, you've just scored and he's running around like there's a tsunami coming. His nonsensical shouting and muttering appear totally inappropriate and actually unnerve people.

The Self-abuser. Screams violently at themselves when they miss a half-chance others wouldn't have even tried to take. This bloke is tormented by the fact his body can no longer carry out instructions from his brain based on his memory.

Occasionally Irritated. Nine weeks out of ten he's busy with his game, very calm and trying hard for the team, so when he starts getting ratty it's quite unnerving. Like being snapped at by a psycho terrapin.

Anger Management Classes Needed. It's only a matter of minutes after you've kicked off inside the hot, sweaty gym when this chap totally loses it with the same blokes he loses it with every week. Old personalities and grudges have just worn away the fuse. And it's comical. You can only hope that the frustrated duo are on the same side and it's not yours. Balls are caught and thrown while AMCN chases the other bloke round the gym shouting at him. If the bloke who annoys AMCN is on the opposition the torment might not emerge until he's losing in the second half and it all flares up about a head-height, handball or D-infringement decision. Then he just cracks and erupts. Strangely our AMCN has calmed down; must be since he's become a magistrate.

Grudge-based Giant. Thinks his size excuses him from doing any work so gets totally riled if you try and encourage him to actually play for the team and chase back or go in goal instead of just standing around waiting for the perfect ball to his feet and then hammering it over the crossbar or even a throw-in on the opposite side of pitch. If you're playing against him and keep dribbling round him, look out for a Pepe-style hacking. Looks as still and moody as a volcano until he erupts.

Hothead International. Some people's game is based purely on intensity and when other players 'interfere' by tackling them or expecting a pass, they see it as just wrong and unacceptable. Stand back and watch when two players like this come into contact. The only time I can remember seeing a punch thrown by regulars in our Sunday game was in such a clash of the battling tops. Good players, intense, not dirty, just combustible when put together. By the time they've finished with the sloppy fists flying around, everyone's forgotten what it was about.

Slow Pan Boiling. Friendly at the start of the game, concentrating during first half, frustrated near beginning of second, furious by end. Nothing's going right, he's feeling his age and people are letting him down with passes that are just a little too long for him. Temper frays. His idea of a relaxation tape is Michael Douglas in *Falling Down*.

Visiting Nutter. No one will admit to having invited him but he's here and taking it far too seriously, chopping people down, clattering them into the walls, pushing, disputing everything. Usually prompts lines like, 'You tell him . . . He's on your side!' and 'I didn't fucking invite him!'

There are so many degrees of mistake that can prompt responses from irate teammates. I've wondered about this and I think there's the

Right Decision, the So-so Decision, the Wrong Decision and No Decision.

The Right Decision is obvious: it results in something positive like a goal, a good pass or a ball being made safe. The So-so Decision has a result that's not bad but another move could have been better. It doesn't matter, though. The Wrong Decision is obvious: you made the wrong call, a shit pass, a failed tackle or a weak save; or your shot is still travelling towards Mozambique instead of nestling comfortably in the back of the net, while a teammate is stood in front of the empty part of the net with their arms, eyes and mouth wide open in disbelief.

Of that list, though, the worst decision is No Decision and I think seeing people frozen and unsure what to do with the ball, despite vocal encouragement, just triggers the exasperation button. Do something. Even if it's wrong, at least you made a decision. The great England goalscorer Gary Lineker once said that hitting the post or the crossbar wasn't as bad as it seems because you'd actually hit the target, just the wrong bit of it. I often feel like that about a greedy striker. I like to think they're getting their range in and eventually it will come good. That's my excuse anyway.

Someone can miss a sitter or hammer a shot into the hanging cricket nets and you'll go, 'Oh well, he gave it a try,' but another time a shit pass or one of those weird 'I just thought I'd handball it instinctively' penalties people give away can just tip you over. At least the striker is trying to score. Mistakes forced by endeavour are tolerated but mild errors forced by indecisiveness aren't.

It's definitely strange how different levels of error can prompt inverse levels of criticism. Why does something small wind you up when something large and extravagantly bad doesn't? Or is that just me? I find myself constantly thinking, 'Oh, for fuck sake,' about small mistakes when I know full well that if you encourage a player it can help them. The big challenge is keeping the 'FFS' to myself.

Some moments are so appallingly bad they actually puncture the tension by provoking laughter. One week in the outdoor eight-a-side game there was a big lad in a bandana, football shirt, tights, Man U shorts, full-length socks and boots. It was a boiling April day and he was dressed like Axl Rose in Lapland. After ten minutes he clearly kicked the ball out and then went to take the throw-in. When the opposition politely pointed out his error he just looked a bit surprised. I started to wonder if he knew the rules, but his ball control wasn't too bad. Just his decision-making was weird.

Shortly afterwards he had the ball on the right wing with space opening in front of him, then he jerked left suddenly and hammered it all the way across the pitch to the left back, who was stood with his hands in his pockets grumbling. It felt like someone pressed the wrong button on the PlayStation handset.

Even weirder was to come when he was in goal. Their guy was advancing down the left wing and the attackers and defenders, sensing a long cross, surged as one to beyond the far post. Our Man in Bandana went with them, leaving a totally open goal for the winger to look up and pass into in amazement. It was so inexplicable everyone just laughed.

Give a new player the benefit of the doubt, I'd like to think, but in this case give him a basic explanation of the rules too.

It's your regulars you have to bite your tongue with. If you want to meet weirdos, play Sunday football or five-a-side. If that sounds unfair on your game, come and play with my lot.

There's one player, George, who just dribbles and dribbles around going nowhere, like a courier without the exact address. He shuttles past teammates galore, who just look on in wonder at what the fuck is going on and how come they have to torelate (yes torelate) this every week. And when he does finally pause for breath, like someone who's just sat up because they realize they've fallen asleep leaning on a computer keyboard, he turns and plays you a hospital ball when you're heavily marked.

At moments like this other players tend to shout, 'George why didn't you just pass it to one of the six teammates you just ran by?'

It's like playing with one of those local community buses that weave in and out of every street going. Here we have a key problem for people with short tempers: often it's the people who think they are doing some good when they're not that wind you up most.

Someone who's shit (and George isn't) either can't help it or can improve. But someone who just plays weirdly is inexplicable.

It's this repetition of bad team play that seems to wind people up. Don't include your teammates and they'll get irritated. Keep shooting too early without looking up or taking your time and they'll get irritated. Playing a Hollywood ball twenty-five yards away but overhitting it off the park or above head height when there was a better pass two feet away will guarantee frustration and probably, again, irritation. Missing a sitter when you need the goal – irritating.

Being fast, young, overconfident and losing the ball repeatedly in the same way is irritating. Not even trying to save the ball if you're in goal will annoy people who've been busting a gut trying to win the game. Staying on your line in goal but not closing down the angle is the same. Repeatedly hitting it above head height will cause irritation. Stepping in the fucking D when you could have shot from outside will cause irritation.

These are all reasons why you need to pack any real-life niggles away before you even start. If you don't zone it and be positive, then the irritant factor exemplified by a disappointing ongoing score will eat away at you.

All of these are genuine factors guaranteed to bring stress to others. More torelance is required all round. We're supposed to be enjoying ourselves – even if everyone is shit, ourselves included.

Injured

A first-degree strain is damage to a few muscle fibres

A second-degree strain is damage to a more extensive number of muscle fibres

A third-degree strain is a complete rupture of the muscle itself

If you'd asked me two days ago what a quadriceps was my guess would have been something to do with Marvel Comics. Maybe a giant four-armed beast that looks like a cross between a terraced house and an octopus. Arms flailing up high over the comic logo as a normal Joe in a grey suit leans back in terror with his hat popping off, wondering where a superhero is when you need one. No one wants to die at the many hands of a home with homicidal tendencies.

If you'd got more specific and asked me what 'rectus femoris, vastus lateralis, vastus intermedius and vastus medialis' are I'd have sent you off to get a copy of *I, Claudius* as vastus you can.

But after two days of research, watching horrible videos of operations, reading documents for doctors on how to treat a torn rectus femoris, learning how these things work and the best way to look after them, I can tell you a quadriceps is in the front of your thigh.

Mine is killing me and this is how I ripped it. If we really care about five-a-side we should make some attempt to try and do our best, occasionally. It's the difference between enjoying it and not. After the last time I played, I realized I was making really simple errors in my game and I ought to sharpen up. So this time I had actually gone about trying to improve. Like James Kyllo, I had undertaken a walk round the local park, twice in two days. Like Ray the *Men's Health* trainer suggested years ago, I had cut out desserts, sweets and chocolates.

I started eating smaller portions and smaller meals. And for three days between Thursday and Sunday I seemed to be making some headway. I know, I know. Three days! But listen I didn't become a fat, lazy bastard overnight and I'm not going to become a fit, running Slim Jim overnight either. They say from little acorns mighty oaks grow, so I've cut out the acorns too.

I also vowed to think more about what I was going to do on the pitch in my Sunday game – get it and give it. Simple stuff. This was partly because I was conscious that during the last week three different people had mentioned my historical habit of shooting from the halfway line. Occasionally with spectacular results, but often firing wide.

Martin McVeigh, a skilful midfielder I used to play with on Sundays until he ballooned up and floated off to New Zealand, asked on Facebook, 'Are you calling your book *Shooting from the Halfway Line*?' To which I replied, 'Yes, and your chapter is called "Shooting Back for Seconds"'.

So I didn't set out to get injured, I actually set out to try and improve my performance. I don't normally do that. I normally just show up and see what happens. I decided to try at least some degree of planning.

Maybe not rushing around last minute would help. What about if I actually took folded kit and got there on time? I might feel better beforehand. I started going to bizarre extremes to try and get an edge over the others, like washing my hands and face at the end of the day in the possibility this might somehow wash weight off. That's how desperate and deluded I had become.

Come Sunday I prepared properly and then jumped on my bike and cycled to Kentish Town. Miraculously I got there first, just before the proposed kick-off time of 11 a.m. For a moment I wondered if the game had been cancelled. Then twenty-two people turned up. For a game on an eight-a-side pitch. I looked at this ever-increasing group of players and immediately thought, 'How the fuck am I going to be able to write about a twelve- versus eleven-a-side game when it's supposed to be a five-a-side book?' Isn't that cheating? Well, it's on a flat hockey pitch not mud so, you know, it's amateur football . . . Stay with me.

The teams were picked, our team of attackers versus the opposition's team of defenders. Twelve versus eleven. How did it get like this, I wondered? I noticed that we had three players on our team who won't chase back from their chosen strike positions, and that the opposition had the two best young players. How did that happen? Aren't they picked opposite each other? 'I'll have Joe', 'OK, I'll have Hamish.'

Seeing the way the teams were stacked I offered to go centre back, then slugged from a bottle of Gopro amino drink, and we cracked into a really good game. Despite there being so many people, it was a little like being back in the street, proof you can actually play with too many people outdoors. Whereas too many players on a tiny indoor pitch is a pain. As Martha Reeves sang, there was nowhere to run, so lots of short passes and interrupted dribbles ensued, which made for a good contest.

Fortunately for us Darren, the decent player I'd left on his arse because of 'Peter Reid needing a tackle' months before, arrived late and joined our team to even the numbers. At half-time one of our team-mates moaned to me that Darren wouldn't release the ball soon enough and kept demanding it back, but, as I said, 'He shows for me every time I have the ball at centre back and will take it and keep it regardless of who is on him, which is fine by me with so many players out there.'

Interestingly, Darren had Villa shorts and socks on. This was the morning after they'd been relegated, so Gabby Agbonlahor was probably still partying hard on the balloons in a Park Lane hotel, while Joleon Lescott was dabbling in the art of 'bad PR' with his pronouncement that it was a relief to finally go down and various Villa board directors were busy drafting resignation letters. But Darren had worn half his Villa kit. Just the bottom half, which I thought was apt, as they hadn't been out of the bottom half of the table all season.

I remember doing the same thing when Leeds got relegated. When your team's in trouble real fans wear the colours; it means more than when you're winning things. Fair play to him, I went over and welcomed him to the Championship wilderness.

It's a busy game in our back three, but it's very enjoyable and we're holding our own, with lots of clearances and interceptions. Meanwhile up front our two strikers get out the deckchairs and fetch a picnic, waiting for the ball to be delivered on a plate for a tap-in. The lazy bastards.

With about ten minutes to go, I am over on the left-hand touchline. A bit imbalanced and without putting much strength into either my standing position or the clearance, I chip the ball over their midfield and full backs and into the space where our strikers are having their picnic.

As the ball goes so does my right thigh. I can feel it tear, pop, rip, strain . . . call it what you want. It goes and as soon as I put my passing foot down it bounces back up gingerly with pain as I make contact with the ground.

I hobble back to go in goal in agony and pull another bloke into my position at CB. That's me for the last ten minutes of the game. One good left-hand save from the opposition's best striker of the ball and a really painful hurried right-foot clearance.

Darren had already taken a nasty whack on his ankle and limped off, so we were two men down. We lose the game, shake hands, say hi to Keir's lot coming on and then I just lie down next to the sports centre wall. My leg is really painful and feels as heavy as an anchor. Someone warming up for the next game hammers a shot so wide that it sends the water bottle by my head flying. I'd be safer just lying in goal.

Marlais is still booting a ball against the wall, as only kids can do after a seventy-five-minute game in the hot sun. The rest of our players drift into the changing room and I'm still lying there on the sandy Astro surface. Slowly I realize that my leg feels so bad I might not be able to get up.

By a genuine stroke of unplanned good fortune, Lisa and Billy have followed us over from home and for the first time ever are in the centre's soft-play area. I hobble down to the car, chuck my bike in the back, climb into the front seat and feel the pain.

'We watched you for about ten minutes. Billy was screaming, "Daaddy!" but you didn't hear. I saw you kick one ball away over your shoulder the other way without even looking, that was impressive. Then we went to the soft-play area, which was crowded and Billy got caught in the face three times.'

Our mornings sounded similar. My leg just seemed to be getting heavier and heavier with pain. Only pulling faces and smiling at my lovely toddler in the wing mirror kept my mind off it. I'm not sure I've ever had an injury like this before. Still, rather than go to the hospital I decide to plot-up on the sofa and self-diagnose. It will be over four months and three rubbish attempts at a comeback before I finally sort myself out and get proper physio on it. The irony of getting injured while writing a book about playing football is not lost on me. Still, it gives me some time to read about injuries online and ask other people if they've had any bad/funny/memorable ones.

Nowadays, because of Beckham's foot and the way everything else trickles down from professional football, we have all heard about ligaments, metatarsals and sports science. When I was a kid the only time you'd see the words 'sports' and 'science' next to each other was on your school lesson timetable. Back then the injury we feared most was getting a football in the bollocks. This would immediately prompt all players, including the injured party, to roll to the floor screaming, 'HERNIA!' amidst gasping peals of laughter. If it landed hard enough it could make you feel sick. Which was even funnier for your mates. The last time I saw anyone in such agony was when I tried to volley a wall pass off David Baddiel's chest and end up nearly crippling him.

During a Tuesday night game I was in a left-wing cul-de-sac, very close to the wall, with the ball bobbling at knee height between myself and Baddiel. Somehow we were both facing against the way we were playing and I figured if I could just rebound it off his chest it would spin back over my head and I could turn round and set off in the right direction again. This move was not without precedent. At the underground cellars where I'd first regularly played with Kyllo and Gary, I'd once managed to drill the ball off the bottom wall away from the nets but get enough spin for it to rebound back across the keeper and into the far side of the goal. Since then I've managed that a few times against the wall in Hoxton too. I was just thinking along the same sort of snooker-style lines with David's chest.

Unfortunately for him, it didn't quite work out as planned. I cracked the volley much harder than I intended and there wasn't enough space for it to rise to his chest, so the ball fired straight into his bollocks. Baddiel left the ground and then hit the floor in total agony, asking what the hell I was doing. He limped off the pitch and didn't reappear for about three weeks. I felt terrible. It looked like I'd decided to cripple him, but in that split second I was simply trying to improvise.

I have since apologized and explained my intention. Thankfully he seemed to understand.

Plenty of adults have received no sympathy when they've gone down injured. Here's Roger Wilde, a five-a-side player from Hull, who in 1984 found himself on the floor in agony outside a music venue in Leicester, where his band, 3Action, were supporting The Housemartins, featuring Cherry Burton FC's finest, Paul Heaton: 'The teams were Housemartins and their roadies, stereotypical southern ponces, barring Heaton, who carries some credibility, versus 3Action and our mate the poet Swift Nick. After a while I received a hospital pass. A roadie in size 10 steelies, fresh from chucking various Marshall cabs about, goes in well over the top and kicks my kneecap round the back of my leg.

When the ambulance arrives, the driver exits the vehicle and is met by the sight of twelve males all writhing around in agony, claiming to be the injured party. My genuine screams were being largely ignored as the perplexed and increasingly radged medic tried to work out who was hurt. I did the rest of the tour in full-length plaster.'

It could have been worse, as Steve Gallagher from Twitter reveals: 'Working at Rothwell Sports Centre, I saw a guy lose his false leg while playing with kids. The look on their faces was priceless!'

Given that I've been playing amateur and five-a-side football for so long, I've not encountered too many ambulances. We've only needed one once in our regular Sunday eight-a-side game when a guy called Dil went up for a header and landed badly. A builder's skip prevented the ambulance from actually reaching him inside the hurricane-fence-protected pitch.

A semi-serious five-a-side injury can subsequently make you relatively invisible to the rest of the players. Someone gets crocked, they hobble off and they aren't there next week. Then you get used to their absence and it's only if you bump into them away from the game that you realize they've not been around for a month.

Five-a-side is like our body cells: new players just emerge and replace the old. Different shape, different kit, different ability, but essentially they are there to continue the numbers. If they turn out to be good players or funny people, if they add something to the game, that's good.

The formation of a five-a-side game is quite ruthless like this. Someone always appears from somewhere to get the numbers up. Every week I currently play in games with all sorts of ill-planned numbers. Keir's game, which follows ours, sticks to a round sixteen, helping themselves to some of our players to top up until frowned-upon late arrivals appear.

Maybe it's because no one wants an injury themselves that so little time is spent considering other players who miss games in pain. 'Where've you been?' you ask when bumping into a guy who's gone missing. 'I've done my leg in,' comes the reply. Blank stare. Thinks: 'Why are you telling me this? I might catch it.'

One player goes down and another pops up to replace him in a sort of game survival mechanism. A game that seems perilously close to having its regular numbers ebb away can suddenly tap into a new blood bank of players. A pre-game email will say 'and Andy is bringing his mate Will' and before you know it Will's a regular, the guy he's replaced has been forgotten and Will's bringing his mate too. It really is a case of survival of the fittest or, in many games where the slow don't run too hard, survival of the . . . well, you know.

This Sunday when I got injured a guy called Hugh played whom I haven't seen for over four years. Before that he was a regular fixture in our game, a good player, then he got a minor injury and drifted away. Because I was off coaching kids for three seasons on Sundays, I'd forgotten about him. Yet when we met up again I knew exactly how he played – good in the air, fancies his chances at corners, good centre back, brings it forward confidently.

Injuries just rub you out of existence. They are another example of the peculiar way these games roll out. People come and go with anything up to a decade's gap. I would imagine that of the twenty-three players this weekend, only three of us knew Hugh had been a stalwart in the game five years before.

Often these long disappearances have geographical reasons behind them, or the guys have new families and are needed at home more, but an injury has no upside. It's the crack that breaks the routine. You miss three weeks and in that time you realize you've possibly enjoyed the time at home or down the pub.

As you get older it's a gradual negotiation with yourself. Should I or shouldn't I? Thankfully I rarely succumb to not going. In the year before he died our friend James Kyllo did miss a long time, over six months, with an ankle problem. This was a noticeable absence for the simple reason that James was the organizational rock upon which the game was built. He booked the pitches, paid for them, kept the scores, kept his stats chart, told us when the pitches weren't available and where we'd relocate to. These are the guys you can't have injured.

I'd bump into James on his bike in the park and tell him how I fixed my ankle problem, which I'd incurred when some cynical ex-Nottingham Forest trainee stamped on it while I was attempting to tackle him in a game for the *Independent*. The main point I was trying to get across to him was that you don't have to stop because one bit of your body might want you to. You just have to find a way round it.

I bump into too many ex-five-a-side compadres who explain their absence with 'it's my knee'. I'd hate that to happen. I can't imagine what it would be like not to be able to play football regularly. Some of the guys I play with occasionally must be well into their sixties. Given that they're sometimes up against kids in their late teens, I say, 'Well done, mate.' It must be frustrating sometimes. Recently in a changing room on a Tuesday night I commented on the quality of the teenagers and one of our most senior players, Clive Anderson, said, 'Yes, too good.' It was almost a mutter and hard to tell whether he meant it or was just delivering a little of his famous Bee Gee withering wit. Injuries. They're shit, aren't they? Nature's way of saying you're doing something wrong or doing it too late in life.

I don't like not playing which is why I keep coming back from this thigh injury too early while writing this book. At one point I find myself barefooted, shaping to boot a huge metal and glass nightclub disco ball I've got lying on my bedroom floor. Like it was a beach ball, only it's solid and made of glass and steel. Maybe I should just give it one more go.

The James Kyllo Memorial Match

I spray Deep Freeze just below my groin, pull up a thigh bandage, wrap tape around it, neck a load of ibuprofen, swig some amino water, have a go on my inhaler and then realize this is more preparation than I take getting ready for Glastonbury.

Just behind me on a huge AstroTurf pitch in the shadow of an east London flyover, I'm relieved to see only a few of the players gathered for the James Kyllo memorial match are warming up. Those actually kicking balls invariably do so twice and then press their hands and faces into the hurricane fence to shout to passers-by, asking if they can boot the ball back into the ground.

If you believe beauty can inspire creativity it is appropriate that our standard of football is nestled next to an ugly concrete slip road rising twenty feet in the air as it rushes people eastwards past Leyton Orient's ground. Beyond the flyover is West Ham's new home and the Olympic Park with its cycling tracks but we are a world away from all that. It's emotion not motion that will be in play today.

I'm stood at the 'car park end' amidst a choppy sea of sports bags spilling their wares onto the AstroTurf. I'm going fist deep into Geoff Norris's Charlton holdall, looking for plaster strip to tighten my thigh restraint. It's like the Tardis in there, so many scrunched-up plastic bags and packets of half-eaten Dextrose and his age-old beloved red and white Charlton shirts.

I really know I shouldn't be playing. My leg aches with a deep throbbing pain in the front of my right thigh. Despite being an amateur hypochondriac, I do know that I've done something bad to my thigh.

I've rested it for almost four weeks, played no football and been for daily mile and a half walks through the local park. Last Wednesday I tried a little light training and stretching with Dominic and the jogging, squats and star jumps all went OK, but when I tried lifting myself from a bench on just my right leg I struggled. I managed to do it but not without visible pain and effort. 'You mustn't do anything with weights on that leg. No lifting at all and you really shouldn't play football this weekend,' is his summary of the session.

On Thursday night I let my head rule my body and tried to play in my hour-long outdoor seven-a-side game where the other team have four of the six teenage sprinters. After my first punt clearing a ball with a volley I feel my thigh pop again, a searing pain that I try to jog off. I manage one Hollywood pass from the right wing of the halfway line, straight to the foot of Mikey on the far side of the opposition area. He kills it, lays it off and we score, but I'm limping back to our goal in real agony. I spend the rest of the game between the metal posts, clearing it with my left foot. I have a last five minutes playing out and make a couple of hefty tackles with my left, but I can't even kick it in the air with my right.

The next night, with a day to go till we kick off James's memorial game, I catch my foot on a step in Leeds Station and there's a lightning flash up my thigh. It's absolute agony. I now understand why professional players insist on being picked for important games despite being unfit. Jermaine Beckford was heavily strapped up for Leeds in the League One play-off final against Doncaster at Wembley, but his usual sharp attacking threat was blunted by the injury he was carrying and you could see he was half a step off most of the tackles and shots.

I know I'm going to play in the match for James and just hope that, with a reported thirty-seven players coming, we have a mini five-a-side tournament with roll-on, roll-off subs and plenty of rests between matches. You can imagine my delight when I see it's a full-sized pitch, twenty-odd players and only two kits.

If we didn't have football kit on I think passers-by would struggle to guess what activity the assembled men had planned. Maybe some weekend rambling? A gardening club? The local youth who are hammering balls into the five-a-side nets beside the pitch look on with curiosity as eventually twenty-seven middle-aged men don rhubarb-and-custard- coloured T-shirts.

As I pull my shirt on I get my excuses out early. They're genuine and I want to limit the expectations of my teammates, still hoping that once I start everything will be fine and I just won't feel anything.

Given the size of the pitch and a general lack of fitness, I suggest we just play everyone – thirteen versus fourteen. So the pitch is enormous after all, the more blokes on it in yellow the easier it will be to pass it short.

The gathered players all look significantly older than we did when we started playing in the Wednesday and Sunday games that James first organized decades ago. There's a handful of players from Brighton and former staunch regulars whom I haven't seen for years. It reminds me of how people just dissolve away from a regular five-a-side or eight-a-side fixture but the game itself rolls on, slowly evolving personnel-wise. There are three players I used to play with week in, week out whom I'd totally forgotten about. I knew a couple remembered from my earliest games had moved away to the coast. One I didn't even recognize until halfway through the game.

It's strange how easy it is to recall immediately the way these former regulars play their game. Two of them are still branded with Gary's shit nicknames, Little John and Tooting Tim. Tooting Tim is stood by the pitch in a Steve McQueen Barbour T-shirt, straw hat and shades, while Little John is bouncing up and down in his tracksuit bottoms, as ready as ever to kick off. Tim is clearly not going to play, but I almost don't recognize him without his kit on; it's his profile and physique that jog my memory. A shape remembered from years of snatched glances wondering where he is so as to lay the ball in to him.

I thought he was one of the best players in our game, skinny and agile. He has what David O'Leary called 'quick feet'. If you got the ball to him in the area he would score a lot of good goals every game. A great guy to play with, he knew how to move into the right space when you were looking to play him in. I can picture him straight away in his white shirt surrounded by defenders while poking a shot into the roof of the net. I ask him why he isn't playing and he replies, 'I have a prolapsed disc', and points to his back. I don't know what this is but it sounds terrible.

Despite historical folklore, Little John isn't a giant but was simply smaller than another John the original game had. Again as I recognize him I can see John instantly through the mists of time, plugging away in between big centre backs and banging a loose ball fiercely into the net and running back with a grin breaking out across his face. A keen boxer, he was perfectly at home in the close-quarters conflict of a goalmouth scramble.

I've not see either of these guys for almost a decade but the memories are instant. There are others too. Harry, a cartoonist, I remembered from the first game I ever played with James in the dark, dripping railway arches where Shoreditch Station is now. I always thought Harry had a unique style in this cave of a pitch. He'd crab-shuffle inside and outside onto the wing, beating his man and then moving on, like he had croissants for legs. Then there's Howard, the guy I didn't remember for half the game, a tall, commanding centre back who could confidently move the ball around while looking unruffled by anyone attempting to tackle him. In my memory all four were good players. The older we get the better we all used to be.

I've never started a game injured before. I've carried on when I've tugged a muscle or fractured an ankle or broken a toe, the adrenalin and competition just keeping me going. I won't be starting injured again, though. Jogging out felt fine but the moment I had to curl a pass more than fifteen feet and get some air on it I was getting twinges of pain and a slight lack of power. I just hoped people would stay close and not drift away. Lack of stamina across the team thankfully made this the case.

We played a game of three 'halves' with a proper ref and an increasingly large crowd of curiously patient kids and teens waiting to get onto the pitch. I found if I just used the incoming ball's momentum and hit it straight from the top of my foot I could move it some distance without too much trouble. Curling and lofting and placing it were very difficult, though. There are those who'd say I struggle to do any of those on a normal day, but today everything I touched deliberately went above head height.

We lost 4–3, but the genuinely excited cheer from the local kids when our team pulled back to 4–2 was really inspiring and appreciated. 'Come on, yellows,' they screamed, leaping up and down and on top of each other. Even the teens, who were sulking a bit because they had to wait for their own game, seemed to get involved and started shouting encouragement. Maybe I'm not alone in being able to watch any game regardless of the standard.

I played the last hour left-footed, volleying anything that came near me back the way it had come. At one point it looked safer to dip below chest height and steal the ball from two different players with my head than risk tackling that high with my right leg. One of many Andys playing asked me afterwards, 'Didn't that hurt, getting two kicks in the head at the same time?' but in comparison with the sawing feeling in my right thigh it was nothing. Like someone throwing an empty carton at you.

Pleasingly four of the five goals were scored by the older players who play on the tiny polished wooden pitch on Wednesdays, the one exception being a moment of unprepared genius from a guy with braids from Brighton, Michael. With his back to the corner flag just inside the edge of the area near where the D starts, he managed to stumble backwards and away from three defenders in close attendance, spin and get a really great shot off into the top corner as he rolled back and hit the ground. It looked absolutely amazing. Across the two teams twenty-seven smiles appeared instantaneously.

By the end of the game the pitch looked like a sandwich with no filling or a Subbuteo game with all the 'little footbollers', as my eldest son's Welsh mum once called them, clustered round both goals. Each half had a team of defenders and the opposition's midfielders and attackers in their own half. Nothing existed in between, just a big trench of emptiness as the midfielders had given up chasing back and the keepers were punting it end to end.

The hit-and-hope nature really reminded me of the first school match I ever played in for Bedford Field aged nine – no one team in control and only half the players capable of directing the ball where they wanted it to go. I couldn't help think how curious that was. Some of these players clearly hadn't played on a large pitch in decades, and by the end others looked like they'd never play any football ever again.

Playing left-footed with a searing pain down my right leg was strange. People use the phrase 'playing through the pain barrier', but this didn't feel like that; there was no 'through' to it. Twice in the game, one free kick and another timid clearance for a throw-in – when that was all I could manage – I actually had tears in my eyes from the intensity of it. Most of my life I've found the worst pain to be emotional not physical, but this was something else.

As the ref blew early and the teens and kids piled on for their games, one of them asked me, 'Is this a charity game?' When I told him it was a memorial game for a friend who died, he just replied, 'Oh,' and said, 'Well done, then.' I realized that maybe he couldn't comprehend the idea of one of his friends dying, but by then he was diving around saving shots from ten different kids with balls and the guys as old as his grandad trooped off for photos and some much-needed rest and recuperation.

In the changing room we sat and caught up. Geoff Nutter said, 'Phew, that was hot.' To which Little John replied and nodded my way: 'Not as hot as that Sunday when James ran into the Talacre changing rooms and had a shower in his kit at half-time and then just came back out dripping for the second half.' I'd forgotten about that, but thinking back it was surprisingly effective. Like chucking your shaggy dog in the river on a boiling day. I had run the drips off in minutes.

Given that I'd rarely socialized with the midweek team and already knew John was a Leeds fan, I took the time to ask Geoff who he supported. 'Well, I'm a Liverpool player,' he replied, and then, as we all looked up with smiles, he muttered a bit and corrected himself, 'A Liverpool fan. That's who I support.'

But it was there just for that moment, a glimpse into his inner dialogue. The childhood snap-back that told him he wasn't a middle-aged man playing a modest-standard game next to a shitty flyover a few hundred yards away from a rubbish tip and a motorway. That he was in fact Keegan or Hansen or Barnes or Rush or whoever his childhood hero had been. In his mind as he scored his long-range goal and toiled over a field of a pitch, before retiring after twenty-five minutes with a hamstring, while celebrating the life of a huge, recently deceased and much-missed Canadian, James Kyllo, Geoff was a Liverpool footballer. And he was right. That's exactly what we are. All of us. Five-a-side and A side, thirteen-a-side. Above or below head height, we play football because we love it. Because we are footballers.

And that's why it's better than everything else we do.

Wearing the Game

When you have played often enough and as well as you can, when you've beaten the opposition to score great goals, when you've stuck your leg in the way of a shot that tattoos the ball's panel stitching into your leg, when you've deftly cushioned the ball on its way into your goalscorer's path and when you've had your shins and ankles clattered and nicked and your knee go bone to bone and your arse thumping down onto the hard wood floor from some mad collision, when you've done all of these things again and again, then you have the right to wear the game.

Especially to feel it. What looks like a tapestry of bruises is actually closer to the Cub Scouts five-a-side badge – reward and notification of endeavour and skill – or, if you want to be really dramatic, the scars scene from *Jaws*. The strains and stiffness, the grazes and the awkward way your shoulders have settled are proof you've been playing. Carry them and you can go ahead and retell the creation and execution of your last and best goal.

I first felt this at eighteen when the school team was doing so well. It was the start of my final year, one I'd end six months early with no further qualifications to show for the eighteen months in the sixth form, but my ankles told a story.

I walked into my dad's bedroom early one morning to ask him where my shirt was and I could feel the bruises all around my ankles. As I walked it felt as if the lower end of my legs would ring out like a glass if you flicked them. There were no ankle-protecting pull-over shin pads back then. All I had was a shin-hugging moulded-polystyrene pair. They were light because I didn't like the heavier ones, but I don't know if they were much cop. I still don't like shin pads; I feel like they slow me up.

That was a great school team, though. It featured those of us who'd played together through the years, supplemented by the best players from the lower sixth. Richard Solk – a skinny black-haired crow of a boy who had once stood up at a theatre midway through a Rowan Atkinson set and heckled in the style of Atkinson's own heckler character, just as Atkinson had left the stage to lowered lights, intent on relocating to the crowd and doing the same thing. Solkie played one side of me in the midfield and a very skilful lad called Nigel Froggatt played the other. Froggie could twist and turn his way through lunging tackles and play passes in much the way Wilshere does for Arsenal. I knew if I turned left or right away from a challenge I could play the ball without looking and they would be where the ball was going.

Behind us was Sam Bell, a gifted centre back who regularly played with David Batty and Brian Deane for Leeds City Boys. Sam, who was two years younger than me, could bring the ball out from the back into the opposition's half without any fear of losing possession. On the wing we had 'The Cat', an amazing Roy of the Rovers-style character with a mane of thick golden hair, a brilliant keeper who turned out to be an amazing winger with a lethal shot. At fullback we had my mates Geoff and Ashley, who'd been in those positions every week of school in and out.

I would sit in the middle of them, having moved into the centre from the wings after finally adding tackling and long-distance shooting to my repertoire. I was very skinny, not too tall, but in a city that had Bobby Collins, Billy Bremner and Brian Flynn as football club captains, height wasn't an issue.

A good team wins games and, by the nature of cup competitions, wins equals more games. My ankles were so blue and sore to the touch because we had got to the point where we were playing three games a week.

This was the first time I instinctively knew where players should be, and Solkie and Froggatt knew it too. Also the first time I got to wear the game on my body after we had finished. It's a physical sense of achievement and experience. You can see that feeling in a much more concentrated and heightened way when marathon runners finish, the thorough exhaustion crowded with the pained smile – when you push your body to do what you want to achieve. It's the same with continual five-a-side. Unlike charity distance runners, though, there's less attention to hydration and physical aftercare.

Just after I was divorced, I was training for a *Men's Health* Challenge feature, which meant I had the fitness, interest and (on alternate weekends, when I didn't have my son) the time to play as much as I wanted. I'd play my Sunday morning eight-a-side game with James and Gary in Kentish Town and then, when that ninety minutes in the sun ended, I'd just stay on for the next game with Keir and his guys. Then I'd go home and sink into an afternoon of football on Sky. Next morning I got up to play a very fast indoor game in a deep, long concrete gym at Finsbury Leisure Centre with Matt Tench, then sports editor of the *Sunday Times*.

The playing wasn't an issue, but I'd be so dehydrated after that fourth hour in twenty-four I'd be wiped out for the rest of Monday. Stretching properly wasn't something I bothered with and weirdly, looking back on it, neither was hydration. I should have got some rehydration powders, but you think just bottles of water on the Sunday afternoon will be enough. By Monday afternoon I'd have a headache and feel as heavy as old furniture.

My work situation was all retainers and business talks, so I didn't have to be anywhere in particular during the week. I'd play the Sunday, then the Monday, then I'd have two days off the ball until Wednesday night and then a Friday morning game and possibly the odd appearance at an outdoor game on a Saturday morning. Five-a-side was my life.

The stiffness that came with such a schedule as I got older became a coat of armour to wear – one you wore after the battle but not during. When you're playing you don't feel those bruises; they're surface irritation, a fly on the windscreen. You're too busy avoiding the next one to worry about the physical baggage that you're carrying.

It's not only the adrenalin that numbs that pain, it's the love of the game itself. The avoidance skills first appeared in the street or primary school playground with British Bulldogs or fifteen-a-side matches. Jumping through woods or over fences, being chased out of allotments, you'd feel brambles or splinters grazing you but you wouldn't feel the pain until later.

That sense of movement with the ball is just as exhilarating. Rolling it forward from foot to foot, out of the reach of the opponent, twisting your body to skip the lunge and proceed up the pitch. During those moments you can see where you're running and the opposition look stiff and solid until one lurches at you like a jump-started car.

For me the celebration of a great driving goal on the Talacre eight-a-side outdoor pitch always meant running back to our own half where the move had started from.

All the brief encounters with the opposition which make up the game, the short periods of play when you're in possession, in control of the ball, are changing the game. They give you bumps and bruises and nicks and knocks, but you crack on regardless because in your mind you're whoever you adored as a kid. You're being the player you want to be.

And that is what you take away. Not just the purple badges of pain and experience around your legs, but the stories you can retell like battles from days gone by. To me that is 'wearing the game' and earning the right to recount how the game went for you. And the great thing is anyone can do it. Everyone has a moment when their teammates, maybe even the opposition, applaud: an astounding save, a through ball, a deadly finish from an outstretched leg or a lovely curved shot.

Shorts, Socks and Coats

I'm travelling back across the Caledonian Road late on a cold black Monday night in February when I see three guys in football shorts and big waterproof coats unlocking their vintage racing bikes opposite Pentonville Prison. Two of them have bulging plastic bags in their hands, the third has a modern urban rucksack on. Apart from grocery shopping, the plastic bag was made to hold football boots. The combination of bags, coats and shorts was the telltale sign, these are some of our tribe.

When I point the lads out to the friend driving the car and say, 'They're the guys I'm writing about in my book,' he doesn't understand. 'What, do you know them?'

No, not personally, but I know who and what they are: they're inner-city amateur footballers, five-a-side players, men who will happily travel home in nylon shorts and puffa jackets. There is no other reason to be dressed like that at 10.15 on a cold February night, unless they were planning some sort of sports-related break-in to Pentonville Prison.

From the looks of it they've just finished an after-game drink a street away from the pitches at Islington's Market Road. Perhaps in a descendant of the big four pubs, the Lamb, the Lion, the Black Bull and the White Horse, that used to corner the area now known as Market Road, which in the nineteenth century was a huge cattle market, processing 15,000 cattle a day.

Since I started writing this book I've seen even more of the coats and shorts guys, usually on the road heading to or from an outdoor pitch, but occasionally somewhere unusual, like the three I saw happily chatting away on the Piccadilly Line down towards Chelsea.

It's only when you're involved in something totally physically and mentally engaging that you can walk around with scant regard for what you're wearing. That's why mountain climbers look the way they do. Sure, there are times at an autumnal all-night festival you might see women raving in tiny shorts or a miniskirt from the day smothered in an enormous coat, but you aren't going to catch many men going large up top and brief down below unless they've been playing five-a-side.

Increasingly, there's every chance that apart from the five-a-side sector of the 'Modern Male Lifestyle' Venn diagram they might also fit into another part of it, the 'Men Who Stare at Coats' sector. This is the name I've given to the men, often from the football-going fraternity, who buy magazines like *Proper* and shop in places like Oi Polloi to obsess over the latest styles and fabrics of outdoor winter waterproof wear. The coats usually come from Scandinavia. The grandfather is the duffel. There's a big industry revolving around these garments, with specialist shops in most towns selling the gear. It's not cheap, but it's top quality.

The emergence of the market for quality lightweight waterproof coats over the last thirty years and the explosion of so many five-a-side pitches across city centres have allowed this look to flourish. It is a practical application of the coats, not a pose, but there may well come a time when coats and shorts are hustling up and down the catwalk. If they haven't already done so.

One person who has made me laugh by appropriating football kit for faux fashion means is *Vice* journalist Hannah Rose Ewens, who, in 2015, matched her boyfriend's football kit with stuff she'd found in a skip and a computer power cable for a necklace, and ventured out to London Fashion Week to see how many members of the fashion media would take her look as a cutting-edge fashion blogger seriously. It was a brilliantly funny idea but it was the boyfriend's football kit that gave it an air of legitimacy.

A couple of years into the original British house/rave scene, as the 1980s stumbled into the 1990s, vintage cotton football shirts could be seen in bars and fields across the nation. When I visited Rock in Rio with the Happy Mondays at this same time, Bez appeared in a vintage Brazilian short-sleeved football shirt for the *NME* cover shoot. One night at a bar in Soho around this time I convinced a West Ham fan in a round-neck claret and blue shirt you'd have once seen on Clyde Best that Alan Devonshire, the great West Ham midfielder, was my dad. He was so keen to get in touch with West Ham's roots he didn't notice my Leeds accent.

It was at this time that companies like TOFFS (the old-fashioned football shirt) sprang up and the vintage football shirt market is still going. It's a strong sector of the sports merchandising business, especially among those of us who long for the better days their clubs enjoyed.

This fetishization of historical shirts continues to grow apace with the recent publication of the football shirt bible, *A Lover's Guide*, by Neal Heard. It's an interesting read and I'm pretty sure five-a-side pitches all over the country will start to see a trend in green 1980s St Etienne shirts as a result of its being declared the football enthusiast's football shirt.

Neal was kind enough to ask my opinion on some of my favourite football shirts and the first I noted was the great Leeds United Aertex Admiral long-sleeved away shirt of the mid-1970s, which was yellow with blue and white stripes on the arms and the famous Smiley badge on the left breast. I had that shirt as a kid and it was a killer. In an era when any old stock was worn away from home, Leeds were the first team to introduce a fixed away colour, going for yellow as it clashed with so few other teams' main kit. Liverpool and Arsenal soon followed suit. The other shirt I mention in Neil's book is the fantastic vertically striped Admiral Welsh kit, which has seen a resurgence of late for obvious reasons. I didn't own that shirt as a kid, but I did have the shorts and tracksuit top, presumably drawn to it by the likes of Brian Flynn, Terry Yorath and Carl Harris wearing it when they were away from Leeds on international duty.

As a kid I also had the Barcelona and Juventus kits, cheap unofficial copies from a sale in a sports shop in the Headrow, Leeds. Their presence had been announced by Leeds City Boys player Johnny Paynter, midway through a game at the bottom of the woods, which was cancelled immediately as we all ran off to get money. The combination of the rarity of foreign club kits and the affordability was enough to stop the game and prompt a stampede of kids towards bus stops all along the 56 route. This was an era when Cruyff and co. would be seen only in the pages of *Tiger and Scorcher* and *Shoot*. Or newspapers. The only television you'd come across them on was in a European final or the World Cup. They might as well have been painted images on cave walls.

The wearing of kit is a key element in the world of five-a-side. Without it you are a laughing stock, as Chris Collier recounts: 'Our keeper turned up with his girlfriend, but realized he'd left his kit bag at home and it was too late to go back. She'd been at the gym, so he went in goal wearing his striped, button-down collar work shirt plus his girlfriend's black skin-tight leggings and trainers. Looked like Max Wall. He had size 9 feet, she was a 4 or something and kept bollocking him from the touchline about breaking the back of her trainers. Made him tiptoe so as not to bust them. Had to scramble across the area like a ballerina/baby deer to deal with shots.'

Adam Smith offered me this story via Twitter: 'Our team didn't have enough shorts so we had to play a game of fives to see who'd play in their pants. The ref allowed it.'

Presumably Adam's mate's pants were more concealing than the kit worn by @JamesSymc24's mate: 'A fella arrived to play wearing cycling-skin-tight leggings with no shorts on over them. I repeat NO SHORTS ON OVER THEM.'

Sometimes you can just see too much. I will never forget the lunchtime changing-room sight of a *Jack* magazine colleague called Steve Cadwell, who sat, fresh from the shower, with his thighs wide open revealing a spreading blush of rosy-pink chafing that ran from his bollocks down both thighs towards his knees, looking like a map of the old British Empire. This is one of the more savoury stories I could tell about him.

I once settled an argument with a loud drunken woman about elements of the male physique by firmly stating, 'Listen, I don't care how many people you've shagged. I shower with over twenty different men a week and I've seen more naked male bodies than you.' Which drew strange looks from other people in the restaurant.

As I've said before, if you only see the people you play football with when you're at five-a-side, it can be strange seeing them in their everyday attire. One time I was out with my girlfriend when I saw someone I play five-a-side with. He was also with his wife and we let on to each other across the street, then I shouted, 'I've never seen you with your clothes on before.' Which didn't sound right at all. I could see his wife looking at him inquisitively and Lisa looking at me as if I was mad. He was a recognizable TV actor and she thought I was heckling the bloke. 'It's OK. I play football with him,' I explained hastily.

So it's important to have kit. The presence of bibs in many games means some players don't have to try, wearing whatever they like underneath. But sports centres do insist you wear something. It's health and safety and decorum gone mad. PE teachers of the 1960s, 1970s and 1980s would be turning in their tight tracksuit bottoms if they knew that their sadistic topless non-strip invention, 'skins', is now barred from public pitches on hot days. Not that they'd ever suggest skins and shirts during a month when it was still light at 7 p.m. Only during the winter.

Contrary to what professional football clubs would have us believe about their merchandising, you don't have to spend a fortune to get kit. For the memorial game for Kyllo there were all sorts of emails flying around about colours and bibs until Gary intervened and said, 'Don't worry about it. I've sorted it,' and showed up with eleven custard-coloured T-shirts and eleven rhubarb-coloured ones. They were a weird colour but they were large and comfortable and he didn't even ask for any cash for them.

'Where did you get these?'

'A place on Stoke Newington High Street. They were a quid each. I get all my football T-shirts there.'

Total bargain. People certainly judge players by their kit. You can tell a lot about someone from what they're wearing to play. You can tell who they support from the club shirt they wear, how old from the style and shirt sponsor across the chest, how fit and healthy from the shape of the body beneath the shirt, and you can guess their chosen position or hero by the number on the back.

I think simplicity looks great, like the early Subbuteo teams. This Sunday George, who I play with on Sundays, had his back to me and in his simple long-sleeve white T-shirt, shorts and socks he looked like he had the perfect 1960s Leeds kit on. As I was about to tell him this, he turned round and ruined it with some red Arsenal branding on the front of his shorts. Still, he went on to have a good game, so maybe he was helped by the ghosts of Revie and Bremner. There was, of course, a time when only Celtic had anything on their shorts and that was the player's number.

At the other end of the spectrum you can be too flash. Chris Steele reports on Twitter: 'I played in a league against a team that had full matching tracksuits and shirts with numbers and names on. They had their striker play in a sailor's outfit one week to celebrate scoring 100 goals. They had never lost in the history of the league and cracked the champers out at half-time in the cup final. Which they went on to lose 4–3 on pens.'

I asked my friend Mikey, who works in the sportswear business, if he had ever seen anyone who caught his eye for good or bad kit: 'One time this guy showed up and I noticed he had our best, latest football trainers on, really hard to get, and a great kit, and I thought, "He looks like a proper player," but he turned out to be shit.'

In my experience this is quite a common factor and is the main reason I don't like wearing branded kit. I don't feel I'm worthy of wearing the kit my heroes wore. The flasher you look, the closer the scrutiny you're going to get on and off the pitch and the worse you're going to appear if you don't have a good game.

About a decade ago, when I was in Barcelona with Marlais and Andy Mitten, I did think about buying a shirt at Camp Nou, as they had a great centenary one that reminded me of the kit I'd had as a kid (not that I'm a 110 years old or anything). I looked at it for a long time and thought, 'Nah, you're going to look more like Pavarotti than Cruyff, don't do it.' It was the corporate logos all over it and the label fixed to the washing details by a small chain that stopped me.

As an industry it's the emperor's new clothes, a way to suck more money from the people who pay for the game. Right now my team, Leeds United, have good kits, but last year we didn't even have a sponsor, which was an unexpected bonus of having a cack-handed owner. Again this year the shirts look good, but I'd much rather have the kids' sponsor, Greenpeace, than the adults' one, which is a gambling company. The Greenpeace shirts look great. Support LUFC, save a whale.

Surprisingly, somewhere where there's a fair bit of Barcelona kit in the streets of the northern Indian city of Dharamsala, home to the Dalai Lama and focal point for the Tibetan monks who have escaped persecution in their own country. I was visiting there a few years ago with two mates, Matt Sankey and Miles, from the *GQ* five-a-side team, staying at the fantastic mountaintop Hotel Eagles Nest, when Matt and I came across some young monks and kids playing a small game of football in the cobbled streets leading to the monastery.

We joined in their game and impressed the kids with our spiritual well-being and ball control, and after picking the ball out of a book-shop's open window display a couple of times, we asked them how come they had Barça shirts on but no other club colours apart from their own distinctive burgundy monk's robes.

'Puyol, Puyol, Puyol,' came the little kids' replies, then a monk in his twenties explained that Puyol, the magnificent Barcelona captain (who had just retired that summer), felt some international kinship between the Tibetans and his own Basque people, so had donated money to their cause and had visited the monastery, bringing kits for the kids. The only other team they mentioned when pressed was Arsenal. Legend has it that in the furthest reaches of Tibet, David Rocastle is worshipped as a minor deity. This was a street game but the monks also told me the older ones had their own eleven-a-side team and were fully kitted out in decent footwear and happy to take on all comers.

When I had been to India to make that extreme yoga series for Channel 4 I'd met some guys on top of the mountain who told me about games they played at the bottom of the valley with up to twenty a side and no one wore boots. In the UK five-a-side footwear is of course imperative and the general perception is that adidas Samba are still the best.

Leather uppers and a decent sole are key. I'm yet to succumb to the new-fangled fad of trainers that incorporate mesh socks, which might look cool if you're under the age of twenty-five, but to the rest of us they just look like the Penguin's spats in *Batman*. All are a long way from the plastic bags over plimsolls Ian 'Scampi' Reid once wore to football training back at Lawnswood School, predating Withnail's similarly clad trip to the shops by a decade. I've come to realize that any adult who arrives for a five-a-side game in plimsolls could well be a nutter.

Socks, as I mentioned previously are just a bind. Anyone who can point me in the direction of a decent pair will be rewarded with old Panini stickers from my son's historic swaps collection. Long socks without shin pads is commonplace but questionable, short socks *with* shin pads is ridiculous, while shin pads with no socks has been spotted, held to the leg by gaffer tape.

Whatever you wear is likely to leave an impression, not so much as a fantastic save or an impressive goal count, but an impression all the same. And you never know when your five-a-side kit could give you a step ahead in business, as Liverpool-based five-a-sider John Lunney will conclude in this superb tale: 'A few years ago, I worked in an office with a bit of an odd bloke who had no interest in football at all. He loved any opportunity to go 'networking', though. When he got an invite to a five-a-side networking event, he decided that he would enter a team and went round the office recruiting the lads who regularly played five-a-side. We were a bit surprised by him asking us, because as far as we knew he'd never played football before in his life. We put our names down anyway and didn't think much more about it.

'The tournament was held at the Pits in Liverpool. This is a load of five-a-side pitches at the end of Scotland Road, near Anfield. It's not that bad any more, but at that time you would regularly see police cars and ambulances in the car park from games that had got out of hand. There is always groups of young scallies hanging round there looking for a spare pitch.

'On the day of the game, we asked him if he had brought his kit in for the match. He hadn't, but told us he would "sort it out" on his lunch. By "sort it out" we assumed he meant he would go home and get his kit or go to Sports Direct and buy some gear. What he actually meant, though, was that he'd go to his car, find an old pair of jeans in the boot and cut them into shorts.

'I've never had to cut jeans into shorts before, but it must be quite difficult to judge the length, because he drastically underestimated the length of his legs. His outfit consisted of a work shirt (fully buttoned up to the neck), brown brogues, grey socks and a pair of Kylie Minogue-style denim hot pants. The reaction of the gang of local fourteen-year-old lads as he walked out of the changing rooms was priceless – a mixture of disbelief and fits of laughter.

'The game was ridiculous too. He hardly got a kick, but every time he did both teams and the group of scallies now watching were reduced to uncontrollable laughter. At the end of every game, he stood by the exit handing out his business cards. He certainly made an impression, but I doubt he got any work from it.'

Genius.

Kyllo and the Organizers

When the article about Kyllo went viral, something I hadn't thought of before struck me. During it all people kept telling me, 'We have a guy just like this,' or the article would be tweeted to someone else with a line like 'this reminds me of Sarge'.

What became apparent was that most games have a much-needed and relied-upon organizer, someone who books everything from the pitch to the ref to the pub for the annual Christmas drinks or awards ceremony. They deal with the sports centre, send out the emails, bring the bibs, make sure there's a ball, collect the money. Without them the game is impossible.

For those of us who organize our own games these people are vital. But there are also companies who set up and organize leagues, matches and teams and find individual players games for a living. The more famous existing leagues are of course Powerleague and Goals, but there are others too. I came across 5aside.org on Twitter and initially thought they were a dating service for lonely players looking for a game.

'What do you do for a living?' I asked Nick Frith, who answered the phone when I called them.

'This is my living,' he replied. 'It's a full-time job.'

'Can I come down and see what you guys do day by day?'

He tried to steer me towards coming to their matches, knowing that's where the real fun in what they do takes place, but I wanted to see what went on behind the scenes. I imagined they'd be in a Portakabin with walls covered in whiteboards. In fact, Nick's work takes place in a large four-desk office in a former synagogue turned business centre in Brixton. At first glance the empty metal shelves that greeted me as I walked in looked a little like a sports shop that had just been looted. There were three floor-to-ceiling industrial shelving units with just one deflated football and a box of trophies on them.

'That's normally full of balls,' Nick explained apologetically.

'We get through about 1,500 a year,' added his colleague Amy McClusky.

'Really – that many?' I asked.

'Yes,' she replied. 'We're all out and we're expecting some more any time.'

With the timing of a *Postman Pat* episode, a delivery man followed me into the room with four large boxes packed with deflated Puma King Pro Direct Trainer leather balls. Nick opened it, pulled one out and showed me the company name embossed on it.

'Who's going to pump all of them up?' I wondered.

'I am,' said Nick. 'Because I usually have to work a Saturday or a Sunday, my friends joke that my job is just pumping up footballs.'

Sports equipment was scattered around the room: an open box with goal nets, a stray orange goalkeeping glove on a desk, a surfboard propped behind a filing cabinet, a rail of scarlet 5aside.org branded nylon referee's jackets. Beneath the rail there was a large box with hundreds of used golf balls in them.

'You organize golf matches too?' I asked.

'No, they're Jamie's. He just likes golf.'

Jamie Mascaro's golf balls are next to his clubs and you slowly get a picture of the man who started the company. His bookshelf is full of titles on entrepreneurial endeavour, sports law, the sorts of books that might help someone who has cleverly turned a passionate hobby or interest into a business.

Jamie usually has three staff in the office. When I visited two of them were in: Nick, who is a Hereford FC supporter in his mid-twenties, and Amy, a twenty-four-year-old netball fanatic.

'I spend most of my day looking for new pitches and seeing if we can book them to start leagues,' explained Nick. 'We've currently got twenty-four pitches across London and 354 teams playing on them. The leagues last ten weeks, it's £50 per game for a team and you have to pay up front. That means teams don't drop out and there's a good all-round commitment to the league.'

'The main difference between us and the bigger companies like Goals or Powerleague is they own the pitches whereas we rent them from councils, schools and sports centres.'

'Jamie started it with his mates in south-west London and it just expanded from him organizing those games,' Amy told me. She then showed me an online map of all their sites in London. 'We're looking for new ones in east and south-east London. They originally grew around the Tube lines and there's not many Tube lines heading south-east. We've also got a women's football league at Market Road and 125 netball teams.'

'What's funny about the team names,' said Nick, 'is that captains hand them in and always think they've come up with something funny and original, but pretty much we've always heard them before. One thing that has changed with the names this last year has been the number of Leicester fans who've either started playing or started using the club in their names: 24 Hour Vardy People, No Fox Given, Ranieri's Rangers.'

I eventually caught up with Jamie on the phone and he explained how he went from being a five-a-side player to a professional league organizer.

'Ten years ago I was playing in a league myself and I simply thought I could do a better job than the company running it. I was training to be a lawyer at the time and I thought I'd have a go at running a couple of leagues in the evenings. Then, after I'd qualified and got a job in the

City, I very quickly realized I didn't want to do that. I've played five-a-side for as long as I can remember and it's something I really enjoy doing, so it seemed a natural thing to do, a way of earning a bit of money without having to sit in an office, so about eight years ago I started full-time.'

'What's the best thing about running leagues?'

'Being at the games is the most enjoyable aspect of it. It's nice to go down to the pitches and play and meet people who have the same interests, the players and the captains, people letting off steam in London, which is a serious place a lot of the time. I'd say 99 per cent of the players are nice people.'

'How many games were you playing yourself?'

'At the beginning I was playing three or four games a night sometimes. I'd go down and set up, someone would be short, so they needed you to fill in for ten minutes, then ten minutes becomes a whole game. Then it settled down to about four or five games a week. You know what it's like, playing four against five is a bit crap, so you feel like you want to join in and help. I don't play so much now. I'm thirty-four and have had a few injuries.

'We have had a couple of ex-pros play. Scott Minto played. George Best's son plays in a league, but he's obviously not as good as his dad. Jack Whitehall was playing the other night. He's not a great player and I don't think he'd mind me saying that.'

'Do you have any idea where organized leagues started?'

'I think it started with Leisure Leagues in the Midlands in mid-1970s with indoor sports hall leagues. I think they organized the first commercial five-a-side.'

The 'History' page of the Leisure Leagues' website has a brilliant description of how they started. It's not poetic or anything, just brutally simple and familiar. Reading it, I was reminded of those documentaries on the first men to build and ride surfboards. Here's the way Leisure

Leagues tell the story of how it began back in 1986/7 in Coventry and Bedworth, Warwickshire:

> Many years ago, a group of sports centre managers began running a 5 aside league at their facilities. These managers all knew each other and quickly realized that there appeared to be nobody else doing a similar sort of thing. It also became apparent that the 5 aside leagues were very popular and lots of groups who normally hired sports halls on a casual basis much preferred to play in a competitive league format, particularly football clubs in the off-season.
>
> In those days, there were few if any Astroturf facilities in the UK! So the leagues which first started were all in sports halls, usually with wooden floors and occasionally with paint markings for goals on the brick back walls! The first balls that we used were like big balls of sponge and bounced about in an irregular fashion. If you could dribble one of those balls then you really were skillful [sic]!
>
> The first fixture lists for small-sided leagues was implemented by us and were hand-written on sheets of white card. If a fixture list needed to be changed, it was all done manually and changing fixtures was an extremely time-consuming process. To run more than a few leagues would simply have been impractical. We still have the very first fixtures codes for different leagues, although the paper has gone a bit yellow and the staples holding them together have gone a bit rusty. [. . .]
>
> In the mid to late 80s computers came on the scene and this revolutionized the way league tables and fixture lists could be updated, speeding the process up vastly. The initial group of sports centre managers now began seriously thinking about expanding their operation from just a few leagues to many leagues across the country.

Five-a-side is a such a big deal now it's strange to think its commercial roots were laid just four decades ago. And yet the men who invented commercial five-a-side, which is now a worldwide sport, with a European six-a-side tournament, were a group of unnamed sports centre managers from the Midlands. From little leagues, mighty businesses grow – Leisure Leagues alone now has franchises across Europe and the States and has just done a deal for leagues in Asia and Africa. They have thirty staff at their head office and hundreds more across the UK.

Their site goes on to say that one of the founders emigrated to South America and the others have gradually stepped away, remaining as occasional consultants. When I contacted Leisure Leagues to put names to these mysterious founding fathers, Andy Thorley, their PR guy, kindly replied, 'One of them was honestly called John Smith, another was David O'Connor, and I had to do some digging for this, but the other guy was Matthew Reynolds.' By rights they should have developed mythical status in the five-a-side world. There must be people out here who played with them or certainly competed in their early leagues and yet, like so many founders, they've been forgotten. They should build a statue of the three of them with their hands over their face as a ball flies high above head height.

Goals, one of the big guns in the commercial five-a-side world, started pretty much the same time in Scotland. They too can make a case for being the first to see the commercial potential in small-sided football, Keith Rogers tells me down the line from Los Angeles, where he is now Head of International Development for the company. 'You could almost say this massive game started in the west of Scotland.' Almost. Keith may or may not have been the first to get people to pay to play on fixed, dedicated pitches, but there's no doubting he's been extremely influential in the expansion of the commercial side of the game.

First with Powerleagues and then Goals, his is an interesting story because from the off he understood the tremendous commercial potential and scope for growth, first through hedge fund investment and then a public offering on AIM. Keith went straight to the financial funds that allow you to expand fast if you have the right idea.

Keith Rogers was born in Grangemouth, Scotland, fifty-five years ago, started his professional life driving ice-cream vans and now lives in Pasadena, Los Angeles, where he is building a thoroughly modern football business. Who says 99s are bad for you?

The first five-a-side business he was involved in was called Pitz, which started in 1987, after a health centre in Paisley turned four tennis courts into five-a-side pitches: 'Back then you really struggled to get time on an indoor wooden-floored sports hall covered in dozens of different floor markings, as it was usually taken up for badminton or table tennis. At Pitz, we had tennis courts that were unused for most of the year and saw the opportunity to meet the demand for five-a-side.'

He sold Pitz to investors 3i, who had helped him develop it, and walked away in search of another opportunity. Meanwhile 3i took the business forward, renaming it Powerleague. Six months later he acquired Goals, which was an existing small family business with three centres, operating out of Glasgow, and reached out to the City to help expand it: 'We had built the business up to around eleven centres but needed more capital to take it to the next level. So we decided the next stage was to float on the stock market. We invited a load of fund managers, mainly young guys, down to Goals Wimbledon for a presentation on a weeknight at about 5 p.m. It's an amazing-looking facility, but at that time of day the teams hadn't arrived. I deliberately positioned the room so that as I was talking to them they could see the pitches filling up quickly as people finished work and hundreds of players arrived to kick off their games. The penny dropped and we were five and a half times oversubscribed when we floated.

'We've now grown to forty-six centres in the UK and one in California. It's important that the centres look great so that when you walk onto the pitch all you want to do is kick a ball and have a game. We introduced the 3G turf long-pile artificial grass with rubber crop infill – which looked and played just like real soft grass. This was a big change for five-a-side, as we were the first ones to use it in the UK, so no more carpet burns and scrapes from the old-style artificial grass. We were the first up with a website, the first to be able to book online, we've developed an App now so people can book direct from their phones, organize their players and even match up players with teams and vice versa.'

Rogers prides himself on Goals being a next-generation business and is busy expanding it in California. He's now President of Goals America in addition to his role as Head of International Development across the whole company.

'We launched our US pilot centre in South Gate, Los Angeles, in 2010, right in the middle of the economic downturn. Lots of Hispanics immediately took to it and we started running regular tournaments which drew people in from further afield across LA. We cut our teeth here and it's now our most successful centre. We're building our second centre in Pomona and that's the start of our rollout in the US.

'When we opened in LA we originally got a bit of stick because LA was not a place many associated with soccer. However, the US offers a huge market and soccer has actually been the most popular high school sport in California for over a decade. Soccer in the US has now reached a tipping point, with some MLS attendances not far behind those in the Premiership, and beating some of the European leagues. A decade ago there was very little soccer coverage here, but now there's over a dozen TV stations telling you everything about soccer from around the world, including the MLS.

'I'd been coming to America for twenty years, so I could see these changes taking place. I recognized the opportunity before America went crazy for soccer after the 1994 World Cup and before Beckham came here. There are 18 million people in LA and a huge Latino community that loves soccer. In the seventeen-year-old demographic soccer is their first choice of viewing sport, so it has an incredible future here.

'You've only got to look at the numbers of children registered as soccer players in California to chart that growth. In 1974 there were 100,000 kids registered. By 1990 that had grown to 1.6 million and a few years ago that had become 3 million. These are just the kids who are registered. Most people aren't registered, they just play recreationally.'

Keith is very keen to build a business for the future and he's definitely flying a green AstroTurf flag: 'Business is all about making a profit and the only way you can do that is if you deliver what your customers, in our case our players, want. That's what makes it work: delivering the best experience the people who walk through our doors and onto our pitches want.

'Right now we're developing something called Goals Fit, which is the use of biometric wristbands and GPS so the players can have their fitness tracked when they're on the pitch. We're installing cameras so you can download your personal highlights from a button on your wristband. We're installing that technology now in both the UK and the US.

'There are three main reasons why people play five-a-side: they love the game, there's the fitness aspect and then the social side. You've got guys who are between eighteen and twenty-one years old for whom the fitness is all about looking good, then there are the forty-five-year-olds keeping their cholesterol down.

'With Goals Fit you can get that sense of self-gratification, you can track yourself game on game and you can compare with each other, which is a source of banter as much as anything else, especially if you've run a mile and your mate has only run ten yards.

'We're trying to make the pitches as realistic as possible, so right now we're making synthetic grass look like striped turf as part of a huge returfing operation in the UK, so it actually looks like stadium turf.

'We name the different pitches out here after famous stadiums. You can play at Hampden Park, San Siro, Wembley, Camp Nou. We provide the historical stats, the look of the stadiums. We theme our sports bars with soccer memorabilia. We've even found that players in the US love the British accents, which adds to the authenticity of our centre, because England is viewed here as the home of the game. The players love the heritage here.'

A Horse

Thousands of miles away from the Californian technology of Goals, our late organizer James Kyllo would track our weekly performance in his own computerized league system. It fitted his mental outlook to do this, James being an unlikely footballer. In fact, he was quite an unlikely person. I first met him in the mid- to late 1980s in Parfett Street, Whitechapel, on the doorstep of an East End terraced house huddled between, on one side, the neighbouring mosque and Rowton House on Fieldgate Street and, on the other, the Commercial Road.

For many years that street was a London home to me. Parfett Street was full of Bangladeshi toddlers, and all sorts of people came and went from the houses where John, Bernie, Martin, Alison and Terry lived. When I first stayed there these run-down houses were squats; then they evolved into housing trusts. The older buildings still had tarpaulin flapping off their roofs. I can remember sitting there on a tiny back ledge that came out of the top-floor window – it was just big enough for a deckchair. I was typing up my singles reviews for *Sounds* from my handwritten notes there (Janet Jackson was single of the week, in case you're wondering). Looking down the row of Victorian backyards, little had changed since they were built.

Rowton House on Fieldgate Street had featured in George Orwell's *Down and Out in Paris and London*, and in 1986 was still a huge red-brick shelter for the homeless, the transient and the dispossessed.

Kyllo arrived on the doorstep of 43 Parfett Street one day looking for Terry. He was a huge bloke with a large head and glasses whose dress sense owed more to the library than the catwalk. His faint Canadian accent rustled around in his dialogue. He had arrived in the UK with his parents as a child and gone to school in Surrey, where he played rugby in PE and developed a big interest in playing and listening to music.

At the University of East Anglia he met my friend Terry, and Charlie, Simon and Colin, who were collectively known as The Higsons, a John Peel punky funk band who needed a manager. James's organizational skills and interest in music made him the perfect candidate. He combined a notable intellect with an obsessive attention to detail, he liked stats, he liked logging things, he liked finding obscure aspects of life that interested him.

When he died some of his friends from university put the words 'A Horse' in Facebook comments under the news. James had once represented UEA on *University Challenge* and the only time he spoke during the whole half-hour quiz was to answer one question with 'a horse'. I don't know if the answer was correct or not, but it was a unique enough offering to become associated with him for the rest of his life and beyond.

Over the years I would see James regularly at gigs and birthday parties. As the 1990s turned into something resembling Keith Moon's never-ending birthday party, one of the strangest things to happen was this bookish, immensely intelligent and interesting figure with a tremendous amount of knowledge about literature and obscure music was working at the heart of the wildest, most drugged-up, happening record company of the day – Creation. I could never get my head round that at all; he was so unlike the rest of the maniacs dangling from the windows of Valhalla.

While Alan McGee, Oasis and Primal Scream were brilliantly reintroducing excessive behaviour and ambitious arrogant music to the mainstream, James was quietly working away behind the scenes with McGee's main sideman, Dick Green, making sure everything that needed to be done with contracts and distribution and so on got done.

I could never really marry these two personalities, the excessive success that McGee and the Gallaghers had delivered and this really calm, quiet, bookish bloke I played football with.

When word sadly rolled round our group of football-playing friends that James had died, three of them subsequently informed me, 'I thought they meant you.' I had been a more likely candidate for death than James. He was just there, always had been, and we assumed always would be. Quietly getting on with organizing two football games every week and continuing to work in the music biz.

When I rang McGee to tell him James had died he was as surprised that he had played five-a-side football as I had been twenty years before that they were working together.

Andrew Innes, the musical heartbeat of Primal Scream since its inception and a smart observer of football himself, told me, 'We'd be out the front taking drugs and having a big party and doing the gigs and he'd be one of the guys just quietly pottering away upstairs, making sure all the things you had to do to actually get the music out had been done. In this way he was key to the success of the label, but I always felt he would have preferred it if it hadn't been quite so big. If it had been a bit more obscure.'

Certainly that element of finding the little known and cherishing it would see Kyllo regularly taking budget flights on short-break holidays to obscure European towns, where he would take in a home game and buy their suitably strange football shirts. If conversation ever stumbled across a team from the German fourth division, James would undoubtedly have visited there, could tell you which famous player's dad had played for them and show you their shirt from his collection which would look like a cross between jockey's silks and the flag of a Central African dictatorship. He could probably also make an interesting music connection too. 'Oh, that's where Lou Reed's mum was from.'

This wasn't some sort of noisy hipster affectation, though. He would simply present his knowledge and interest like a minor footnote. He just seemed to enjoy the discipline of exploring unknown destinations based on them having a modest football team, a local brewery and some second-hand book and record shops. He was a very keen Brentford fan. The season before he passed away I went with him to watch Leeds at Brentford. We sat on the front row, where the grotesquely large and terrifying Brentford bee mascot looked down on us from pitch side. Brentford filleted us 2–0.

Whether or not the appeal of a lurid kit informed his choice of European destination I don't know, but he rarely came back from his travels with something as simple as a solid coloured shirt and matching shorts. If it didn't have the sharp colours of a punk single sleeve it didn't make the cut.

James would appear on a Sunday with a shirt as pink as a 1970s ladies' hairdressing salon paired with Amazon green shorts and scarlet socks. He wore it well, because no one blinked an eyelid at a six-foot-plus obelisk masquerading as Willy Wonka. This was just James and His Amazing Technicolor Away Kit. When James died his family sold the shirts to members of our playing group. It seemed a pity to split them up as they would have made a peculiar addition to the National Football Museum in Manchester. 'In this cabinet twenty-nine shirts from across the lower levels of European football. Sunglasses are provided.' But people wanted a memento of his love of football and I'm sure they did something good with the money.

Now on Sundays and Wednesdays regulars show up in Hoxton and Kentish Town in the shirts James sported for so long. The most surprising thing is they all fit, because he was so much larger than most of us. It's a nice tribute to see them on display.

As bright as his football shirts were, his own clothing would be as simple as an off-white fleece, large khaki shorts and sandals.

The summer before he died I'd gone to the Indian restaurant that sat midway between both our houses with my dad, Marlais and my former flatmate Matt, only to find Kyllo sitting there quietly on his own with a book. There were only three tables in use in a large dining room and he was on the next one, but he was so still and focused on his book that it took until the poppadoms arrived for me to realize it was him and to invite him to join us.

James never wanted to impose himself on anyone, on or off the pitch, but he joined us, and listening to him talking with my dad about the topic of his book was interesting because although I'd seen him almost every week over the previous seventeen years, we'd been playing football rather than chatting.

It was another reminder of how five-a-side players meet to get what we need from playing small-sided football together and then go our separate ways. Our game undoubtedly lasted so long because of him. It was as simple as that. There are capable deputies but the organizer sets the tone for the game.

Guys like James Kyllo, and Charlie Dawson and Will Rayner, who run my other regular fixtures, are the lifeblood of the game. You all have your own. Their houses are full of stinking bibs spewing in or out of the washing machine, they make up the financial shortfall when people don't pay their subs, they bring needles, pumps and half-inflated footballs, and they do it for the love of the game.

In James's case, he took the time and interest to create our individual player league table, which actually gave us some sense of achievement or improvement. Charlie, who organizes our Tuesday night game, also did this for a while: 'I tried adding a bit of left-field interest by keeping track of who played for which side each week, and running a fantasy football league table of our individual results. Fascinating. Like *Lord of the Flies*. After a few weeks the character of the game had changed, people were getting competitive, grumpy and a bit obsessed, so I stopped again.'

Those traits were for many years prevalent in Kyllo's Wednesday and Sunday games, when the league standings were closely followed.

Our organizers get nothing from it but personal satisfaction, so make sure you take the right change for your subs this week and buy them a drink in the pub afterwards. If nothing else, they might be predisposed to put you in a good team next time they select the sides in advance, and they won't allocate you the bib that fits like Jessica Ennis's running top. And make sure you thank them for organizing the match. If it's anything like when I was coaching kids, they'll appreciate it.

Recreativo Juniors. Ekow, Marlais, Stan, Felipe, Cal, Jem, Freddie, Ritchie. A great team.

If the Kids are United

In the eighteen years since I stopped drinking I've only seriously wanted to drink four times, as in if there'd been a pub in sight I'd have gone straight in and ordered many. Two of those times came straight after watching the kids' team I coached play competitive matches, and neither of them was even a defeat. I found the games so intense I needed something to knock the edge off the adrenalin coursing round my body, or perhaps to propel it faster. Old habits don't die, they're just lying in wait ready to pounce.

Coaching the Recreativo Juniors Under-10s for three years was like nothing else I've ever done. It was fantastic, all-consuming and super-intense.

A few weeks after I'd started coaching the kids, Peter Hooton from The Farm came to stay with us while we were working together on *The End* fanzine reissue. I invited him to come along and watch a match and as I did so my girlfriend, Lisa, looked up and said, 'You might as well, because you'll hear all about it in great detail for hours afterwards anyway.'

'I know it well,' said Peter. 'I used to do it myself. Does he sit up in bed late at night writing formations down and ask you whether you think he should play one, two or three at the back?'

Lisa looked at Peter in amazement. 'YESSSS! EXACTLY THAT. Only it's not only at night, it's when we wake up, when we're in the car going somewhere, when people come round. Is it just because it's the beginning? Does it calm down?'

He looked at her, laughed and shook his head. 'It gets worse. At some point he'll be up all night wondering where he's going to get a new goalkeeper from. I had to stop doing it in the end, it was getting too much.'

This is what I had let myself in for. The old coach, Michael Jackson, left to live in France with his family and Jimmie Gregory, who ran the club, was happy for me to take over. James Brown followed Michael Jackson, Recreativo's very own Soul Train.

To me Jimmie is a true local hero. His dad and his elder brother had both played professionally, his elder brother Johnny had even played for England, but Jimmie never banged on about any of that. He'd rather discuss a demo he once went on that turned into a riot. He's got some great stories from his 'political days'.

Every Sunday he was getting out there in our local park with his bag of balls, bibs, cones and snap-together nets, doing the training, having a big match mixing the age groups at the end, and then the finale would be a penalty competition against his youngest son, Storm, in the nets. They were great mornings, the kids were really funny and keen players, and in many ways it was like being back at school.

One morning so many kids showed up in my age group that I sent a handful of our better footballers over to train with Jimmie's older boys. I had a big group of about eighteen kids gathered round in front of me and I explained what we'd be doing and how important it was they kept drinking their water and responding quickly to directions. They all nodded their heads and then scrambled off to get bibs, balls and bottles. All except one kid called Noah. He was standing dead still, looking at me quizzically. Then he averted his eyes downwards and his friend James was lying on the floor holding Noah's ankles like he was rugby tackling him. He'd been like that all the time I'd been talking. That he resembled Harpo Marx made it all the more comical.

Two of the next three years were so brilliant I gave up my own Sunday eight-a-side morning game for it. By the time I came back to play again I could read a game much better than before.

If you think you know what's going right and wrong in your five-a-side game, then you'd probably enjoy coaching the kids – well, the tactical side during games anyway. Unlike your mates, kids might actually listen to you. And if you do know what you're doing tactically, they'll respond and make the game better in whatever way you'd asked them.

The boys I inherited were great. I'd been watching them for the year as Marlais was in the team so I already had a good idea what each was good at. They had survived in the top division by a point after the last game of their first season together, sixth out of eight, but that wasn't bad, as the top three were set in stone and the boys had no fixed keeper to speak of, they just took it in turns like you do with mates in the park.

Given that I had no experience of teaching or coaching kids and hadn't done any badges or anything, all I could do was try and get some sense of order into what they were doing, try them out in positions they seemed to do well in and find a fixed keeper. I managed to do all that, a couple of really talented new kids arrived and we were away. What I hadn't expected was the intensity of the games and how much the boys would give their all for each other and the team. They were brilliant. A kid called Cal went in goal; he'd never played there before, but he was a very brave tackler so I figured he'd have the guts for it. He turned out to be a very good shot-stopper.

We had three clear defenders, a very strong centre back called Sal, who could weave his way out of an attack with the ball and charge back down the field, turning defence into attack. There was the little right back, Stanley, who would ping about like a SuperBall, popping up everywhere, a really excellent tackler and reader of the ball, which I assumed he'd developed by being a keen tennis player. Then there was a tall centre back called Freddie, who on his day could defend like Tony Adams.

We had loads of good midfielders, really good players. Felipe was an extremely skilful boy from South America who could jink his way around the opposition, lay off a pass and finish brilliantly. We had

Arron, who went down the wing like he'd been shot from a catapult. My own son Marlais could tackle, pass, shoot and would run every minute from start to end. Ritchie was a tall, angular boy who could play anywhere and had the sort of skills that come from studying Ronaldo for weeks on end, which is, I'm guessing, what he would do. Ritchie had a such a lethal shot that his free kicks looked like fighter jets leaving an aircraft carrier before frequently ending up in the roof of the net. In his first ever competitive game he executed a perfect 360 on the wing.

Up front we had a couple of goal machines called Echo and Jackson who would bag almost forty a season between them. Jackson looked just like Tony Currie. Echo was a law unto himself, scoring goal after goal after goal but often losing possession rather than playing his teammates in. One game Jimmie and I offered him a quid for every assist and he promptly changed position from striker to right wing and cracked in three excellent crosses that resulted in goals.

Then there were Jem and Rory, who took three years to become two of the best players in the team. By the end of it Rory would show up with mud on his knees from a school rugby match on the far side of London and then score four in one match. Jem was such a quiet kid but he had something and after three years he could take the ball from the keeper and do the whole length of the pitch on the wing before crossing it. Then there were Matteo and Harry, were great kids who, in retrospect, I wish I'd given more game time to.

Marlais once went round to Matteo's for tea and he had built a free-kick set-up in his back garden with chairs as defenders and goalposts and everything. Harry was a blinder in training, diving headers with his eyes open, volleyed finishes, the lot. But in the league games the standard was so high and so physical that it was difficult for them to get stuck in and get a touch. It's my main regret that I didn't stop worrying about the results and just include them more.

We finished third in our first year, then second the next, two wins off the top. When we started, those top-three positions had seemed totally unassailable but the players were so good and they worked so well together as a team we just got better and better. Too good. Like Bayern Munich poaching from Dortmund, the team who finished above us nicked our centre forward. Half of the boys were selected for the Hackney District Schools team and never came back, joining an eleven-a-side set up by a District Schools coach. Better coaching for them but difficult for us to replace four of our best kids at that age.

The next season we often didn't even have a full side to kick off with. We crashed and burned, but there were some upsides. I learned a few things from it. It makes your own professional football team's results seem secondary, which can be a relief. You can read and set up for a seven-a-side game of your own better for having managed a team playing in one. And that thing that managers say when you've been hammered 4–0, 'We can take one or two positives away from that,' is true. The result might be terrible, but that quiet kid who had lost a bit of form might have done everything you'd asked him to do to get his game going again. Or maybe someone had scored their first ever goal.

My greatest moment as a dad while spending time as the coach was seeing my son Marlais score his first goals. He'd played two years for Michael and then half a season for me in midfield until he decided to unleash a belter from so far out I saw him squinting to see if it had gone in or not. The celebrations on the touchline overshadowed those on the pitch as Jimmie and I leapt up and down, and he said, 'It's great when you see your kid's first goal.' Ten minutes later in the second half he got another in a goalmouth scramble. Fantastic moments. And more were to follow throughout the next two seasons. Seeing your own child running away jumping in the air with happiness is one of the best things going. Much better than scoring yourself and you know how good that feels.

*　　*　　*

Do you remember what I said about being deluded regarding your five-a-side abilities? A few years later I was out with Peter Hooton and we mentioned coaching kids and someone said, 'Was James any good?' Perhaps the fact that I'd helped The Farm onto the *NME* cover way back helped, but without embarrassment he said, 'Yes, I had my doubts, but the two games I watched up close he was like the Jose Mourinho of Camden Town and his kids were brilliant. He had them running for each other, improvising, scoring great goals and his half-time team talk was excellent. The whole game was fantastic.'

Sure enough for about thirty games those Recreativo boys had it. One of the best things I've ever done. With a baby on the way, Lisa asked me if I'd pack it in. It wasn't the six hours a week I was out with the team that worried her, she just couldn't handle discussing team selection every waking hour.

So I was back to playing Sundays. And I have to say they were relaxing by comparison. Jimmie's restarted the Sunday morning kickabout and when my leg gets better I'm going to go and join him again.

Have You Been in Yet?

They say you have to be mad to be a good goalkeeper but that's not true. You have to be adept at stopping goals. Charles Manson is considered mad but he is shit in goal. No, you just have to be able to stop a ball from going into the net. It's that simple. Making sure it doesn't rebound towards the striker so they can have another shot is also important, but first and foremost you have to protect the line. Do that and your team mates will love you.

And yet strangely most rotated five-a-side keepers – i.e. you and me during our five-minute turn – protect the wrong line, the goal line, when we should be standing just inside the D line. Close the attacker down, fuck up his angles and you're more likely to stop a goal.

Staying on the goal line is a weird thing. It instinctively feels like you should stand right against the crossbar, but it's the least effective place to defend the goal from. The good keepers know that, it's you and me that let the side down, leaning with our backs against the post, ball watching, having a drink like a spectator at a cricket match.

It's a solitary position and one that endures the most intense encounters during a game. Sabotage Times contributor and author Rob Kemp has been a goalkeeper for decades. He told me, 'At five-a-side this week, I kept a mental tally of how many shots came at the goal I was protecting. In an hour it was over forty – most of which from a distance you could shake hands in. I lost count of the actual number after my knuckle dislocated for the umpteenth time and I had to resort to the tried and tested formula for treating this particular injury. Two parts Lucozade Sport poured over the affected swollen finger, one part "give it a shake" to get the blood flowing again.'

You can handle the gloves with grace, confidence, cockiness or out and out arrogance, five-a-side player Clive Leighton told me: 'When I was about eighteen, nineteen, my mates and I used to play with some really old guys of thirty-five to forty who used to piss us off with lots of condescending shite. One time the biggest mouthy middle-aged arsehole was in goal for a penalty against my mate. He's giving my mate big noises of how wealthy and successful he is, about his cool girlfriend and how we're all losers. My mate cracks the ball. Hits the bar. There's a split second of dejection as the arsehole's face lit up. The ball hits the arsehole on back of the head and bounces back into the net. Goal. Yahoo. The force of impact pushed the arsehole's previously unrevealed wig into his "about to clap" sweaty hands. Game over. Night over. We crawled, crying, to the pub without getting changed.'

You see, there's always someone watching and remembering when you're in goal.

The best eight-a-side keeper I played with regularly was Dave 'The Cat' from the North-East – Hartlepool, I think. He played for about five years in our Sunday game before someone with a decent team spotted him and actually said, 'Hey, come and join a proper quality eleven-a-side Sunday league team, we need you.'

His ink-covered arms were as muscle-bound as other people's legs, his own legs were permanently hidden by trackie bottoms, but despite this they could propel him around the goal area like he was made of rubber.

These were the years when I was at my best and I looked forward to playing against Dave more than anyone. I'd spend the whole game watching and waiting for an opportunity to score past him. If you got two or three in a ninety-minute eight-a-side game you'd done very well. It wasn't just that he was the best of our bunch, he was at a different level to us. And he stayed in goal for the whole game, which was another bonus for whoever's team he was on. No constant outfield personnel changes.

They didn't name him for his goalmouth ability, but for the speed with which he scaled the side of the sports centre when the ball went onto the roof. No one knew much about Dave's past, but he once told me that he'd punched out a famous zero-tolerance police inspector.

It was hard to catch Dave unawares. If you were coming at him straight you had no chance of scoring: his arms, legs or body would shoot out and deflect the ball wide. The way to beat him was to move the ball down the wing really quickly and put in a devastating cut-back so the advancing teammate could finish it as Dave was spinning round to follow the ball in from the wing. You needed to be fast and accurate.

It was because Dave was such a good keeper that I know the best goal I ever scored in that game. Chelsea Michael with the massive grin and the multiple knee bandages had banged the ball out to me on the left wing from centre back, a bit harder than was needed, so when I took it on my chest off a bounce it sat up nicely and I thought, 'Ah, fuck it, I'm going to just hit this now with the outside of my right foot.' I was miles away from the opposition's goal in the midfield/wing area, but I leathered it and as it flew away I could almost see the comic strip-style speed lines follow it in. It shot straight past Dave's astonished face and nestled devilishly inside the far side netting. I won the battle that day, but there were plenty of Sundays when he came out on top. I imagine he remembers the ones he saved, but I can remember the ones that beat him. Every regular five-a-side player has the right to remember and cherish those favourite goals. Anyway, I miss playing with Dave. He was a good bloke and a brilliant, proud goalkeeper.

It's unusual how the importance of the goalkeeper changes between childhood and adulthood. As a kid it was the last-on-the-shelf position, but in five-a-side a decent keeper is vital. And they either come along ready-packaged like Dave 'The Cat' with a good reputation or appear as a complete surprise. Fans of the TV show *QI* might be surprised to know that the curly-haired slouch in the floral shirts who captains one of the teams is a surprisingly agile and frustrating goalkeeper. You think you've whipped one round him and his fingers just stretch that bit further and lift the ball away from danger. It surprised me, because I'd played with him on and off for well over a decade before I ever saw him go in goal and do this.

You can elevate yourself from being just a bloke stood in the D getting the ball out of the net to a half-decent keeper by doing a few simple things. Narrowing the angle is obvious. Not passing the ball to their centre forward is another simple tip. Actually, trying to stick your hands between the on-rushing ball and the net is another, and it doesn't really hurt. You didn't need to spend a minute struggling into those big padded professional keeper's gloves someone always brings along.

And then you do your shift without the gloves and occasionally it does sting. One Thursday a few months back Wiel struck a fierce volley to my right from about four feet away just as I was moving to my left. I managed to get my right arm out and strong enough for the ball to slap my hand furiously and bounce wide for a corner. It probably looked better than it felt – he's a great striker of the ball and my hand was lined with ball-stitching marks for some time to come. But you know what? I'm not sure gloves would have made any difference. The save felt better for the sting. Proof of purchase.

One week I accidentally fractured a regular player's wrist with a really long shot. I'm not sure gloves would have helped John, I think it was just the angle of ball and bone that caused the problem. I was way out, but the ball must have gathered momentum and caught him at a bad angle. No one even realized he'd fractured the wrist until he showed up the following week with a light cast on.

The other simple move anyone can do that genuinely makes you a better keeper is to lie down as the opposition striker is approaching the

D and readying to shoot. Lie down, bring one arm up high and make the other one long, raise your free leg into a massive K shape on its side and suddenly it's a lot harder for them to score. You look stupid, obviously, and they just might find a way to dink it beyond you, but believe me they're not expecting it most of the time and the fall will put them off as much as the outstretched limbs might actually stop the ball.

I like good goalkeepers, they make a massive difference. Some people love doing it too. I've only ever been of the 'New keeper needed, whites, you haven't been in yet' variety, but others have been through the mill to protect the scoreline. Rob Kemp again: 'From a goalkeeper's perspective five-a-side is on a par with a stint in the medieval village stocks. You're being pelted with shots from such a short range that the term "off target" is irrelevant. All my knuckles have snapped at least once and I now come fully taped-up for a game. The close-up impact has taken its toll on my wrists too – again, they're locked into place with bandages and reinforced with the cuffs of the gloves before I start. The overall effect from years of shot-stopping is that my gnarly, misshapen hands would even elicit a sympathetic "ouch" from Sir Ranulph Fiennes.

'The worst five-a-side pitch I ever played on was surrounded on all four sides by walls constructed of upturned railway sleepers. Along the top of one wall was a bar area and veranda where the teams waiting to play could watch the games or hurl down abuse, bottle tops and lit cigarette butts. The pitch was concrete with an interesting, gravel-like veneer to it, contributed by the nearby cement works. I spent the bulk of the warm-up scraping fragments of bottles and pint pots out of my area using the side of my shoe.'

Those are the thoughts of a proper keeper, someone who endures the hardships and functions at the stress levels created by forty shots an hour. Thank fuck for people like Rob, say I. On a five-a-side hour-long indoor game I'll try and go in about forty minutes in, when there's little chance of having a second go, which is weird really because I quite like going in.

I like the heat of the goalmouth scramble. I like the opportunity to ground the game when you've got the ball in your hands. The opportunity to watch attacks build for or against you, and the direction you can give a defender to close it down without having to do anything yourself. With the pens you've also got roughly a 50:50 chance of saving, so long as you actually make an attempt to save them.

I've played with and against a load of good keepers and I love the lot of them. Even when they unexpectedly stop you with a moment of genius, you find you have to respect them for it. And how many times a game do they actually save you? Every night someone pulls off something miraculous and sometimes they don't even realize it.

Rage Against the Dying of the Light

Sometimes something like this happens. It's the Thursday eight-a-side game and as usual a mixture of not bad middle-aged blokes and super-fast late teens are playing on the large local comprehensive pitch with its old-school artificial surface. I'm right by the centre spot when the ball spins across from right back and bounces in front of me. Knowing their keeper is way off his line in the sweeper position, I keep my eye on the ball and cushion it in the air with my left instep, then clip it with my right and use the spin to send it goalwards. It travels the half of an almost full-sized pitch and passes over the keeper, and as everyone is wondering if it will make it, it bounces up perfectly into the roof of net. Audacious, though I say so myself, and I've a massive grin instantly.

The reaction is rare. The seventeen-year-olds who normally streak past me like I'm a bollard turn and run towards me in delight and amazement. The whole goal took two passes and one clip and I was side-on to the direction of play. It was a rare glimpse of what I believe is in there, what keeps me going.

'I maybe fat,' I say out loud, 'but I can still make it look like I once had it.' Even Marlais, who's at an age when he doesn't want to be seen with his dad in public, says, 'That was a great goal.'

And then seven days later you can come in from the next game and write this:

Some days on a big hard AstroTurf pitch where the ball is too hard and the bounce too high and the teams have too few players, and the combination you do have is wrong and passes are too wayward and the shots high and wide and no one is tracking back or tackling, and you think there's a man on, so you hurriedly hammer the ball into nowhere without any thought, and you're guilty of all of this and more . . . on these days you just have to hold your hands up and admit that sometimes you're shit.

And I have to say that for me, in that game, it's the inconvenient truth. Massive pitch, massive age gap, massive reality check.

Of the four or five regular games I play in this is the one that reminds me most of what life was like as a teenager and what it's like now. For the simple reason it started as dads and lads and now it's a given there'll be anything up to six or seven teenagers and anything up to sixteen adults. And as a chap I was chatting to in the pub this weekend, who has played once or twice, said, 'The thing about that game is the massive age gap.'

It's a good thing, though. The kids get to skin the old men, the old men can match themselves against the young men we once were. And despite the age gap the standard is pretty well balanced.

This game isn't a league or pure five-a-side. It's closest in format to our Sunday game: show up and we'll pick sides. Then, once he's divided the sides up, Will Rayner, who organizes it, hands the bibs out and we kick off. There's only an hour and five minutes have already passed. At the other end of the hour, as the clock hits 9 p.m., we'll be bullied into finishing by darkness or the caretaker. It's a really enjoyable game to play in. When numbers drop off seasonally and it's down to five-a-side we play across the pitch and the standard is good enough for really fast, controlled 'one touch to shoot' games.

Right now, though, the game ended a few hours earlier and it's dark outside. The street's quiet and even the restaurants, takeaways and late-night shops on the main road have shut. It's gone midnight and I'm still awake. This is what happens when you play after 8 p.m. You stay up, adrenalin still ticking over, thinking. It's why the Strollers, after their even later kick-off, go for a curry and a drink to soak up the human fizz whizzing round the body and mind.

Tonight there were six good teenagers playing and ten dads. I scored one goal from distance with the outside of my foot after turning and losing one of their best players. It felt great. It's one moment like that, where something really good comes off, that makes it a successful evening.

But I was almost run down while attempting to get a loose ball from Kobi, a giant seventeen-year-old who used to play in goal for Jimmie's team at Recreativo Juniors. Then I actually was run down by Kobi ten minutes later, competing for another ostensibly easier ball to win. Up, up, way up in the clouds, as I lay on the floor, I could hear him politely and softly say, 'Sorry, James.'

Let me tell you about Kobi, because he's worth a few paragraphs of your time. He's not always so quiet as he was when apologizing. When Jimmie Gregory and I coached the two Recreativo teams Kobi was one of the club's true stars. Not the best player but one of the most influential and certainly the biggest, loudest, funniest, most spirited kid. There'd not be a week of training when he wouldn't crack everyone up with his sense of humour or his mad play, diving around like an acrobat and coming back up from the mud with his mouth still going. He was constantly making all of us laugh.

He was a tall, strong, gangly outfield player who was emergency goalkeeper for the older team when the regular goalkeeper was asked to move on. Then he was spotted by a scout and QPR asked him to come in for a trial. Jimmie and I both really hoped he'd do well and thankfully after the trial game they asked him to come back in for a two-week-long trial. That's quite unusual for a fifteen-year-old, as he was then. The clubs normally have the players they want for that age group by then. So it was testament to his character and potential that they invited him. A few of the boys had been at clubs, so it wasn't unusual, but Jimmie and I were really pleased for Kobi. One of the rules was no lateness, no excuses, they're strict like that, but the training ground was right over the other side of London. Sadly, on the third day the person giving him a lift couldn't get him there on time and that was it. Trial over. Thanks, goodbye. I was gutted for him. I'm still sulking about getting dropped from the cup final by Lawnswood twenty-three years ago, so fuck knows how he felt.

So many of these boys have been in and out of different academies or trial situations and it's great to see them still playing with so much love for the game, despite not being kept in. Kobi's head didn't drop. Back at Market Road, he continued to deliver his constant encouragement to his teammates from his position back in the nets. It was a great thing for him to do, Mr Positive, like having another player in the team. All teams need players like Kobi, all clubs or five-a-side games where you play for the love need a Kobi to keep everyone laughing. Personality is king. If you're not laughing at some point during a game or afterwards there's something wrong.

Isaac is another of the older Recreativo guys who can make you laugh with an unexpected finish, celebration or, as is more likely, some mad piece of bizarre play. It's great getting to spend an hour a week with kids ramped up with expectations of what might happen in life but still infused with the fun schooldays can foster.

We're at a tipping point now, where the older boys we coached at Recreativo are legally men. By the time this book comes out they'll be eighteen. All bigger, all still playing so fast and regularly fantastic to watch, regardless of whose side you're on. Weirdly one of them, Saul, has improved significantly since he went to Camden Girls' School mixed sixth form to do his A-levels. Maybe he's just maturing as a player or maybe there's something in the canteen there that gives him an extra spring in his step. The girls probably. He's one of the best players in our Thursday game, outclassing the adults and haring past them with ease, whereas three years ago he was a sub in Jimmie's Under-15s.

Wiel was captain of the Recreativo older boys, and whether he's got the ball or not he always accelerates into the action like he's been fired from a rubber band. At club tournaments I'd watch this tall, skinny kid drive his team on, pulling goals back on his own when the opposition were obviously stronger across the team. He's possessive with the ball, but is clever with what he does with it; he's inventive and has a great shot.

These are some of the best players I play with every week and they're still in the sixth form. Another boy, Robert's son Louis, loves running rings round the opposition's ageing midfield. He likes to drift in possession across the pitch, so you can force him away from a direct route on goal, but he just keeps going. It's the best you can achieve, because when he runs directly at you at speed it's hard to play him at all. His touch is so precise, you think you're reaching a ball between you and him and then it's just fucking disappeared and he's off like a motorbike on the horizon behind you.

My son Marlais and Josh's son Sal were in the same Recreativo team, and they're the younger fifteen-year-olds who play with us. Both are easily good enough to hold their own against their dads. Sometimes it's fractious playing with your own kids, but it means you can also see them grow and develop. Tonight I was watching Marlais pass to Louis, who is two years older than him. Three-quarters of Marlais's passes reach their destination now, most of them are good passes, some really good. Seriously, it's enough to make you believe in the power of genetic inheritance.

The older boys are involving him in the game, which they wouldn't have done so much three years ago back at the club. The first time I took Marlais to the Recreativo training session, aged about eight, I saw this kid sweeping around at the back, mopping everything up, flipping his way out of defence and through into the midfield, a different class. I told Marlais, 'Just watch that boy when you can. He's a very good player.' At an age when all the really good kids want to show it by scoring goals, he was showing his class in his defending and dribbling.

After that first session I asked Jimmie who he was and he said, 'Oh, that's Robert's son Louis. He's at Spurs.' Two years ago, when we first started playing on the floodlit school Astro pitch on Thursday night, Louis moved the ball past me with his foot in a way I'd never seen before. Just sort of offered it, then swished it away without his foot even touching the ground. It was like a magic trick, but it just felt unfair. Not only do they have youth on their side but they have all the new skills too. And they have less appetite. I probably eat in a day what they eat in a week.

As I watch them flying past old blokes with ease, I realize I did the same thing when I was in my late teens with my neighbour Alan, in Scott Hall Road, Leeds. Back he'd look in disbelief as I jinked in and out and sped past to score. It's life's great trade-off, experience replaces youth, but you only know about it once you've passed from being teenage wunderkind to fifty-year-old.

The great thing is these boys don't know what's to come. None of us did, for the true strength of youth is believing you won't end up like the old blokes. You won't give in. What I didn't realize when I was eighteen, and couldn't conceive of being a father, was that it's creating new life that so radically alters yours. You hand the baton over basic-ally, straight away.

A good deal is when both parties are happy with what they've got. I'm not sure if I've got a good deal right now. These seventeen-year-old boys I play against have their lives ahead of them. There are thirty-three years of football to come before they reach my age. Will they still be playing then? Who knows? One of them, Dannio, a superb player who was on semi-pro forms with a league club when he was still messing around with us, didn't believe I was fifty when I told him; it's too old to comprehend. But let's hope they are still playing when they're fifty – there are examples everywhere in the five- and eight-a-side worlds.

A few years ago I was online looking for Gary Lovelace, an old mate I used to go to gigs with, and I found him at the Old Modernians Football Club in Cookridge, Leeds. Browsing through their website, I was surprised and pleased to see the head coach of the club was a guy called Mick Birch. I looked at team photograph Mick appeared in, but it was too small to identify the largish bloke in the tracksuit dead centre on the front row as my mate from Ash Road forty years before. Back then he never went anywhere without a tartan cap, even when we were playing football. There couldn't be two of them, though.

When we'd played at the bottom of Queenswood Drive as kids, Mick had been the best player who didn't get taken by Leeds. It was inspiring to think of him at a football club, not only still playing but, more importantly, coaching. The deal with the higher power they call nature is if you've got it you need to nurture it and stick with it. If you can keep your body onside you can keep going well past fifty.

My contribution to the Thursday night game is I can thankfully still move the ball accurately to where a player's sprint is taking them. Tonight I sent one long guided cross from the right midfield position in our half directly onto the penalty spot. Wiel had set off down the left wing, calling for it moments before, directing where he wanted it with his head and eyes, and actually seeing him meet this long ball and hit it at an angle was life-affirming. There are simple highlights to this game every week. Tonight seventeen-year-old Wiel performed a really impressive volleyed one-two with Josh and then hammered an amazing left-foot volley off the return pass that dipped and curved away from us and hit the bar. Marlais lobbed a nice finish over our keeper and for me my dummied turn away from Sam meant I actually escaped his close marking and was able to drive on and score. Who doesn't go home and mull over the best bits of their game every week?

But maybe teenagers just take it for granted. They charge around with spring-heeled optimism, capturing balls from bylines others had given up on, racing a real distance to meet a cross that could allow them another goal. If they're generous they'll pretend not to notice you've not much pace or stamina and they'll work to reach your passes. But so often they'll just leg it through and hold on to it for ever. They're teenagers. Thank God they still want to play football and not just go to the pub and start pretending to be older men, like so many of my mates did.

They do have immediate inspiration, though, in one of the guys who plays with us. One minute Sean Clare's having to play with me and the next he's signed for Sheffield Wednesday. Strange but true.

Sean was a little different from the other unstoppable nineteen-year-olds who have since left our game for uni because he had the skills to go past anyone, but he preferred to bring you into the game, using his teammates to orchestrate getting from one end of the pitch to the other rather than just legging it solo.

A few weeks after he'd last played with us an email came round from the park kids' club two of our regular players run, saying Sean had scored at Wembley for the Nike Academy in a victory against Barcelona Under 21s. That was a very exciting thing to see on YouTube.

Within days he'd been snapped up by Sheffield Wednesday and was sent out immediately on loan to Bury, where he made his debut against Bradford City that week. The stuff of dreams. Now he's back with Sheffield Wednesday and in their development squad.

The Thursday game isn't all about fast kids, although if you tracked their movement it would look like someone had scribbled over the pitch. The older players have some proper ability. There's a picture-framer called Sam who could probably hit a two-foot-square watercolour from thirty yards and a film writer called Karl who can shoot and score from the touchline. These are old guys with stamina and ability. One of them, my immediate neighbour Richard, has a handful of kids he brings up on his own. He must have passed forty but he's an absolute class player, probably the best on the park. Despite his age he can keep up for pace and ability with the older teenagers who are already playing semi-pro.

In the other 'dads' you can see runs and passes you'd expect from decent players. There's a lot of footballing intelligence in that game and it makes a difference. It's fun, it's relaxed and it's very energetic rather than competitive, but it's not without the odd physical moment. There are giant twins called Charlie and Chris who will think nothing of teaming up to take you down. Imagine if both Charlton brothers had been like Jack – the only hope you've got when they pincer in on you is to take them down with you. At the other end of the scale, we had a really good but quiet Spanish left back for a while called Adrian. After he left, Will told me, 'He wouldn't talk about it much, but I think he played for Barcelona as a kid.' His ability and modesty suggested this was more than likely to be true.

As far as the bigger outdoor pitches I play on it's the best selection of players. Eight-a-side games regularly finish with five or six goals scored. There's no head-height rule, you get Astro sand in your boots and you regularly have to chuck the discarded school jumpers onto the sidelines from that day's schoolbreak. I think one of the reasons I like it is I don't actually have to spend every day there studying.

The best thing about it, though, is the loop of life we see going on before our very eyes. It's at this game that I now see my son is a more productive, fitter player than I am. He scores great goals, regularly – long shots, lobs, drives from balls spilling out of corners – and he can pass very well. The other adults are surprised when I say he's not in the school team any more, but he insists he's not physically big enough to compete with the lads he played with four years ago.

I grew up playing with older, bigger kids, so I didn't have that size awareness. Everyone had always been way bigger than me and the team I grew up idolizing helped. No one knocked Bremner about and Brian Flynn didn't have any problem dictating a game. But I've seen Marlais's old teammates in the park and they are indeed now giants.

Everything just goes around. You feel better about getting on when you see the kids playing so well. This Sunday I was walking through the park when I saw some of the adults I play with coaching young kids. I went over and asked one if it was OK for Billy to start aged three. He said, 'Not really, it's four. But if you come with him we'll see what we can do. We have good coaches with the little ones.' Who? 'Wiel and Kobi.' And I just turned around laughing. The cycle rolls on.

Picking Sides

You know the scene: you're playing with your mates, not in a competitive league, and need to divide the group into two teams. All over the pitch different clusters of players are chatting and warming up with a curious display of exercises ranging from the useful to the pointless.

Someone is jogging round the pitch then breaking into shuttles. Someone else is holding the goalposts and grabbing a foot up behind him to his arse. For just a few seconds. Triangles of players pass the ball around. A loner dribbles the ball forward then whacks it at the goal but slices it wide, just missing someone else's head as they bend over to put their boots on after packing their normal clothes into an old leather sports holdall.

A headband is being adjusted. Someone is grudgingly stamping their feet into trainers without untying the laces. Pre-match bananas, Dextrose, water and sports drinks are being ostentatiously consumed. You have to be seen to be prepared, even if really you're not.

If you're outdoors someone in the far corner is having a fag. Big Chris is trying to chip the ball in a Soccer AM-style crossbar challenge.

Away from the main group two players stand close together. They mutter conspiratorially for a few seconds and then one crosses his left arm in front of his stomach and supports his right arm, which is folded up to his mouth. The classic thinker's pose. The automatic first few choices of the best players have been made and now the pickers are working out whether they need attackers, defenders, runners or a keeper.

I play a few games where the teams are assembled in advance because the group of players involved has been recruited and confirmed by email, but picking live this way is much more interesting because there's an element of competition and guile in planning on the spot who you need to make up the team.

Get the wrong balance and you're fucked for the next hour. There are always endless numbers of midfielders, people who move the ball from one end of the pitch to the other, chase back, pass, tackle, shout, run in either direction – although forwards is more usual than backwards.

However, after the picking has ended, should you find yourself without a decent centre back or striker, then you are essentially just moving the ball from people who can't defend to people who can't score. If this happens you lose no matter how good the midfield is, for the simple reason that the pitch can be covered from one end to the other with a goal kick.

It's the exact tactic Neil Warnock used at Leeds, despite the fact that he didn't have a very good defence or attack, because he had loads of midfielders. Many of these had to retire early from the game with aching necks brought on by watching balls flying overhead, like soldiers trapped in no-man's-land.

If you've any sense you get the best striker first (no one ever won a game without scoring), then you get the best all-round midfielder or the best centre back – that's if you're playing in our outdoor eight-a-side game. If it's inside on a single basketball-court-sized pitch or on an Astro pitch you need a precise finisher, fit players and very quick clever passers. If they're in short supply just choose whoever you fancy playing with.

The combination of players is vital. As is the choice of picker. You have to have two players selecting the teams who are matched ability-wise. Last Sunday Gary, who likes to pick in our game, was doing it with Glynn, who before he joined us had 'mainly been kicking it around in the garden with the kids' – his words. Glynn wouldn't mind me saying that Gary is a more experienced player than he is, but perhaps more pertinently Gary has been picking teams for years. He knows the balance required and importantly he knows who will work hard for the team.

When I saw them stood together picking I raised my eyebrows and after they'd finished I asked Gary if he thought the teams were fair. 'Yes, I think so, pretty fair.'

I feel that fairness is important, if you're playing with your mates. If you're not, then anything goes. Here's an example. Fellow Leeds fan Mike English told me about a time his team were taking a hammering until their star player, a former Ipswich youth player, turned up late: 'He watched the end of the first half as one of the opposition was torturing us. Then he came on at the beginning of the second half and asked for the ball immediately. He then went to the lad and told him he was going to nutmeg him, which he duly did. He did the same thing a second time, telling the lad, "You know what I'm going to do," but despite the warnings he still managed to 'meg him. After the third time the referee booked him and when we asked why he said it was "for taking the piss".'

So, we lined up. We had the most intense midfielder, the two fastest, youngest and most accurate finishers, the best passer, plus two decent defenders. The opposition weren't bad, but they didn't have a goal-scorer among them. When I asked Gary how that had worked out, he said, 'Well, I gave him first pick and he chose Danny.'

That is understandable. Danny is a mountain of a man, very strong, very fit, a powerful runner with a shot you don't want to have to get in the way of, but the pitch is small for him. He's a must-have in an eleven-a-side. I've played with him on a larger pitch and he looks and plays like a pro. But there are more accurate finishers in our eight-a-side game and Gary chose both of them. Within fifteen minutes we were 5–0 up.

The tone of the game is defined by the picking. For a long time I played with one very competitive bloke who was an excellent player, probably the best all-rounder. He had pace, a low centre of gravity, a strong tackle, a great shot, but for years if his team went behind he'd just shut up shop and start sulking like a kid.

Then he realized he could do something about the teams by picking them himself. Both of them. One time I was picking against him and he started explaining why I should pick certain new players, trying to manipulate who I picked so he could have who he wanted rather than me.

In another game I play two of the organizers create a mutual selection committee and divide the players up between them, largely guided by shirt colour – white or dark.

Picking sides is like playing cards with one suit – both players want the only ace, the king, the queen and so on. Only one man can have them, so if you're taking the second pick you've got to gamble on whether to get the best defender when the first picker has taken the best striker or simply get the second-best striker.

By the very nature of trying to pick from the best players downwards you don't always end up with the best team. So many games are already won at the picking of the sides. Then again, sometimes I look at the teams, make an assessment of who will win and am totally wrong. It often comes down to how the team gel together and work rather than who has better players. And who starts taking their chances first.

So there you are, while everyone is doing the mad warm-ups they've vaguely copied from watching pro teams before kick-off, you are arranging their imminent destiny. If you're lucky you pick the best player first, the one who can dominate the game and score, then you pick the fittest, who can keep the game running, or perhaps the best keeper or defender. If you get to pick second you are invariably just playing catch-up.

With the division of light and dark shirts yet to take place and everyone moving around doing their own thing before kick-off, it's quite easy to miss someone you should logically have picked. Then there are the latecomers. A really good player arrives as the picking ends and either totally unbalances or evens it out depending on who has the final choice.

When you're down to the last three players, you need to know clearly what those players can do to complement the rest of your chosen team. Because they can be the difference, they're as vital as your first picks. I'd say the common denominator for the last players picked is mobility or lack of it.

Two players in our game who probably knew they weren't first to fly off the shelves when the picking started were the late James Kyllo and a lifelong Charlton fan, Geoff Norris. Or, as Gary calls him, Old Geoff, even though (perhaps because) he's only two years older than Gary.

It dawned on me after a few years of playing with these guys that both were pretty useful if you didn't play them at fullback. Fullback is the place captains or managers put someone they're not sure about, which is fucking nuts when you think about it, because it's also the first person who's likely to receive the ball. Put them under pressure and you've a good chance of stealing it.

In the indoor Wednesday game Geoff Norris would move onto the left wing because he has a pretty lethal curving shot from the inside of his right boot. That was his number one strength, he knew he could score from there with a little cut-in first, so whenever I picked him I'd stick him there and know he'd score goals.

It was the same with Kyllo in the outdoor game. Putting him on one of the wings meant we had extra width, a target, someone to hold the ball up, and when the play was over the other side someone who could silently slip in and score at the back post. Both were much more effective in these positions than in the fullback roles they'd often automatically adopt.

Another reason for not getting picked is if you're roughly the same ability as the bloke doing the picking. Or maybe he just never fancies you in his team.

Fullback is one of the most important positions in a small-sided football game when there's an above head-height rule, because the keeper can't just hammer it upfield. Someone skilful has to be able to show for it and take the ball. Your teammate playing right in front of the D invariably has the opposition striker on them, so you need a player who can read the movement of the opposition, create some space to receive the ball and then adapt accordingly to either dribble or make the right pass out, starting your possession or attack.

That's why I don't like putting a weaker player at fullback. I really think a basketball-style feed at fullback on a seven- or eight-a-side outdoor game is vital.

Feed is certainly a very important word in proper five-a-side. No, my fat friends, this isn't about food, it's about basketball, the game that is closest in structure to five-a-side.

At school, when it came to basketball, at first I didn't even think about going to the trials as I just assumed it would be a land of giants – blokes the size of ladders or giraffes throwing the ball to each other, while us smaller guys wondered if there was a lift to take us up into their orbit. But when we rotated to doing basketball in PE I discovered there was this position where you had to be small, fast and good with a ball to move it out from the back and take it up to the attackers, who would score the baskets. This was the feed and without the feed they couldn't get the ball to score. Five-a-side is the same.

So who you pick, where they play and the order you get them are all vital. Unless of course you've had the sense to join a league, in which case you only have to make sure your own players get to the actual game on time. Even then it's not that simple. We all know someone who has arrived late, grabbed at the leftover socks in a pile on the changing-room floor, dragged the last remaining shirt on, still slightly wet from the captain's or organizer's washing machine, and then run out to looks of astonishment from everyone playing and the ref, looked down and said, 'Ah, fuck, shorts.'

Above Head Height: Why Five-a-side Should Waive the Rules

O ne of the biggest points of dispute in five-a-side is, unsurprisingly, the rules. They really get on my tits. In fact, the rules and the ragged side netting that seem to exist in half of all goals must be the reason for 90 per cent of all on-pitch disputes.

The implementation of the specific five-a-side rules concerning playing height, shooting distance and goal-area infringement often make me feel like I'm back in the fifth form at school, the dubious rule callers being tedious law-crazy teachers. The names Simpson and Dunning still spring to mind. 'You seem to be at an age, Brown, when you want to question every rule.' 'You seem to be at an age, sir, when you're too old to realize that half of them are fucking stupid.'

Even the influence the five-a-side rules had over the naming of this book has prompted a fairly heated row with myself. I didn't know whether to call it *Above Head Height*, as I'd originally intended, or *Below Head Height*, as technically it should be.

Above Head Height sounds better, it starts with 'Ab', which will place it at the beginning of any alphabetical listing, and the name suggests an aspirational quality, along the lines of 'Reach for the Skies'. On the other hand, it doesn't actually make sense. It's a bit like calling a snooker memoir *Under the Table* – which, come to think of it, is a really good title for a collection of scurrilous tales from the green baize. So maybe *Above Head Height* works.

I hate the playing-height rule in my Wednesday game because, along with its brother the in-the-area rule (which we'll come on to later), it robs us of several minutes each game, which add up to hours a season and days per year. If you accumulated all the time spent over the last seventeen years or so arguing the toss about whether a ball was above or below head height you'd have enough to go on a decent summer family holiday or get a search party out for some value in Coldplay.

One of the reasons I enjoyed switching to Charlie's Tuesday night game in Somers Town was the absence of the head-height rule. Also, with no goalmouth D at either end and no shooting line, it felt like total football freedom. No arguments at all. Really.

For many years, suffering the weekly rows in the Wednesday night game about the head-height rule felt like being the child of arguing parents. There was no way to penetrate the repeated cyclical madness of the conflict. In borderline cases, above head height is as difficult to prove as the offside rule in professional football, which involves a long ball from deep inside the attacker's half. The linesman cannot possibly look in two directions at once, he physically can't see where the offside player is at the same time as he sees the ball being released, unless he has eyes that sit at forty-five-degree angles to each other. Everyone sees the ball from a different angle and personal height, so if the 'Above head height' shout is questionable, as it often is, especially to interrupt an attack or rule out a goal, then no one can call it accurately. If it's really high, fair enough, but . . .

Here lies the root of my frustrations, like those of fans troubled by referees in the pro game: it's the total lack of logic or consistency in applying the above-head-height rule. As I see it, I come to play football, so the fewer stoppages the better. In the Wednesday game, during approximately fifty-five minutes of play, the ball probably goes above head height about twelve times. This means we stop once every four or five minutes. Each call takes approximately thirty seconds from the shout to starting to play again, once we've got the ball back to where it was when it went above head height. We've had the row about whether it was or wasn't above head height and, in the case of tackles and blocks, about who touched it last before it went above head height. And then a subsequent ten seconds or so is wasted when the opposition, who caused the offence but lost the appeal, stand too close to the ball to allow the free kick to be taken. Times that by twelve and it's seven minutes or almost 15 per cent of the actual playing time being taken up just arguing the toss.

Because of Kyllo's performance league, whereby each player would receive three points for a win, one for a draw and none for a loss, throughout the years the Wednesday night players in particular have become over-competitive, worrying about not slipping down that season's rankings, or even the all-time rankings.

James's 6aside.net league generated such an intense level of competition that every rule infringement was challenged with the sort of mad fury that people reserve for demonstrations against fracking. It surprises me that this never escalated to a sit-in, a boycott or a demo. Six fairly rotund middle-aged men in a hotchpotch of kits sitting down with placards in the middle of the gym, chanting, 'Above head height!'

Had we just dispensed with the rule, none of this would have happened and we'd have had somewhere in the region of fifty times nine minutes extra to play a year: i.e. 450 minutes! That would have been seven and a half more games a year. If there's an average of twenty-two goals a week that would have been over 150 more goals scored a year. Imagine how much happier everyone would have been. Apart from the keepers.

As far as I can tell, the rule is there to preserve the quality of the game and keep it fast and low and on the move. This is great if you have the skill to do that, as I'm sure many of you who play have. Watching a YouTube clip of the Thames Valley Indoor 5-a-Side League from the 1980s, the ball just sticks to the ground like it's been heavily weighted, while the pros move it around.

But in our game we usually have too many people on too small a pitch with too broad an array of abilities to maintain this level of play. So much so that the ball spends more time in the air than below the knee. If it's purely for skill management why not keep it at below the height of the five-a-side goal's crossbar – for me, that's rib height. Above crossbar height could actually be universal. Importantly, the crossbar is the same height for everyone playing. It's consistent and so would allow for no arguments about whether the ball was above or below head height.

In the Wednesday game we have Dan and had James Kyllo, both about six foot four. Then, at the other end of the scale, we have Pete, who is about a whole foot shorter. A foot is neither here nor there in a golf drive, but at the edge of a cliff or on a railway line it's the difference between life and death. And it is over this level of apparent importance the toss is argued.

To bring some uniformity to the Wednesday game it was decided that the marker would be the top of the heavy plastic wrapping holding the cricket nets that hang from the roof and are bunched up against the wall. But there are just two of these, they're only on one side of the pitch and if you're all looking away from them it's even harder to claim the ball is high. The whole set-up provides the perfect ingredients for an exasperation festival. To make it even worse, the top of the blue plastic was above James's and Dan's heads. So what was the point?

The frequency with which the ball flies above head height means the rule clearly has no influence over the style and quality of play anyway.

A secondary argument in favour of the rule was that maybe it was below head height – i.e. below shoulder height – to help people with glasses. This is pointless again because five-foot-something Pete's shoulders are around six-foot-something Dan's ribcage. Even if these measurements were taking place in a calm, considered manner they'd be confusing, but they happen during the height of battle, when someone's trying to claw back a two-goal deficit.

And it's not as if the ball is just flying up accidentally through deflections, blocked shots, tackles, saves or crossbar rebounds. I'd say half of our wayward balls come from shit shots, mad goal kicks, rushed hacked clearances and perfectly weighted lobs delivered with perfect brain-fade – when you see a great pass on but inexplicably forget the height rules. Sometimes it's even deliberate. Martin Eales of the long-standing Old Robsonians five-a-side team told me this of his competitive league: 'One year we won our league with a 1–0 victory, during which we concentrated on booting the ball over the fence whenever we had it to waste a full eighteen minutes. This drove the opposition mad.'

Yet another version of this spoiling tactic comes when someone on the opposing side calls, 'Above head height!' deliberately because they want the game to stop – they're winning and they want to interrupt the opposition's attacking comeback momentum – but the side in possession disagree with the verdict, carry on and score while half the players on the pitch have stopped.

This then becomes a moral argument about whether you should stop for a rule infringement against you, if it isn't to your advantage, you haven't called for it and have actually played on. This goes on every week. It's frequently impossible to measure what is and isn't above head height.

One week a ball whizzed past most of us at chest height, well within the limit, and someone small got their head onto it and scored. Great goal, everyone applauds, until the opposition defender goes, 'No chance, it was above his head height, he had to jump to reach it,' and it was so difficult to disagree, the goal was wiped out despite being below the agreed height. Fractured logic prevailed.

Another time I was stood on the left wing when the ball was curled out across the pitch from our goalkeeper and it came perfectly for me to swivel, get my right leg up, over and through it, and hook the volley straight into the net. A goal that everyone applauded until Gary, laughing, said, 'Above head height,' which was questionable against the wall marker but the ball clearly dipped to reach the high level I kicked it at. In my mind it should have been allowed to stand just because of the quality of the pass and finish. In some perverse, inflexible respect for the rules, everyone seemed to agree with the shout, though, and it was ruled out. Maybe it was just funnier to disallow it on a technicality because I was so obviously delighted with it.

Not long after that I was watching Leeds play on *Soccer Sixes* on Sky and Jon Newsome of all people, a robust league championship-winning defender when he was at Elland Road, scored the exact same goal, but in his game they let it stand. Young Ronaldinho can also be seen scoring the same goal in hazy footage on YouTube. Again, his goal stands. Bastards.

In both the Wednesday and Sunday games we still allow back passes to be collected by the keeper, even though they were outlawed last century – over twenty years ago, in fact. That's before our youngest players were born. So that's the total ball-breaking pain in the arse that is the head-height rule. Next comes the D.

The D is the goal area. It is marked out on the pitch in coloured paint. Only the keeper is allowed in it. And the keeper isn't allowed out of it. However, the law of momentum makes this impossible. If you hit a shot near the D after running with the ball, or try to block one, you frequently carry on over the line. Anyone with any flexibility and imagination would allow a degree of leeway here. Does this exist in our Wednesday game, and many others across the land? NO. FUCKING. WAY. JOSE. NO. LEEWAY. AT. ALL. IT'S A PEN!

As many rows erupt about whether the keeper or striker has crossed the line as whether the ball has risen higher than the fringe. That's another eight minutes wasted a game. Another possible six games a year we could be playing instead of rowing. Another 120-odd goals. More joy. Fun.

Only it's longer because every time the row is decided in favour of the attacking team you have the build-up and execution of the penalty. That's ten hours a year the Wednesday lot spend arguing about head height and D infringement. Get rid of the rules or relax them. Allow people to overspill into the D if it's a genuine attempt to hurriedly block or shoot rather than goal hang or defend.

Tom Findlay tells me his Friday morning game has dealt with this to some extent: 'To stop so much rowing the guy who organizes the game has changed the rule. He's invented his own rule and it's definitely cut back on the arguing. The defender can go inside the area and take one touch. They can't all pile in and block and defend the goalmouth, but if you're defending and are forced to step into the D because of how close you are, you can carry on in and play the ball. That's where most of the rows come from, a penalty being awarded for a defender going into the D. It's helped keep the game going.'

Good idea, but there's a third moan we must attend to, which is the controversy around the shooting line. Often you can only score inside a designated line: in a gym it's usually a line that's been painted there as part of another sport, invariably known as 'the red/black/yellow/blue or green line'.

When you pause for a half-second during a run and shape to shoot as it passes that line, it feels on a par, if not better than, making the perfect pass. Know you've shot and scored from the right side of the line and no one will argue; if you've any self-doubt everyone sees it and the goal is ruled out. It's the one rule where usually the argument is dissolved almost immediately as your own team find it hard to argue the toss.

You can, however, use this rule to your advantage if you're yet to cross the line. I've had people shout, 'Outside the line,' when I've deliberately fired one in, hoping either the keeper will spill it into the net or the path of a loitering striker or it will get a deflection and fly in. Both are totally feasible actions given the standard of keepers we have and the power and swerve you can get on a ball from what is really nothing more than about fifteen feet out. The rule says you can't score from outside that line, not that you can't shoot.

It's as easy to place it to brush the side of a player's calf as it is to place it into the corner of the net and it can often pick up a touch to legitimize the goal. You have to then take the time to point out you can't score from outside the line but you can shoot from there. Many a frustrated keeper has had to pick the ball from the net after such a deflection. It's always worth a go if you're in the lead and looking to demoralize the opposition with tainted luck or if you are desperate to get a goal back and confronted by a wall of legs. Different tactics get different results.

And if you want to know how maddening they can be, here's a guy I've occasionally played with, Stuart Gyseman: 'Someone once snatched the ball off me to take a pen. They smashed it against the crossbar and it came back and broke his nose. To make it worse the ref gave a free kick against us as our guy had touched the ball twice without the opposition touching it.'

These are the rules. They're fucking pointless, but we play by them.

Tuesday Night Strollers

A few years ago I was in a pub in King's Cross chatting with the music writer Pete Paphides about five-a-side and how I needed to take a step back from my Wednesday game because of the number of stoppages and arguments about the rules. He invited me to join his game, but I knew I would struggle to make it because of the kids' bed times. Then the bloke sitting next to me said, 'We've got a Tuesday game that starts at 10 p.m. if you fancy it.'

The bloke in question was author and comedian David Baddiel, who had been on the bright orange *loaded* Euro 96 cover, a particular favourite of mine. We'd met occasionally over the years when he was doing *Fantasy Football* and we had a couple of mutual friends. More recently I'd been enjoying his short-lived column in *Esquire* magazine.

'At 10 p.m. where?'

'Somers Town, just behind Euston.'

That was only a couple of miles from my house, so it sounded ideal. Ever since I'd stopped drinking I'd had these slack hours between when the rest of the family went to bed and the other side of midnight, when my natural energy and green tea combination would allow me to eventually calm down.

Most of those hours were spent either dicking around online or, if I could actually get into bed with my girlfriend by half ten, watching Garry Shandling as Larry Sanders, Larry David in *Curb Your Enthusiasm* or my animated life reflection Peter Griffin in *Family Guy*.

'Yes, definitely, I'll come next week!' I told Baddiel.

It really did sound like an ideal time. Everything else had finished and I figured Lisa would probably appreciate the extra sleep and prefer that I was actually out doing something healthy rather than just sitting on Twitter.

A week and a few hours later I arrived home at half past midnight stinking of curry with a bag full of totally sodden kit. I probably smelt like I'd enjoyed a takeaway in a sauna. Lisa rolled over, looked and sniffed at me through half-closed eyes and asked, 'How was it?'

'Really strange. Everyone was really positive and encouraging, and no arguing at all.'

It genuinely couldn't have been more different from the frequently fractious Wednesday game. I liked the guys I played with on Wednesdays, but the interruptions and disagreements over infringements were really stopping us actually playing football. In Somers Town there had been no head height, shooting line or goal area rules to row about and the pitch was massive. Come to think of it, there wasn't actually a goalkeeper's area at all. Where you could or couldn't pick the ball up by hand was just judged on goodwill. It felt a little like the feel-good finale to a Dickens TV adaptation.

Before she drifted off I felt compelled to tell her, 'Some of them were so posh and enthusiastic it felt like playing with the Escape Committee in *The Great Escape*. Lots of them were good players and, most impressively, there was lots of space to play in.'

She said, 'Oh, that sounds good,' and went back to sleep. But I really had enjoyed it and couldn't sleep for ages from the adrenalin still pumping round my body. I lay in bed thinking back over the game. It would become a weekly fixture for me, my new favourite game. The kick-off time in particular made it unique.

All in all, it was a complete revelation. The size of the pitch – two basketball courts – and the lack of rules meant we just ran and ran and rarely stopped. We played solid eight-a-side for seventy minutes, like being back in the school playground. I was utterly fucked afterwards but had kept going for the whole game.

There were a few very good players I'd played with before on a Monday morning, including Richard 'The Whippet' Smith, a lovely winger who had played in my adidas World Cup tournament team, and Ross, who looked and played like a cross between Bill Oddie and *Tiger and Scorcher*'s Hot Shot Hamish.

Ross's great skill was to twist left and right and left again, like a dog who can't make his mind up, and then, when he'd shaken his marker/ tackler off, he'd unleash a shot from the tank barrel of his left leg and watch from distance as it bulged into the back of the net – powerful and exceptionally damaging to the scoreline if you're on the receiving end. The only way to stop him was to mark him so tightly he couldn't receive the ball in the first place. He's a lethal finisher to play alongside or against.

There was a much younger guy than the rest of us called Barnie, who could easily skip from one end of this large pitch to the other to bury the ball. He also had what looked like serious goalkeeping skills. He could pretty much land the ball on your feet from thirty yards away. Like all the best players, there were suggestions he'd done very well as a kid at a pro club, in his case Portsmouth. In my experience of going to Portsmouth, just staying sober for the evening would give you a head start.

There was a giant goal hanger in a Fulham shirt called John, who specialized in missing his first shot and then making sure with his second or third as the ball bounced back off the back wall. There was organizer Charlie in his Palace shirt, David in his Chelsea strip and a whole variety of other vintage Arsenal, Everton and sky blue and red shirts from Manchester. The ages seemed to range from late twenties to mid-sixties, but the ability spread didn't embarrass anyone, the teams were well matched and a lot of great goals were scored.

Apart from the actual games, what I liked most about it was the perverse pleasure I could take in mentioning to non-players that this was a game that kicked off at 10 p.m. and didn't finish till after 11.

'You play at 11 at night?' they'd ask incredulously.

'Yes, it's a great time to play. It doesn't clash with anything.'

At the end-of-the-year Christmas dinner they kindly gave me an award for Most Thunderous Shot, commending me on my left-footed sharp shooting. Which was nice given that I'd deliberately been trying to score with both rather than rely on my traditional right foot.

With the camaraderie, the lack of conflict, the kick-off time, the size of the pitch and the option to go long and high from one corner to another or to just simply push it down and run, this soon became my favourite game.

Like many long-standing games, it had its own history, legends, routines and ritual. All games would be followed by a curry, there were no careless fouls or arguments, everyone would arrive with a white or a dark top, teams would be divided up as fairly as possible and we'd be off.

It was only when I showed up for the Christmas dinner and they all arrived in ties and started referring to the club as the Strollers that I realized I'd been co-opted into what seemed like an Oxbridge society. So long as we stuck to eight-a-side and didn't attempt to re-form the Cambridge spy ring, I was fine with that.

Ironically, the week the book was commissioned they moved to a much thinner, slower pitch with a low-netted height restriction and earlier start time, and although it was walking distance from my house, after just one game I knew it wasn't for me.

But what of the Strollers' history? I asked organizer Charlie Dawson to explain: 'It was originally organized by Jonny Brock, an eccentric/characterful barrister who had been to Cambridge with the group of people who formed the nucleus of the Strollers when it first started, in the 80s at some point – ex-Footlights people and friends, I think. Jonny ran it like a kind of private members' club, with no explicit rules but lots of implied ones, where he was in complete control but guided by taking "soundings from senior Strollers". He had a sheet of paper that had become like parchment and listed everyone who played, what they'd paid and who had moved from being a casual, paying weekly, to being asked to join the club properly and pay a debenture. This was a big deal, lacking only some kind of secret handshake.

'Jonny had a heart attack that wasn't caught quickly enough, so he was in a coma, brain-damaged, and effectively disappeared from the Strollers overnight. Eventually, after months, he died, in his early fifties. So sad – so much life and charisma. I was already organizing the Sunday football team we had, so I stepped in. It just seemed to carry on from there, never with a sense that I'm in charge or anything like that. There's an unofficial bunch of Senior Strollers who get consulted still if difficult things need to be addressed, like asking someone to stop coming or change the way they're playing. Pretty rare, though. The bottom line is we all love the Strollers – the football, the spirit and the group – and we want it to keep going, I guess for ever, although, as Prince said, that's a mighty long time.'

I then asked Charlie what he thought the best aspect of playing was.

'Losing yourself in a weekly game where nothing else matters. Being part of highlights – a great pass, seeing a great goal or save or tackle, stuff to run through in your head going to sleep – that puts work and family hassle and money and all that a million miles away.

'Doing this within a group that has togetherness – not close friend-ship, but something important, shared, where we all connect on a level. It's also a great way to stay a bit fit – totally enjoyable, unlike the run that I also do every week. I remember a goalkeeper's throw to the right wing behind me, it bounced, I back-heeled it over my head forward down the line over Martin, who hit it as it dropped on the volley into the opposite far corner like a bullet. We could try for another six months and not repeat it.

'We have a good age mix and I can see that when sons play something special is happening. You can also see evolution in action – most of them are way better than their dads.'

I then asked my Strollers recruiter, David Baddiel, how he thought playing affected him: 'I do feel – and I may well feel this in life – a constant sense of unfairness about my performance. A sense that I'd have to beat every player on the pitch and score a hundred volleyed goals to get Angus Deayton to say, "You had a good game."'

And the funniest thing he'd encountered playing five-a-side?

'When I was a teenager I was in a game and my mate Dave got a ball kicked incredibly hard in his face. He had literally just looked up when the same player, having received the ball back from Dave's face, kicked it incredibly hard in his face again. He got very cross but it was hilarious.

'One of our larger players – not you – once fell over and, because Somers Town was a polished floor, travelled quite a long way on his back, but quite slowly, like a stately boat. That too I couldn't stop laughing about.'

On a different note, David then talked about the death of their previous organizer: 'Jonny Brock was the top banana when I started. He was a QC and ran the game with a rod of iron. If someone pissed him off they were out – he would write them a letter. Anyway, he died . . . I didn't go to his funeral, but I heard it was a complex affair, as both of his wives were there and so it was all very tense and fractured. But then the week we convened after his death, Martin Redwood said before the game, "Shall we have a minute's silence?" And so it went, fourteen knackered old blokes standing around in a not very well-rendered circle in a smelly-with-just-left-basketball-players'-sweat gym in Somers Town actually observing it – actually standing there for a minute – and then spontaneously applauding, all of us, when it was over. It was very moving.'

And his favourite experience of playing?

'The above. And the Italian trip we do. Playing our unbeautiful football in very beautiful places.'

Next up was fellow stroller and author John O'Farrell. I asked him how much five-a-side means to him.

'I've been playing in our Tuesday night game for over twenty-five years and it's sort of ridiculous how much it means to me. I never accept an invitation on a Tuesday night, and I always hope they don't ask why, because the truth never goes down very well. My wife asked me what I wanted to do on my fiftieth birthday and I replied, "It's a Tuesday. I want to play five-a-side football." But then my friend Tim had arranged with the curry house to bring out a cake complete with candles at the end of the night.

'I love the fact that we all turn up with such dedication every week, even though we are of such mixed ability and fitness. We don't care, we just come together to completely forget about everything else in our lives for that hour or so. Here is a bunch of blokes from various walks of life who you could never organize to meet with such regularity for any other reason, but we have this universal operating system which is football. Like millions of other groups of football fans all around the world, we are just completely in the game for that period we are on the pitch. The motto on the Strollers' crest is "*Amici ludique tum Standard Tandoori*", which means "Friends and the game, then . . ." I'm not sure about the third one, I never did Latin.'

John's an out and out striker, so I asked about his favourite move or goal.

'Recently my grown-up son has started coming along, so of course I love it if we manage a creative one-two that culminates in a well-worked goal by either of us. But my favourite goals are when I foresaw how the play was going to pan out and made a creative run which a teammate anticipated – Charlie is good at that, and will sometimes thread a lovely ball through to where he knows I'm going to be and it may just be a tap-in. It's the sense of the unspoken communication and understanding between us that is almost spiritual! That higher mental plane that sport can bring – there's a great speech by Paul Newman in *The Hustler* about this. That's what I love most, whether it's a goal, a pass or a first touch, when I didn't have time to stop and think what I was doing and yet I attempted something ambitious and, without me knowing quite how, it came off. When you are in that zone and your feet seem capable of independent thought.'

Did he think this Tuesday night game was typical of five-a-side?

'I don't think ours is a typical five-a-side in that it has a fair sprinkling of celebrities, writers and producers. Alexei Sayle came to our game once and based a scene in one of his short stories on it, in which an ambitious new writer was man-marking a top comedy producer so that he could pitch his programme idea to him as they ran up and down the wing. That doesn't really happen of course, although creative collaborations and mutual support do come out of the friendships made on the pitch.

'But once we are out on the pitch, status is regraded according to how good at football you are. We had Woody Harrelson turn up a couple of times. He was one of the lowest-status players on the pitch. I also think ours is a particularly well-mannered game – we stamp down on other players slagging teammates off on the pitch or showing flashes of temper. We joke a lot about what it means to be a true "Stroller", but there is genuinely something quite gentlemanly about our game which is very precious and I have seen missing from other games I have played in that were not so well nurtured.

And the funniest thing he'd experienced playing five-a-side?

'There isn't much comedy during the game, just the usual embarrassing mishits or players falling over, but, like all the best comedy, the laughs come out of the characters. David Baddiel brought Ian Brodie along once not so long after Euro 96 and I said to Jonny Brock, who had just been made a QC, "Oh look, that's Ian Brodie."

' "Who's Ian Brodie?"

' "You know, The Lightning Seeds."

' "No?"

' "You know, the Euro 96 song 'Three Lions'?"

' "No?"

' "Jonny, you are going to make a great judge . . ." '

'That's what Johan Cruyff said'

So I go back to the Tuesday game, still injured, to fill in for them. I live near Highbury and they had uneven sides. My leg's still twingey but I was missing it, so I offered to go in goal.

Guess what? It was like a different game, amazing pace and skill, much more suited to the thinner Astro pitch with a low hanging net instead of a high ceiling. I realized I have to now park the memories of the huge, high and wide Somers Town gym, the polished floors and the space that allowed me to run there, and get fit and get back involved on Tuesdays. I'll become a better player for it.

The new Tuesday is like a sci-fi sequel to the one game I played at the Arsenal Hub. It has regenerated in just three months or so. For a start it was seven- not nine-a-side, or whatever the first week was. So there's genuinely more space to move into. Secondly, the players have all transformed into young men, lots of them, and it's amazing watching them stream through the opposition like X-Fighters attacking opposition defender Omid Djalili's Death Star. There are plenty of one-twos, fast sprints with the ball and numerous darts into position without, plus quite amazingly controlled long passes that reach their destination without interception. There's an abundance of dummies and drag-backs, and plenty of rolling the ball under the feet. It felt a little like when I watched Peter Crouch playing with the Chelsea coaches on holiday at Forte Village this summer.

It was fast and furious, in fact it was fast and furious 10. One guy in particular was very strong. I realized for the first time in many years that if I genuinely wanted to try and tackle this guy I'd have to tackle him really hard to make an impact and that would probably make the injury worse. There was going to be no nicking the ball off this kid, as he was skilful *and* strong. I felt my age, my weight, my injury . . . and he sidestepped round me.

This kid was amazing. They were all very good, but this one could pass twenty yards over everyone's head without clipping the net hanging from the ceiling. Perfectly weighted balls. He could skip round everyone. He was tall, very strong and very mobile. It was only when I saw him taking such delight in rounding regular centre back David Seemungal that I realized it was his son, the one at Charlton Athletic. Different world. It's basically called the future. It took them ten minutes when I'd come out of goal to realize if they passed it to me they'd get it back in the space it should go into. It was exciting to be in the middle of it and it's a target to get properly fit for.

A few days later I was looking at the huge brown shapes in our back garden where some old raised flowerbeds had until recently been, wondering how long it would take to reseed them. It was a big space and, coming over all McCreadie-ish, I was running through my mind whether to buy fresh turf or grow the grass from seed. I mentioned this to my dad on the phone and he said, 'Why not try AstroTurf? Loads of people with kids seem to have it now.'

I said, 'It's actually really expensive and besides it will hurt the kids' knees if they skid on it playing football.'

'Yes,' he replied, 'that's what Johan Cruyff said to me.'

I was stunned. I stopped for a moment to think about what I'd just heard, because for someone who doesn't have any interest in football it was a hell of a name to drop. The mad thing was, I knew it was true.

It's strange that I had got almost all the way through writing the book for my dad to remind me of this. It hadn't really occurred to me before that my dad had worked on the original development of Astro Turf. But he had and, what's more, we had two square tiles of it in different lengths and thickness in our house. I had them in my room as a kid, in fact. This was the late 1970s, so I'm guessing just as Cruyff was going back to Ajax. It seemed such an alien concept, long plastic grass. Certainly my mates thought it was truly mad when I showed it to them.

Before he became a writer, my dad worked in market research and he would sometimes come back with bounty. One was research into Batman and Superman branded sweet cigarettes, which meant we had about a hundred packs of each. Our kid and I were on forty white candy stick fags a day for about two weeks. Glowing red tips and all.

The other was AstroTurf, which looked and sounded like something NASA might take to the moon. It was an oblong of long green plastic grass about the size of a shoebox. My dad had been to Amsterdam for a fortnight and come back with all sorts of stuff from Ajax signed for me. When I pressed him further on this recently, he said he'd worked with Cruyff and co. over four visits and had spent the same amount of time at Dortmund.

'I went three or four times to Amsterdam and Dortmund. It was all paid for by Monsanto and the interviews were subcontracted to me by a consultant. It was in the late 1970s. My main memories are of being a bit wild in Amsterdam, staying up all night, being treated like shit in Dortmund because I "looked like a terrorist", and getting a real liking for Genever gin. I also remember seeing a lot of what I think you footballers call "silverware", talking to a few footballers through an interpreter called Gabby Gash, and that one of the managers or trainers was a Yugoslav. Also I saw the prime minister of Holland smoking roll-ups in the press club.'

It was perhaps inevitable that one day I would be sitting staring at a fully grown lawn (I went for the seed option), writing a book about a life on AstroTurf.

I'm not the only one who has dreamed of playing football all their life, I know. We all have. The dream of playing professionally is obviously something to aspire to, but it's also such a short-lived dream – little more than a decade if you make it. But just hitting fifty and still playing is a dream achieved.

A couple of years ago I had the pleasure of having dinner with Rod Stewart and his wife at his manager's restaurant in West Hollywood. It was a good night set up by my promoter mate Phil McIntyre and while the other four diners chatted among themselves, Rod and I spent the whole night talking intensely about playing football. So much so that we seemed to forget why we had gathered in the first place. Despite having made a bundle, Rod has had the sense to buy his own football pitch to play on and decent tickets to games he wants to see, rather than a professional football club. He's still got his own team and loves the game.

In the middle of the chat, when I was asking him about how his love of football developed, his wife, Penny, leaned over and said, 'Rod, tell James about the kitchen.' He gave me that famous grin that befits a singer who apparently has had it all but is about to disclose a secret, and said, 'When I was a little kid, really young, in north London, my dad used to run a local football team, which he and my brothers played in. Every Saturday they used to congregate in my mum's kitchen and I'd be sat there in the middle of them, a whole team of about twelve blokes, just taking it all in. Boots being polished, balls being pumped up, pre-match chatter and excitement. I can still smell the atmosphere in that room. I was tiny but that has stayed with me for life.'

I know exactly how he feels. We didn't have a whole team in our kitchen but once my mum and dad had bought me my first pair of new football boots from the Woolworths in the Arndale, my dad insisted I cleaned them after every game. They had moulded soles and laces the length of the M1, but I sat on newspapers spread out across the small kitchen floor in Headingley and set about them with a knife, scraping and prising the caked mud off them, making sure not to cut through where the upper met the sole. One time in particular I polished them for the whole radio commentary of a mid-week Leeds versus West Brom match, which ended in a draw. I can remember the disappointment of not winning. I say polish, but the stuff I used was dubbin.

The 2016 boots don't seem to need polishing, but dubbin was like a cross between treacle and glue: a transparent catarrh-coloured wax that came in the same type of tin as polish but didn't really disappear as you rubbed it in. The laces were lacquered in it, my hands were covered in it, my boots would slip about in my fingers. But it worked. It kept my boots so supple, other kids would bend and marvel at them from heel to toe. And, as Rod said, it remains a smell that takes me right back to that kitchen.

I don't use dubbin any more but it still exists – still going strong, like the culture of five-a-side.

Few novels have featured five-a-side, but I thought I should get a word from a man I know who has written about it. Stories like *Trainspotting*, *Skagboys* and those in *The Acid House* defined a generation and an outlook on life. Five-a-side was a given in the conversations of characters in all these books and more. Like those of us who've lived a five-a-side life, understand it can be there for ever, Irvine Welsh's still not written himself off. If anything, he sees it as a mirror to how a man's life changes.

'It's such a huge culture, due to the way it dovetails with pissing it up. You start playing elevens when you're younger, and you can go on the piss with eleven people easily in your teens. You're just shouting at each other, talking shite, telling jokes and arguing about where the best places to pick up fanny will be. Then you get older and the egos, intellect and preferences kick in, and you want more conversation and time to discuss the big life changes. People, and teams, naturally divide into smaller cliques, thus fives. I love it when fat cunts like myself, who haven't kicked a ball in elevens for years, get asked to play and think, "It's only fives, piece of piss," and are then blowing out their arses the entire game and crippled the following day.'

It's a harsh reality check. If five-a-side was a racquet sport it would be squash. There's no hiding on a five-a-side pitch, not if you're serious about giving it a go. You give your all and then relax afterwards. And with that in mind, I decide it's time to take my 'fat cunt Irvine Welsh reading self' to Falkirk Street to see how the Wednesday night boys are getting on since Kyllo's departure.

Back to Wednesday without Kyllo

I get in the car at 8.45 p.m. and go down to the Wednesday game in Hoxton for the first time since James died, five months ago. I'm not sure why I've left it so long. Every time I ask Gary about numbers he says it's six-a-side so I give it a miss. But I've finally decided to just go. A physio friend called Liza has started to loosen my thigh up and it no longer hurts when I shoot.

Before we start the other indoor pitch next to us is empty for once and given that there are sixteen of us someone wisely says, 'Why don't we use both pitches and play two games of four-a-side?'

To which someone else replies, 'No, we're playing six-a-side, with two off from each team for five minutes at a time.'

This seems wrong. Across the whole gym there's space for us all to be playing all the time. Why keep stopping mid-game and changing the teams so much? There'll be no continuity. We could have a four-team tournament, keep it competitive.

'No, we'll rotate. It will be fine.'

Madness. Some things never change, but amazingly some things do.

Frank, the guy who could have fallen from a Lowry painting, is positively neon. He has a bright lemon, unbranded, short-sleeve shirt and equally bright blue shorts. Apart from the clashing black socks, he looks totally un-Frank, he is lacking Frank-ness. He is dressed like a fast-food wrapper. He has adopted the modern footballer's uniform and now looks like a footballer, and looks more competent for it. He'll be getting an agent and braids in his hair next. Did he play better or is that just my imagination?

Ish, who is Geoff Norris's son, is back from wherever life took him after uni. When he first played with us he was a skinny thirteen-year-old. Now he's twice that age and has a physique like Ibrahimović. More than any of us, Ish growing up is a reflection of how many years we've been at this. At the other end of the life scale you drop out of the game or, in James's case, pass away, but here's Ish over a decade on and now he's in charge. Ibrahimov-Ish dominates the game with his strength, but mixes it with softer assists to his dad and teammates, setting them up to score again and again. It's a masterclass in how to win.

Unfortunately, I'm on the receiving end. He repeatedly uses his power to drag the game and our team one way and then gently rolls out an assist into the space he's created the opposite way. Excellent stuff and very hard to play against when there are so many people on the pitch and so many off it.

As our goalkeeper plays weak balls out, Ish intercepts them immediately and bangs them back in again and again. So we play too many people on too small a pitch and each player sits out eighteen minutes in the hour. It's a strange, awkward game but one that's been my five-a-side home for the best part of twenty years. Like a marriage you moan about but know well. And the guys are still up for it, still keen, still going strong. The same petty clashes, softened now with age into hilarity rather than anger. The competitive drained away with the end of Kyllo's 6aside.net player league. It's disappeared from the internet and I've no chance to screen-grab the year I came top or my place near the top of the all-time rankings. The most points won from the most games played. Knocked down into fifth place by people with an impossible percentage gained from appearing just a handful of times.

On the pitch, unplanned rolling subs means two of our best players are off at the same time as two of our less skilful players are on. I realize we are playing against ourselves as much as the opposition. A little like life. With people going off every six minutes there are too many personnel changes, too many skill and fitness levels, too many bodies, so it's impossible to find and maintain a balance to compete.

The combination in our team isn't as effective and balanced as the opposition's. They have Ish, who provides power and finishing skill and passing, and Pete the Oil, who ticks along, constantly creating space and looking for opportunities to move the ball around. They also have an American keeper with his own gloves who distributes the ball fast and effectively like a basketball feed, maintaining a bit of stability in their team by staying on for almost the whole game. Gary is the new James. With Geoff, he's been here since the beginning. He gives lifts, organizes the games and has a good perspective on it all. He's had time to develop that from the many hours he's spent waiting outside my house for me to be ready. His signature move is to stand dead still and then try and whip it away as you lunge in. Tonight the ratio of success to failure is in his favour.

By comparison we've a defender who surges from a static ball-watching position to occasionally win a tackle and hammer a clearance, but it's not five-a-side, it's pinball, and he's the last-gasp flipper.

We've a battler, Marquel, who forces his way past one man from our left back position and then gets stuck against the boards. When he is in space he scores two cracking goals, but the wing is a cul-de-sac.

We've the best defender, Derby Dave, who can force his way forward out of defence and shoot when it's only four- or five-a-side, but the overcrowding is preventing him making headway beyond the shooting line. At the back he makes one amazing lunging block, and when he does that I can't help thinking that in his own head he's back in the days of Roy McFarland and Colin Todd.

Up front we've two younger players who can and do score, but with less frequency than Ish. If there's something to be learned from the line-ups it's 'Have children, train them for five-a-side combat against adults when they're young and make sure they're on your side when they're twenty-six.'

Something becomes apparent to me as I see one of our players run into an opposition roadblock when a nice simple pass would have kept the ball alive in our possession. It's easier to play against their better players than it is to play alongside some of our own players. Even though he's dominating the game, there is a predictability to Ish's style that means I can tackle the ball from him. I know he's going to do something really good with the ball, he's going to go left or right and it will be a strong step and rush past or a decent pass to someone else, but because I know he'll select something good to do, it's easier to think what the best move would be and anticipate him. The challenge then is to summon the strength and balance to make sure he doesn't edge me off the ball as I try and steal it from him. His challenge is to act before I get to him.

On the other hand, some of the players on our team are far less predictable, but also less effective. They stand with the ball at their feet for a long time. When they release it everyone's been waiting so long they've stopped moving and the ball is intercepted. We lose a lot of possession, because the ball must keep moving. To me that's the basic law of five-a-side. Let it stop when it's in the back of the net.

After such a long break it's easier said than done for me. I realize I'm trying to find space, drifting like a crewless ship. I make a wing-to-wing pass through a crowded midfield that gets a round of appreciation as it reaches Andy, who buries it. Yet I also snatched at a left-foot shot on the turn with my back to goal that was just really poor. I thought, 'I must look really bad.'

As usual, I am over-analysing and thinking about the game instead of pushing myself harder. I know that the greatest incentive is to be slim, fit and up to speed. We all face that, everyone of us playing five-a-side. However, if I haven't got some of my old stamina, core strength, pace and ability back by the time this book comes out, I'm just going to sound like I'm totally consumed by the five-a-side delusion, where our dreams and self-commentary become our own truths, where we're nowhere near as good as we thought we were. The new players here with can't see past games, only present – the missed passes and weak shots – and the old players are too busy wondering about their own game to remember when someone else used to be good, way back in the era of sharp passes and powerful goals.

As a five-a-side player you need the sharpness that playing weekly will give you. Play five times a week and your body will fuck you up. Thankfully, help is at hand in the form of a visionary and a Ventolin pump.

It's strange playing without James. I think about the last time I spoke to him at length, on the benches in Clissold Park. About the last game, when we swapped positions at the back of the area at a corner kick and he walked in unmarked and scored. He was the ungainly super-keen fixture this game revolved around. The core group of the midweek game is much the same as it was a decade ago and we wouldn't have been here if he hadn't kept it going week after week. We owe him the game and I owe him this book. It was Kyllo's game. It would be too much of a stretch to suggest it's like a band without an original singer, though it certainly feels a little different. However, the game goes on. What score is it? Kyllo always kept the score, always accurate, only ever challenged once in the seventeen years I played with him. Now it's not quite so clear.

In goal for our team is Alex Hardee, who's wearing mauve knee-length drainpipe yoga gear and sporting a Chris Bonington at base camp beard. He looks a little older since I last saw him and weirdly you can see wealth in the lines on his face. Like he's been to a spa for a facial, then slept in a hedge at a festival. He doesn't look so fucked as he used to. A mutual friend of ours has told me that after doing well with his music agency he's thinking of buying himself a brewery. None of this has affected his approach to the game: dribbling and slipping and stumbling and scoring or missing and laughing.

At one point I'm stood next to Alex, while I'm having my five minutes out sucking on Ventolin and swigging tap water from my bottle. I'm leaning against the wall between the ragged side of the goal net and the edge of the D, where our bags are creating a dead spot. I'm not interfering with the game but am close enough to talk to him.

We are a few goals down and it's coming to the last few minutes of the game. Alex has possession. He is in the goalkeeper's D, ball at his feet, no pressure, but he just goes right ahead and chips it high and wide down the pitch into the curtain. Above head height *and* out of bounds. It's a double infringement and gives the opposition a chance to make a huge cry and take a throw-in from their right back position. That's how shit his pass was, it bypassed everyone in our team. We didn't even have a player near there. It's a terrible bit of distribution.

It's so bad I can't help but laugh and say, 'What the fuck was that, Alex?' and he laughs too at how terrible it was, shrugs and then says, 'Just killing time.' 'But we're losing,' I say. 'Well, we'll lose by less,' he answers, and we both laugh again. It's hard to argue with that type of logic.

Alex has accidentally seen through the false hope of elusive glory in attempting to bridge the three-goal deficit and is now just working on damage limitation.

He is clearly some type of savant. I stand there and laugh hard for the remaining minutes of my break. I'd like to be able to say that I come on and score a winner, but I don't. We lose by three, or maybe two – without Kyllo I'm not so sure. I'm giddy from Alex's really shit clearance and the fact that he's said something surreally profound. Our shared laughter is the best moment of the night. A good guy died but the game goes on, and the upside is we're losing by less.

Two Lists

Local Rules Apply

1) In the summer the showers will be hot and in the winter they will be cold. Wherever you play.

2) All pitches must have used plastic Powerade energy and water bottles around the edge of the playing area.

3) All players must empty little black rubber seeds all over their house when they get home despite banging their boots together after the outdoor game.

4) Used kitbags must be left in the hall until the next match or wife/girlfriend/boyfriend demands, 'Is that going to be left there all week?'

5) If there is a roof next to an outdoor pitch someone will put the ball onto it.

6) However, someone else will always be able to scale the wall and fences up to the roof like a cat burglar.

7) Every indoor wooden gym must have a rolled-up dividing or cricket net hanging from the ceiling that will feature a haul of different sports balls in the top of it.

8) If you use the indoor wooden floor pitch straight after basketball players there will always be deadly water spillages on your wings.

9) All indoor goal nets will dangle down over the goal line and have a gap in the side behind one post, allowing for goal in/not in controversy.

10) The above-head-height level will be argued about constantly between smaller and taller players.

11) One participant must bring energy-giving bananas for themselves before the match and half-time but not actually do any running during the game.

12) If playing outdoors the ball that has been booted over the fence will be waited for despite there being four other balls by the bags.

13) If the out-of-court ball is retrieved by some willing passer-by it will never make it back over the fence at first try. When it does arrive it will be cheered.

14) Indoors, all sports bags will be clustered around one goal, thus preventing bounce-back opportunities for the team attacking that end.

15) Indoors, there will be no half-time.

16) No player will arrive wearing the exact same shirt as another.

17) At least one player will sport a retro team shirt.

18) A pair of decent football socks, like a good heart, is hard to find.

19) Most of us aren't as good as we used to be.

20) Most of us have always thought we are better than we are.

21) There will always be one bib that is inexplicably kids' size. This will be worn like a snood round the neck or under the armpits like a gun holster. That's after the wearer has struggled into it and joked about it being a sports bra.

22) Each week someone will say, 'If that had been on TV it would have been Goal of the Season.'

23) One player will arrive with his kit ironed and folded.

24) One player will arrive with his kit in a plastic bag from a supermarket that doesn't even exist any more.

25) One player will always arrive late and apologize like it's the first time it's ever happened.

26) The shouting of utter nonsense to each other in triplicate during the game is allowed and will be encouraged.

27) The brain-to-foot thought will rarely be linked to brain-to-foot action.

28) Only 30 per cent of a team will be capable of chasing back.

29) An outfield player will always unexpectedly turn out to be a far better goalie than the guy who fancies himself as keeper and has the gloves and all that.

30) Incursions into the goalkeeper's D must be argued about.

31) Ditto the shooting line.

32) If you cohabit your football boots will be treated like rubbish by your wife/girlfriend/boyfriend and left under the sink, in the garage, under the stairs, with your tools, in the laundry room etc. 'because you didn't put them away'.

33) Fat players can't run but they can shoot.

34) Any goalie wearing gloves is unlikely to ever stop the ball with his hands.

35) Indoors, the ball coming back off the back wall or crossbar above head height must always cause rule confusion.

36) In a competitive league there will always be a team called Inter Your Mam.

37) At least one row about the score is allowed per high-scoring game.

38) No matter where you stand or how good you were at maths, someone will always beat you by playing a one-two with the wall.

39) Getting changed after the game there will always be an item of clothing left that wasn't there when you came in.

40) Every outdoor eight-a-side game will have someone who refers to themselves in the third person to claim an incoming ball, e.g. 'Jack's ball', but will then usually miss the header.

41) Every game will have a defender who tells everyone else what to do but doesn't actually do it themselves.

42) When paying the organizer not enough players will ever have change.

43) Every long-term organized game must attempt an awards ceremony at some point. With really shit certificates.

44) Rain must never stop an outdoor game.

45) The people on the court before you will take ages to get off but the people after you will come on bang on the hour.

46) The people on after you can be quietly encouraged to come on early if you are struggling to defend a tight lead.

47) Post-match analysis will take place in the pub.

48) All arguments must be left on the pitch.

49) Moaning can take place in the car home.

50) All goals you score are brilliant and can be described in detail for weeks afterwards, even when everyone else has forgotten them.

The Cultural Shaping of the Player – the stuff that made me

1) *Tiger and Scorcher* – Nipper Lawrence, Billy's Boots, Hotshot Hamish, Roy of the Rovers – endless football strips

2) *The Blinder*, Barry Hines's great semi-autobiographical football novel

3) The PE lesson in *Kes* – the greatest televised football match ever

4) Don Revie's Super Leeds – the heroes

5) 1970 Esso World Cup coins

6) *Goals Are My Business*, Allan Clarke

7) Johan Cruyff and Johan Neeskens – the skill

8) Paul Breitner – the hair

9) Subbuteo – hair-raising end-to-end stuff with pre-teen knee-high managers and fingertip-high players

10) The Leeds United sock tags

11) The Smiley badge

12) The Wembley Trophy ball

13) Filey beach – the best pitch ever

14) The animated football match in *Bedknobs and Broomsticks*

15) Sports Corner and Norman Hunter Sports – Headingley's finest shops

16) Paul Madeley paints – paint it white

17) Cheap Barcelona and Juventus nylon shirts from a sports shop on the Headrow, Leeds

18) Football cards with pen-portrait stats on the back

19) The Colourbox unofficial 1986 World Cup theme – the best football theme never commissioned

20) 'Kicker Conspiracy', The Fall – the great truckabilly football rap

21) *Shankly Speaks* – a must-hear album

22) Saint and Greavsie

23) *The End* – a music fanzine read by football fans

24) New Order and Keith Allen's 'World in Motion'

25) The *90 Minutes* magazine Predictor League

26) *Steak . . . Diana Ross: Diary of a Football Nobody*, David McVay – the players sold eggs in the summer to top up their wages

27) *The Damned United*, David Peace – great novel, poor film

28) Strachan, Batty, Speed, McAllister

29) 'Love on the Terraces', Serious Drinking

30) *Sports Breakfast* – who wouldn't want to wake up with Alan Brazil?

31) When I turned French club manager Claude Bez into *loaded*'s Dr. Mick

32) Scarves on wrists

33) The LUFC balaclava in the stands at Paris 75 as seen in *Mundial* magazine

34) Robert Snodgrass – a throwback to the 1970s

35) David O'Leary, Paul Hart, Eddie Gray and Neil Redfearn's kids

36) Leeds vs. Stuttgart replay at Camp Nou

37) Scoring from our half in Eight-a-Side and with a snooker style rebound off the wall in Fives
38) The red brick walls and garage doors of Leeds 6
39) A million other great footballing moments
40) Rory Smith's *Mister*, a great football history book

Dreams FC 1–Reality Rovers 0

Acknowledgements

Thanks to the following for their stories, time, games, photographs, help and lifts.

Armstrong Sound System, David Baddiel, Glenn Banks, Paul Buck, Mikey Chetcuti, Glen Chicorydorf, Chris Collier, Cathal Dolan, Billy Duffy, Hayden Evans, Tom Findlay, Nick Frith, Darren Hare, Peter Hooton, Micky Hughes, Craig Johnstone, Paul Kelly, Gary King, Johnny Lake, Catherine Lascelles for writing space, Jeremy Lascelles, Richard Luck, Jamie Mascaro, Amy McClusky, Andy Mitten, John O'Farrell, 'Orrible Ives, Penhalligan & Morph, Kevin Sampson, Matt Sankey, David 'Tigerman' Smith, Irvine Welsh. Everyone who gave me stories that did or didn't make the cut. I keep thinking about other great stories I could put in, like seventeen-year-old South African school mate Andy Cox who, fresh off the plane, saw real ice for the first time ever in his life playing five-a-side on an outdoor concrete pitch. I'll just have to tell these stories in full at a later date. I'm too fucked to get them in now. It's 2.53 a.m.

Thanks to Fred and Abbi Kindall, Ray Klerck, Dominic Benjamin for attempting the impossible job of getting me fit. Many thanks to Liza Payter for fixing my thigh and making me laugh in agony. To Alex for being first pick when we were kids.

Special thanks to authors and good friends: Charlie Connolly, JJ Connolly, Hunter Davies and Tony Parsons for constant encouragement and advice.

Big thanks to Gary King, Charlie Dawson, Will Rayner, Matt Tench and Jimmie Gregory, without whom there'd be no games to play in nor teams to manage. And of course to everyone I've played five-a-side with, you know who you are. I honestly didn't hear you screaming for the ball.

Thanks to David Luxton at DLA and Richard Milner at Quercus for making the book happen. On on on.

In memory of the late James Kyllo, the great Paul 'Gillsy' Gill, and young Jonny Roberts, our Sunday game misses you all massively. Thanks to Paul Davies and Jonny Cooper for commissioning the original article about James Kyllo for *Telegraph Men*.

Most importantly my own special 3aSide team: Marlais, Billy and especially the long suffering but utterly lovely Lisa Baker. And Terri, Charlie and the late great Alan Baker for letting me sign Lisa on a free.

Finally thanks to my school friend Tracey Bridges who, as *Above Head Height* was being edited, coined the phrase 'Headingley Wallers' on Facebook. It is a brilliant description of what my childhood mates and I were. The roots of my five-a-side life started with the Headingley Wallers.